Test Prep & Admissions Consulting

Turbocharge Your GMAT: Critical Reasoning Guide

part of the 6th Edition Series

April 20th, 2016

- ☐ *Discussion of eleven different question types*
- ☐ *Over 200 practice questions with comprehensive solutions*
- ☐ *30+ questions on rare to super-rare categories: Flaw, MoR, and Parallel Reasoning*
- ☐ *Explanations of key differences between confusing question types: Strengthen & Weaken, Strengthen & Inference, and Weaken & Flaw*
- ☐ *Concept illustration through info-graphic strips and graphic aids*
- ☐ *Three qualifying tests: conclusion test, negation test, and evaluation test*
- ☐ *Discussion on how to predict a qualifying answer*

www.manhattanreview.com

©1999-2016 Manhattan Review. All Rights Reserved.

Copyright and Terms of Use

Copyright and Trademark

All materials herein (including names, terms, trademarks, designs, images, and graphics) are the property of Manhattan Review, except where otherwise noted. Except as permitted herein, no such material may be copied, reproduced, displayed or transmitted or otherwise used without the prior written permission of Manhattan Review. You are permitted to use material herein for your personal, noncommercial use, provided that you do not combine such material into a combination, collection, or compilation of material. If you have any questions regarding the use of the material, please contact Manhattan Review at info@manhattanreview.com.

This material may make reference to countries and persons. The use of such references is for hypothetical and demonstrative purposes only.

Terms of Use

By using this material, you acknowledge and agree to the terms of use contained herein.

No Warranties

This material is provided without warranty, either express or implied, including the implied warranties of merchantability, of fitness for a particular purpose and noninfringement. Manhattan Review does not warrant or make any representations regarding the use, accuracy or results of the use of this material. This material may make reference to other source materials. Manhattan Review is not responsible in any respect for the content of such other source materials, and disclaims all warranties and liabilities with respect to the other source materials.

Limitation on Liability

Manhattan Review shall not be responsible under any circumstances for any direct, indirect, special, punitive, or consequential damages ("Damages") that may arise from the use of this material. In addition, Manhattan Review does not guarantee the accuracy or completeness of its course materials, which are provided "as is" with no warranty, express or implied. Manhattan Review assumes no liability for any Damages from errors or omissions in the material, whether arising in contract, tort or otherwise.

GMAT is a registered trademark of the Graduate Management Admission Council.
GMAC does not endorse, nor is it affiliated in any way with, the owner of this product or any content herein.

10-Digit International Standard Book Number: (ISBN: 1-62926-068-1)
13-Digit International Standard Book Number: (ISBN: 978-1-62926-068-6)

Last updated on April 20th, 2016.

Manhattan Review, 275 Madison Avenue, Suite 1429, New York, NY 10016.
Phone: +1 (212) 316-2000. E-Mail: info@manhattanreview.com. Web: www.manhattanreview.com

About the Turbocharge your GMAT Series

The Turbocharge Your GMAT Series is carefully designed to be clear, comprehensive, and content-driven. Long regarded as the gold standard in GMAT prep worldwide, Manhattan Review's GMAT prep books offer professional GMAT instruction for dramatic score improvement. Now in its updated 6th edition, the full series is designed to provide GMAT test-takers with complete guidance for highly successful outcomes. As many students have discovered, Manhattan Review's GMAT books break down the different test sections in a coherent, concise, and accessible manner. We delve deeply into the content of every single testing area and zero in on exactly what you need to know to raise your score. The full series is comprised of 16 guides that cover concepts in mathematics and grammar from the most basic through the most advanced levels, making them a great study resource for all stages of GMAT preparation. Students who work through all of our books benefit from a substantial boost to their GMAT knowledge and develop a thorough and strategic approach to taking the GMAT.

- ☐ GMAT Math Essentials (ISBN: 978-1-62926-057-0)
- ☐ GMAT Number Properties Guide (ISBN: 978-1-62926-058-7)
- ☐ GMAT Arithmetics Guide (ISBN: 978-1-62926-059-4)
- ☐ GMAT Algebra Guide (ISBN: 978-1-62926-060-0)
- ☐ GMAT Geometry Guide (ISBN: 978-1-62926-061-7)
- ☐ GMAT Word Problems Guide (ISBN: 978-1-62926-062-4)
- ☐ GMAT Sets & Statistics Guide (ISBN: 978-1-62926-063-1)
- ☐ GMAT Combinatorics & Probability Guide (ISBN: 978-1-62926-064-8)
- ☐ GMAT Data Sufficiency Guide (ISBN: 978-1-62926-065-5)
- ☐ GMAT Quantitative Question Bank (ISBN: 978-1-62926-066-2)
- ☐ GMAT Sentence Correction Guide (ISBN: 978-1-62926-067-9)
- ■ GMAT Critical Reasoning Guide (ISBN: 978-1-62926-068-6)
- ☐ GMAT Reading Comprehension Guide (ISBN: 978-1-62926-069-3)
- ☐ GMAT Integrated Reasoning Guide (ISBN: 978-1-62926-070-9)
- ☐ GMAT Analytical Writing Guide (ISBN: 978-1-62926-071-6)
- ☐ GMAT Vocabulary Builder (ISBN: 978-1-62926-072-3)

About the Company

Manhattan Review's origin can be traced directly back to an Ivy League MBA classroom in 1999. While teaching advanced quantitative subjects to MBAs at Columbia Business School in New York City, Professor Dr. Joern Meissner developed a reputation for explaining complicated concepts in an understandable way. Remembering their own less-than-optimal experiences preparing for the GMAT, Prof. Meissner's students challenged him to assist their friends, who were frustrated with conventional GMAT preparation options. In response, Prof. Meissner created original lectures that focused on presenting GMAT content in a simplified and intelligible manner, a method vastly different from the voluminous memorization and so-called tricks commonly offered by others. The new approach immediately proved highly popular with GMAT students, inspiring the birth of Manhattan Review.

Since its founding, Manhattan Review has grown into a multi-national educational services firm, focusing on GMAT preparation, MBA admissions consulting, and application advisory services, with thousands of highly satisfied students all over the world. The original lectures have been continuously expanded and updated by the Manhattan Review team, an enthusiastic group of master GMAT professionals and senior academics. Our team ensures that Manhattan Review offers the most time-efficient and cost-effective preparation available for the GMAT. Please visit www.ManhattanReview.com for further details.

About the Founder

Professor Dr. Joern Meissner has more than 25 years of teaching experience at the graduate and undergraduate levels. He is the founder of Manhattan Review, a worldwide leader in test prep services, and he created the original lectures for its first GMAT preparation class. Prof. Meissner is a graduate of Columbia Business School in New York City, where he received a PhD in Management Science. He has since served on the faculties of prestigious business schools in the United Kingdom and Germany. He is a recognized authority in the areas of supply chain management, logistics, and pricing strategy. Prof. Meissner thoroughly enjoys his research, but he believes that grasping an idea is only half of the fun. Conveying knowledge to others is even more fulfilling. This philosophy was crucial to the establishment of Manhattan Review, and remains its most cherished principle.

The Advantages of Using Manhattan Review

- ▶ **Time efficiency and cost effectiveness.**
    - For most people, the most limiting factor of test preparation is time.
    - It takes significantly more teaching experience to prepare a student in less time.
    - Our test preparation approach is tailored for busy professionals. We will teach you what you need to know in the least amount of time.

- ▶ **Our high-quality and dedicated instructors are committed to helping every student reach her/his goals.**

International Phone Numbers and Official Manhattan Review Websites

Manhattan Headquarters	+1-212-316-2000	www.manhattanreview.com
USA & Canada	+1-800-246-4600	www.manhattanreview.com
Argentina	+1-212-316-2000	www.review.com.ar
Australia	+61-3-9001-6618	www.manhattanreview.com
Austria	+43-720-115-549	www.review.at
Belgium	+32-2-808-5163	www.manhattanreview.be
Brazil	+1-212-316-2000	www.manhattanreview.com.br
Chile	+1-212-316-2000	www.manhattanreview.cl
China	+86-20-2910-1913	www.manhattanreview.cn
Czech Republic	+1-212-316-2000	www.review.cz
France	+33-1-8488-4204	www.review.fr
Germany	+49-89-3803-8856	www.review.de
Greece	+1-212-316-2000	www.review.com.gr
Hong Kong	+852-5808-2704	www.review.hk
Hungary	+1-212-316-2000	www.review.co.hu
India	+1-212-316-2000	www.review.in
Indonesia	+1-212-316-2000	www.manhattanreview.id
Ireland	+1-212-316-2000	www.gmat.ie
Italy	+39-06-9338-7617	www.manhattanreview.it
Japan	+81-3-4589-5125	www.manhattanreview.jp
Malaysia	+1-212-316-2000	www.review.my
Netherlands	+31-20-808-4399	www.manhattanreview.nl
New Zealand	+1-212-316-2000	www.review.co.nz
Philippines	+1-212-316-2000	www.review.ph
Poland	+1-212-316-2000	www.review.pl
Portugal	+1-212-316-2000	www.review.pt
Qatar	+1-212-316-2000	www.review.qa
Russia	+1-212-316-2000	www.manhattanreview.ru
Singapore	+65-3158-2571	www.gmat.sg
South Africa	+1-212-316-2000	www.manhattanreview.co.za
South Korea	+1-212-316-2000	www.manhattanreview.kr
Sweden	+1-212-316-2000	www.gmat.se
Spain	+34-911-876-504	www.review.es
Switzerland	+41-435-080-991	www.review.ch
Taiwan	+1-212-316-2000	www.gmat.tw
Thailand	+66-6-0003-5529	www.manhattanreview.com
Turkey	+1-212-316-2000	www.review.com.tr
United Arab Emirates	+1-212-316-2000	www.manhattanreview.ae
United Kingdom	+44-20-7060-9800	www.manhattanreview.co.uk
Rest of World	+1-212-316-2000	www.manhattanreview.com

Contents

1 **Introduction**   1

2 **Critical Reasoning Concepts**   3
   2.1 What is Critical Reasoning? 3
     2.1.1 What is an Argument? 4
     2.1.2 Not all arguments have conclusions 6
     2.1.3 Placement of conclusion 6
   2.2 Drill - Identifying Premises and Conclusions 8
   2.3 Only the author can conclude 8
   2.4 Markers of Conclusions and Premises 9
   2.5 The Conclusion test 10
   2.6 Counter-premises 11
   2.7 Intermediate conclusion 12
   2.8 Application of basic knowledge in GMAT CR questions 12
   2.9 Premises cannot be challenged, but the conclusion can be 13
   2.10 CR question types 16

3 **Find the Assumption**   19
   3.1 Find the Assumption question type 19
     3.1.1 Predicting the assumption 21
     3.1.2 Beware of new information 22
   3.2 The process of solving CR questions 23
     3.2.1 The Negation Test 27
     3.2.2 Quantity Words and Their Negation 27
   3.3 Examples 30
   3.4 Practice Questions 42
     3.4.1 Questions 42
     3.4.2 Answer-Key 46
     3.4.3 Solutions 48
   3.5 References for Official Guide Questions 54

4 **Strengthen the Argument**   55
   4.1 Strengthen the Argument Question type 55
   4.2 The Process Of Solving Strengthen The Argument Questions 58
     4.2.1 Predicting the qualifier 58
     4.2.2 Predicting the Strengthener 58
   4.3 Examples 61
   4.4 Practice Questions 71

	4.4.1 Questions	71
	4.4.2 Answer-Key	74
	4.4.3 Solutions	76
4.5	References for Official Guide Questions	81

5 Weaken the Argument — 83
- 5.1 Weaken the Argument Question type 83
- 5.2 The Process Of Solving Weaken The Argument Questions 86
  - 5.2.1 Predicting the Weakener 86
  - 5.2.2 Weaken Vs. Flaw Questions 87
- 5.3 Examples 89
- 5.4 Practice Questions 102
  - 5.4.1 Questions 102
  - 5.4.2 Answer-Key 107
  - 5.4.3 Solutions 109
- 5.5 References for Official Guide Questions 118

6 Evaluate the Argument — 119
- 6.1 Evaluate the Argument Question type 119
- 6.2 The Process Of Solving Evaluate The Argument Questions 121
  - 6.2.1 Predicting the Evaluator 121
  - 6.2.2 The Evaluation Test 123
- 6.3 Examples 126
- 6.4 Practice Questions 134
  - 6.4.1 Questions 134
  - 6.4.2 Answer-Key 136
  - 6.4.3 Solutions 138
- 6.5 References for Official Guide Questions 142

7 Find the Flaw in the Argument — 143
- 7.1 Find the Flaw Question type 143
  - 7.1.1 Differences between flaw and weaken question types 143
  - 7.1.2 Assumption vs. Flaw vs. Weaken question types 145
- 7.2 The Process Of Solving Find The Flaw Argument Questions 147
  - 7.2.1 Predicting the qualifier 147
  - 7.2.2 Predicting the Flaw 147
- 7.3 Examples 150
- 7.4 Practice Questions 157
  - 7.4.1 Questions 157
  - 7.4.2 Answer-Key 159
  - 7.4.3 Solutions 161
- 7.5 References for Official Guide Questions 166

8 Method of Reasoning — 167
- 8.1 Method of Reasoning Question type 167
- 8.2 The Process Of Solving Method of Reasoning Argument Questions ... 170
- 8.3 Examples 172
- 8.4 Practice Questions 178

Critical Reasoning Guide ix

        8.4.1 Questions 178
        8.4.2 Answer-Key 180
        8.4.3 Solutions 182
    8.5 References for Official Guide Questions 184

9 Parallel Reasoning Argument   185
    9.1 Parallel Reasoning Argument Question type 185
    9.2 The Process Of Solving Parallel Reasoning Argument Questions 187
    9.3 Examples 191
    9.4 Practice Questions 196
        9.4.1 Questions 196
        9.4.2 Answer-Key 197
        9.4.3 Solutions 199

10 Boldface Argument   201
    10.1 Boldface Argument Question type 201
    10.2 The Process Of Solving Boldface Questions 206
    10.3 Examples 208
    10.4 Practice Questions 216
        10.4.1 Questions 216
        10.4.2 Answer-Key 218
        10.4.3 Solutions 220
    10.5 References for Official Guide Questions 223

11 Resolve the Paradox Argument   225
    11.1 Resolve the Paradox Argument Question type 225
    11.2 The Process Of Solving Resolve The Paradox Questions 228
    11.3 Examples 231
    11.4 Practice Questions 239
        11.4.1 Questions 239
        11.4.2 Answer-Key 241
        11.4.3 Solutions 243
    11.5 References for Official Guide Questions 247

12 Inference Argument   249
    12.1 The Inference Argument Question type 249
    12.2 The Difference Between Strengthen And Inference Question Types 251
    12.3 The Process Of Solving Inference Questions 252
    12.4 Examples 257
    12.5 Practice Questions 264
        12.5.1 Questions 264
        12.5.2 Answer-Key 266
        12.5.3 Solutions 268
    12.6 References for Official Guide Questions 272

13 Complete the Argument — 273
- 13.1 The Complete the Argument Question type 273
- 13.2 The Process Of Solving Complete The Argument Questions 275
- 13.3 Examples 278
- 13.4 Practice Questions 284
  - 13.4.1 Questions 284
  - 13.4.2 Answer-Key 286
  - 13.4.3 Solutions 288
- 13.5 References for Official Guide Questions 292

14 Summary — 293
- 14.1 Approaches for different question types in a nutshell 293
- 14.2 References for Official Guide Questions 296

15 Practice Questions — 299
- 15.1 Practice Questions' Answerkey 341
- 15.2 Practice Questions' Solution 344

16 Talk to Us — 405

Chapter 1

Introduction

Dear students,

At Manhattan Review, we constantly strive to provide the best educational content for preparation of standardized tests, putting arduous effort into improvement. This continuous evolution is very important for an examination like the GMAT, which also evolves constantly. Sadly, a GMAT aspirant is confused with too many options in the market. The challenge is how to choose a book or a tutor that prepares you to reach your goal. Without saying that we are the best, we leave it for you to judge.

This book differs in many aspects from standard books available on the market. Unlike any book from other prep companies, this book discusses as many as 11 question types. This comes directly as a result of students' feedback after finding that there is a scarcity of enough material, and questions with detailed explanations on rare to super rare categories of questions like Find the Flaw, Method of Reasoning, and Parallel Reasoning. Out of over 200 questions discussed in the book, over 30 questions belong to these categories. Another distinctive feature of our book is that each question is explained in a three tier structure—understanding the argument construction; predicting the qualifying answer beforehand; and explaining each option with an emphasis on why the correct answer is right and the incorrect answers are wrong.

Additionally, GMAT aspirants find that a few question types are usually confused with other question types, such as Find the Assumption being confused with Strengthen the Argument, Inference with Strengthen the Argument, and Find the Flaw with Weaken the Argument. This book highlights the key differences between such pairs of confusing question types, and presents their salient features in a tabular form to help students understand their nuances.

Every question type's core concept is also illustrated through an info-graphic strip and other graphic aids to make its gist memorable and easy to relate to. One of the best tools is three tests discussed in detail: first, the conclusion test - a test to correctly identify the main conclusion from between two; second, the negation test - a test to correctly identify the necessary assumption between two seemingly correct assumptions; and third, the evaluation test - a test to correctly identify the correct evaluating question between two seemingly correct such questions.

In a nut shell, Manhattan Review's GMAT-CR book is holistic and comprehensive in all respects;

it has been created this way because we listen to what students need. Should you have any queries, please feel free to write to us at *info@manhattanreview.com*.

Happy Learning!

Professor Dr. Joern Meissner
& The Manhattan Review Team

Chapter 2

Critical Reasoning Concepts

2.1 What is Critical Reasoning?

Critical Reasoning (CR) is one of the three types of questions that make up the verbal section of the GMAT. A CR question comprises a logic-based argument and a specific instruction followed by five options, only one of which is correct. A typical CR question looks like the followoing.

CR Argument

Premises "The new subway line, opened barely a year ago to alleviate traffic congestion, has already been deemed insufficient in satisfying demand. The State Transport Authority (STA), commissioned by the Mayor's office to come up with solutions, has admitted that even if more trains and carriages are added, the demand is such that only a 23% reduction in congestion would be feasible. **Conclusion** For this reason, the city council is now considering building a new highway linking the downtown business district with the East Canton suburbs."

Premise(s) + Conclusion = Argument

Question Stem Which of the following would most weaken the conclusion of the above argument?

Options

(A) One year is insufficient time to judge the viability of the subway.

(B) A ride-sharing program has been successfully operating for more than a year.

(C) The business district suffers from a chronic shortage of parking spaces.

(D) Some residents in the business district are opposed to the program.

(E) The cost of the proposed highway would severely strain the city's budget.

2.1.1 What is an Argument?

An argument is a composition of reasoning and conclusion designed to make some point. The writer of the argument is called the author. He is not to be confused with the test-maker – GMAC. The author wants the reader to believe in a point called the **conclusion.** The reasoning on which he bases his conclusion is called the **premise.**

There can be more than one premise in an argument, but there can be only one main conclusion. In some arguments, you may see an intermediate conclusion as well, but keep in mind there will only ever be one main conclusion.

Let us examine an argument to better understand this point.

> Companies Pinnacle and Acme provide round-the-clock email assistance to any customer who uses their laptops. Customers send emails only when they find the laptop difficult to use. Since Pinnacle receives four times as many emails as Acme receives, Pinnacle's laptops must be more difficult to use than Acme's.

What is the author's purpose in writing this argument?

The author provides information about two companies — Pinnacle and Acme. These companies provide 24/7 email support to their customers regarding laptop usage problems. The author further states that customers send emails only when they face problems using their laptops.

The purpose of the argument is to <u>conclude</u> that **Pinnacle's laptops must be more difficult to use than Acme's,** and the reasoning advanced by the author in support of that conclusion is that **Pinnacle receives four times as many emails as Acme** and that **customers send emails only when they face problems using their laptops.** Since customers send emails only when they face problems in using the laptops, more emails sent to Pinnacle implies that its laptops are more difficult to use than Acme's.

Break-down of the argument

Background Information: *Companies Pinnacle and Acme provide round-the-clock email assistance to any customer who uses their laptops.*

Role: This statement is to introduce the reader to two companies, their businesses, and their service to their customers.

Premise1: *Customers send emails only when they find the laptops difficult to use.*

Role: This is a statement which tells the reader that customers send emails only when they face problems. This is a **premise.** There is reasoning hidden in this statement. If this premise is missing, and one company receives a higher number of emails than the other from customers, you cannot necessarily conclude that the emails are related to customer concerns over laptop problems. You might assume that most emails are related to sales inquiries or for other purposes, hence the motive behind writing premise 1: **Customers send emails only when they find the laptop difficult to use** is to help us to conclude something.

> A **premise** is any **statement, information, fact, evidence, or viewpoint** the author uses to reach his conclusion.

Premise2: *Pinnacle receives four times as many emails as Acme receives.*

Role: This statement is easy to understand. This is also a **premise.** It means that the number of emails received by Pinnacle = 4 x the number of emails received by Acme. Based on this reasoning, that Pinnacle receives more emails than Acme receives, the author concludes something.

Conclusion: *Pinnacle's laptops must be more difficult to use than Acme's.*

Role: This statement is also easy to understand. This is the purpose or the **conclusion of the argument.**

Premises and Conclusion

Identify premises and conclusion

1. Humidity has been rising for the last 10 days. Therefore, sales of air-conditioners will rise in coastal areas.

   Premise: Humidity has been rising for the last 10 days.
   Conclusion: Therefore, sales of air-conditioners will rise in coastal areas.

2. The floods destroyed groundnut crops this season. A rise in the prices of their oil is inevitable.

   Premise: The floods destroyed groundnut crops this season.
   Conclusion: A rise in the prices of their oil is inevitable.

3. The floods destroyed onion crops this season. However, a neighboring country has achieved record onion production. "Hence," the inevitability of a rise in prices is false.

Premise 1: The floods destroyed onion crops this season.

Premise 2: However, a neighboring country has achieved record onion production.

Conclusion: Hence, the inevitability of a rise in prices is false.

2.1.2 Not all arguments have conclusions

We saw earlier that each argument had at least a premise and a conclusion, but not every argument has a conclusion. An argument can be devoid of a conclusion, and you may be asked to draw one based on the premises of the argument.

Let us examine such an argument.

> Companies X and Y have clocked almost equal sales this quarter. While company X has surpassed company Y in home computer sales, company Y did the same to company X in the business computer category.

What is the conclusion here? Well, it is not mentioned. What is (are) the premise(s)? These can certainly be identified.

Premise 1: Companies X and Y have clocked almost equal sales this quarter.

Premise 2: While company X has surpassed company Y in home computer sales, company Y did the same to company X in the business computer category.

The question again crops up. What is the conclusion? There could be many conclusions here. Only the author has the authority to conclude. If you had been the author, what conclusion would you have drawn?

Probable conclusion: The industry is likely to see a close fight in the next quarter as well between these two companies.

2.1.3 Placement of conclusion

How do you identify a conclusion? Is the conclusion the last statement of the argument? Not really! Usually it is, but not always. It can be placed anywhere in the argument.

Let us see a few examples of variously placed conclusions.

Conclusion at the end

> The floods destroyed onion crops this season. However, a neighboring country has achieved record onion production. **Hence, the inevitability of a rise in prices is false.**

Conclusion in the middle

> The floods destroyed onion crops this season. **Hence, a rise in prices is likely.** However, a record production of onions achieved by a neighboring country might counter a price rise.

Conclusion in the beginning

> **A rise in prices of onions is likely,** as the floods destroyed onion crops this season. However, a record production of onions achieved by a neighboring country may counter a price rise.

2.2 Drill - Identifying Premises and Conclusions

Q1- Steve was awarded Best Player of the Season by the State Sports Committee. Steve will make his career in sports.

Q2- Now only rain can make things better for the country. Disappointed farmers have utilized their existing water resources to the fullest. The level of water in dams has reached a record low.

Q3- The new course curriculum of Midland High School is praiseworthy. The school maintains a good mix of academics and sports. This is the need of the hour. Many schools have followed Midland.

Q4- Gold prices have skyrocketed this year. However, silver has lagged behind.

Answers

Q1: Premise: Steve....committee. Conclusion: Steve will....sports.
Q2 : Conclusion: Only rain can...country. Premise 1: Disappointed....fullest. Premise 2: The....low.
Q3 : Premise 1: New.... praiseworthy. Premise 2: The school....sports. Conclusion: This....hour. Premise 3: Many.....Midland.
Q4 : Premise 1: Gold....year. Premise 2: However....behind. No conclusion.

2.3 Only the author can conclude

Please read the following argument and find the conclusion.

> Due to frequent accidents occurring at Junction 16 on National Highway 4, the traffic commissioner concluded that the National Highway Construction Company is at fault. However, this is unreasonable. The same highway design was also implemented on National Highway number 7.

What is the conclusion in the above argument?

The National Highway Construction Company is at fault.

OR

This (that National Highway Construction Company is at fault) is unreasonable.

The **conclusion** is: **This is unreasonable.**
You must keep in mind the definition of the conclusion: a viewpoint of the author that he wants you to believe. Only the author can state the conclusion, and no one else. It is clear that the first statement is the conclusion drawn by the traffic commissioner; however, the second statement is the viewpoint, or conclusion, of the author.

2.4 Markers of Conclusions and Premises

Markers are words and phrases that are commonly used to present premises and conclusions. In most of the arguments, these markers help a lot in determining the premises and the conclusion swiftly.

Below is a partial list of words and phrases that commonly precede the premises or the conclusion:

Premise Markers	Conclusion Markers
Since	Therefore
Due to	Hence
Owing to	It shows that
Because	It follows that
For	It can be concluded that
Given that	Thus
For example	So
As stated	Consequently
As reasoned	As a result
Besides	Clearly
In addition	Accordingly
Additionally	
Moreover	
Furthermore	"However"

This list is not comprehensive and there is no need to memorize these markers. The purpose is to get an idea about the conclusion and the premises in the argument.

A little more on identifying conclusions

Some argument may not have any conclusion marker. How do you identify the conclusion in such arguments? To ascertain the conclusion, always pose the question—what is the author trying to conclude?

Let us look at the following argument.

> The revised Duckworth-Lewis system would be a game-changer. For a long time now, it has been debated whether cricket needs an overhaul. Revitalization of cricket will be observed in many cricket-playing countries.

What is the conclusion here?

Is it *The revised Duckworth-Lewis system would be a game-changer*?

or

Revitalization of cricket will be observed in many cricket-playing countries?

The absence of markers makes the conclusion difficult to identify. There are two conclusions in the argument. One of them is an **intermediate conclusion** and the other one is the **main conclusion.** To identify the main conclusion, one must ask "what is the author trying to advocate?" Is it *Duckworth-Lewis system: a game-changer* or *Revitalization of cricket*?. It is the latter.

If you still have any doubt over what the author is trying to advocate, you may apply the **conclusion test shown below**

2.5 The Conclusion test

If you have a doubt over two statements, both being conclusions, and there is no clue which is the main one, apply the conclusion test.

Statement 1: The revised Duckworth-Lewis system would be a game-changer.

Statement 2: Revitalization of cricket will be observed in many cricket-playing countries.

> "If <**statement 1**>, therefore, <statement 2>." makes better sense, then < **statement 2**> is the conclusion.
>
> Conversely, "If < **statement 2**>, therefore, < **statement 1**>." makes better sense, then < **statement 1**> is the conclusion.

> Let us apply this test on the argument we discussed above.
>
> **S1, therefore, S2:** *The revised Duckworth-Lewis system would be a game-changer;* **therefore,** *revitalization of cricket will be observed in many cricket-playing countries.*
>
> **S2, therefore, S1:** *Revitalization of cricket will be observed in many cricket-playing countries;* **therefore,** *the revised Duckworth-Lewis system would be a game-changer.*

Clearly, **S1, therefore, S2** makes better sense, as because of the revised D-W system, cricket will be revitalized in many countries. Whereas **S2, therefore, S1** does not make sense, as revitalization of cricket in many countries will not make the revised D-W system a game-changer. Hence statement 2: *Revitalization of cricket will be observed in many cricket-playing countries* is the main conclusion.

Let us take another argument.

> Mere practice does not make one a champion. Winning is everything. One must strive hard to win.

Let us say statement 1 is *Winning is everything* and statement 2 is *One must strive hard to win*.

Let us apply the test.

S1, therefore, S2; *Winning is everything;* **therefore,** *one must strive hard to win.*

S2; therefore, S1; *One must strive hard to win;* **therefore,** *winning is everything.*

Clearly, **S1, therefore, S2** makes better sense, as the act of striving hard is driven by the objective: winning is everything. Hence statement 2, *One must strive hard to win* is the main conclusion.

2.6 Counter-premises

A few arguments may include premises that go against the conclusion of the argument.

What is the purpose of such premises? If the purpose of the argument is to formulate the conclusion and ultimately convince the reader about it, why does the author present some information that goes against his conclusion?

The author does so because his stated premises and conclusion may invite some counter-arguments. To safe-guard the conclusion, the author sometimes presents counter-premises himself and then argues against those counter-premises. A premise that goes against the conclusion is called a **counter-premise.**

Let us examine a counter-premise in an argument:

> Credited with benevolent behavior, Mr. Jackson must not be fired from the company, though he mishandled the case.

What are the conclusion and the premise?

Conclusion: Mr. Jackson must not be fired from the company.

Premise: He is benevolent.

What role does the statement "*though he mishandled the case*" play?

The statement goes against the conclusion. Therefore, this statement is a **counter-premise.**

As we said above, the author presents a counter-premise because the stated premises may invite some counter-arguments, and he wishes to prevent those from weakening his argument. One could have countered the argument by stating "Mr. Jackson must be fired from the company, because *he mishandled the case.*"

Without the counter-premise added, the argument may look weak. The author has strengthened his argument against criticism by presenting the counter-premise. The conclusion is still valid as the premise counts more than the counter-premise.

2.7 Intermediate conclusion

An intermediate conclusion is a conclusion derived in the argument to support the main conclusion of the argument.

Let us see through an example:

> Since mere practice does not make you a champion, one must learn strategies to win. Since winning is everything, anyone can become a champion.

What is the conclusion in the above argument?

Conclusion: Anyone can become a champion.

Premise 1: Mere practice does not make you a champion.

Premise 2: Winning is everything.

What is the statement *One must learn strategies to win*? This also acts as a conclusion...right! But it is not the main conclusion. We have already identified that the main conclusion is: **Anyone can become a champion.** So, we name *One must learn strategies to win* an intermediate conclusion, one that supports the main conclusion.

2.8 Application of basic knowledge in GMAT CR questions

CR questions require only basic knowledge to solve the questions. There is no bias towards an expert on worldly affairs or one in possession of many facts about any particular subject.

CR questions require basic knowledge that is is universally known and undisputed.

For example: a premise is *The tax rate for the IT industry has doubled.* You should know that tax is a type of cost for the companies and it will negatively impact the profit; however, you cannot infer that the profit will go down for sure.

Another example: Consider this relationship:

Sales = Cost + Profit

This relationship among sales, cost, and profit is a fact and cannot be disputed. Therefore, this basic knowledge is used in GMAT CR.

Some key financial terms such as **budget** and **deficit** are considered basic knowledge. However, high order financial terms and their implications are not expected. If they are used in the argument, the argument will either define them, or, if it does not, the question does not need that knowledge in order to solve it. GMAT does not expect you to know the difference between terms like **budgetary deficit and monetary deficit.**

2.9 Premises cannot be challenged, but the conclusion can be

Most GMAT CR arguments comprise a premise and conclusion. Some may have background information, premises, and a conclusion. Others may have background information, premises, counter-premises, an intermediate conclusion, and a main conclusion. A few may have only premises.

GMAT CR questions are designed to assess your reasoning ability. You must not mix up real world knowledge with GMAT CR arguments. We have already stated that the premises play the role of facts. Since they are facts, we cannot challenge them.

However, we can question the conclusion. This is only because the conclusion is derived by the author after applying his reasoning to the facts—the premises. We also learned that the conclusion can be drawn only by the author. So, in a nut shell, can we doubt the author? The answer is yes! But this does not mean that we doubt the author's integrity. We believe that the facts presented (premises, as well as counter-premises) are true, but author's reasoning could be wrong!

> *Premises and counter-premises cannot be challenged.*
>
> *Conclusions and intermediate conclusions can be challenged.*

Let us understand this with an example:

> Marijuana works well for arthritis and ailments, hence its controlled consumption should be legalized.

Premise: Marijuana works well for arthritis and ailments.

Conclusion: Its (Marijuana) controlled consumption should be legalized.

In the real world, you can dispute the premise: **Marijuana works well for arthritis and ailments,** but for the sake of this question, you cannot challenge it. You have to accept it as it is. However, you may doubt the conclusion: **Its (Marijuana's) controlled consumption should be legalized,** since the conclusion is derived from the premise.

It has been observed that test-makers craft the options in a few questions in such a way that it does not seem like the option is challenging the premise, and you may fall into the trap. Whenever there is an option which goes against the premise, you must discard it as inconsistent with the premise.

Let us see a premise and some statements. We will sort each statement on the basis of whether it is consistent or inconsistent with the premise.

Premise: Motorbikes with less than 150 cc capacity are worthless to speedsters.

Statement 1: Speedsters drive all types of motorbikes for an adrenaline rush: less than 150 cc models as well as those that are more than 150 cc.

This statement is **inconsistent** as the premise clearly states that, for speedsters, motorbikes with less than 150 cc capacity are worthless, implying that they will not drive such motorbikes for an adrenaline rush. The statement says that speedsters do not make a distinction between bikes with less than 150 cc and more than 150 cc because they like to drive all motorbikes for an adrenaline rush. It goes against the premise, and hence is inconsistent.

Statement 2: Many speedsters do not drive motorbikes with less than 150 cc capacity for an adrenaline rush.

This statement is **consistent** with the premise.

Statement 3: Some speedsters drive motorbikes with more than 150 cc capacity for an adrenaline rush.

This statement is also **consistent** with the premise.

Statement 4: Some speedsters drive 125-350 cc motorbikes for an adrenaline rush.

This statement is also **inconsistent** with the premise. This statement is cleverly crafted with the usage of the ambiguous quantity word "some" and an unqualified range: 125-350 cc motorbikes.

Let us look at the following argument, which has two premises.

> Companies Pinnacle and Acme provide round-the-clock e-mail assistance to any customer who uses their laptops. Customers send e-mails only when they find the laptop difficult to use.

Premise 1: Companies Pinnacle and Acme provide round-the-clock email assistance to any customer who uses their laptops.

Premise 2: Customers send emails only when they find the laptop difficult to use.

Statement 1: The number of sales inquiries through email is significantly more for Acme than for Pinnacle.

This statement is **inconsistent** with premise 2. Premise 2: *Customers send emails only when they find the laptop difficult to use,* clearly states that customers send emails only when they have trouble using the laptop, hence there is no question of emails sent by customers for any other purpose.

Statement 2: Acme is far more prompt in responding to customers' emails between 10 pm and 6 am, while Pinnacle responds to emails the next day between 6 am and 8 am.

This statement is **inconsistent** with premise 1. Premise 1: *Companies Pinnacle and Acme provide round-the-clock email assistance to any customer who uses their laptops,* clearly states that Pinnacle and Acme provide round-the-clock email assistance to any customer, hence there is no question of not responding to the emails during the 10 pm-6 am period.

Statement 3: Some customers prefer to raise their concerns on the phone rather than send emails.

This statement is **consistent.** The statement does not conflict with any premise. Even though premise 2 states that **Customers send emails only when they find the laptop difficult to use,** it does not mean that no one can mail a letter or telephone the companies to discuss their concerns.

2.10 CR question types

Critical Reasoning arguments are followed by a question stem (except in one question type; we will discuss it later). There are approximately 11 different types of CR questions. The question stem, followed by the argument, determines which type of CR question the argument belongs to. Each question type requires a different type of strategy to solve, hence it very important to identify the question type.

We classify 11 different question types based on the family of question types they belong to. GMAT-CR question types can be classified into three families.

(1) **The assumption-based family:** Finding the assumption is at the core of solving these questions. Five question types belong to this classification—find the assumption, strengthen the argument, weaken the argument, evaluate the argument, and find the flaw.

(2) **The structure-based family:** Understanding the structure of the argument is the key to solving these questions. Three question types belong to this classification—boldface (role play) questions, method of reasoning, and parallel reasoning.

(3) **The evidence-based family:** Understanding the inference or the evidence from the argument is the key to solving these questions. Two question types belong to this classification—inference questions, and resolve the paradox.

The complete the argument question type does not belong to any family. This question type may have a mix of many question types.

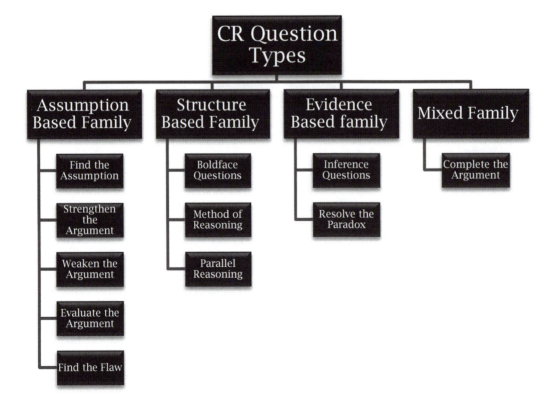

From the next chapter onwards, we will understand, develop an approach to solve, and practice questions of each question type.

Chapter 3

Find the Assumption

3.1 Find the Assumption question type

Find the assumption questions belong to the assumption-based family. These questions require us to identify the assumption made by the author to reach the conclusion.

An assumption in an argument is a premise that the author must assume to be true in order to draw the conclusion. However, the assumption is unstated in the argument.

Assumption questions are frequently asked question types in Critical Reasoning. In our daily lives, we also make many assumptions. Take a real life situation: *You have to fly from London to New York.* How many assumptions do we make during this travel?

You may assume: **The plane will take me to NY only; I will not be asked for additional money on the plane; the food available will be reasonably good; trained pilots will fly the plane; my seat will not be broken.**

In a CR question, you have to find the missing link between the stated premises and the conclusion. Your objective is to think "how can the premises and the unstated premise lead to the finite conclusion?" The act of finding out unstated premises implies finding out the assumption.

Look at the image below. There is a dialogue taking place between two persons. What do you think a necessary assumption is here?

By replying: *Yes, I have cracked the GMAT* to the question: *Can you solve this tricky question?*, there is an unstated assumption: **Those who crack the GMAT can solve tricky questions.** This is the purpose of this question type.

See the next example. What does the author of the argument below necessarily assume?

Messi will score a hat-trick in the match. So, Barcelona will again be the winner.

Premise: Messi will score a hat-trick in the match.

Conclusion: So, Barcelona will again be the winner.

When a player scores a hat-trick, the team wins the match.
Missing link = the Assumption

Most CR arguments will contain many assumptions. Any one assumption will not necessarily make the argument complete, but it will certainly make the conclusion more believable.

Let us examine the following argument.

Companies Pinnacle and Acme provide round-the-clock email assistance to any customer who uses their laptops. Customers send emails only when they find the laptop difficult to use. Since Pinnacle receives four times as many emails as Acme receives, Pinnacle's laptops must be more difficult to use than Acme's.

Let us first deconstruct the argument.

Background Information: *Companies Pinnacle and Acme provide round-the-clock email assistance to any customer who uses their laptops.*

Premise 1: *Customers send emails only when they find the laptop difficult to use.*

Premise 2: *Pinnacle receives four times as many emails as Acme receives.*

Conclusion: *Pinnacle's laptops must be more difficult to use than Acme's.*

Our job is to think about the unstated assumption(s) – the missing link – that connects the premises and the conclusion.

In a find the assumption question, there would be five options, out of which one is correct, but it is always recommended that you predict one or two assumptions on your own. There are two advantages to that. One, you will not be distracted by cleverly crafted options by the test-makers; and two, you will better understand the argument.

3.1.1 Predicting the assumption

To predict unstated assumptions, we must keep an eye on the conclusion—how to make the conclusion more believable. Remember that you must not provide new information to the argument. The assumption is something that is already there in the argument, but is not stated explicitly by the author.

Conclusion: *Pinnacle's laptops must be more difficult to use than Acme's.*

What if Acme receives more letters of complaint than Pinnacle does? The conclusion would seem less believable. So, there is a scope of an assumption.

Predictive Assumption 1: Acme does not receive more complaints through other means such as letters and phone calls than Pinnacle receives.

What if Acme sells significantly fewer laptops than Pinnacle does? It is obvious that Acme would then receive fewer emails than Pinnacle would. The conclusion would seem less believable. So, there is a scope of another assumption.

Predictive Assumption 2: Acme does not sell significantly fewer laptops than Pinnacle.

What if a significant number of Pinnacle's customers are new to using computers? Then it would be obvious that Pinnacle would receive more emails than Acme regarding how to use the laptop.

Predictive Assumption 3: Pinnacle does not sell significantly more laptops to customers who are new to computers than Acme.

Since the author compares the laptops of two companies, their laptops must be comparable in terms of configuration and features. If one company's laptop is high-end, and other is low-end, then the conclusion seems less believable.

Predictive Assumption 4: Both company's laptops are comparable in terms of configuration and features.

There may be a few assumptions that either do not matter or are not necessary. Let us look at a couple of them.

Assumption 1: Emails to Acme are more or less of the same length, on average, as to Pinnacle.

Assumption 2: Acme and Pinnacle have been in business for a sufficiently long period of time.

Remember that assumptions should work toward the conclusion. In a typical assumption question, you may come across such statements, and they may fall under the category of assumptions, but your job is to seek **necessary assumptions,** without which the argument is not believable.

The following illustration depicts your job for an assumption type question.

> Companies Pinnacle and Acme provide round-the-clock e-mail assistance to any customer who uses their laptops. Customers send e-mails only when they find the laptop difficult to use. Since Pinnacle receives four times as many e-mails as Acme receives, Pinnacle's laptops must be more difficult to use than Acme's.
>
> Which of the following is a necessary assumption required by the argument above?
>
> (A) Acme and Pinnacle have been in business for a sufficiently long period of time.
>
> (B) E-mails to Acme are more or less of the same length, on average, as to Pinnacle.
>
> (C) Acme does not get complaints that it can receive through other means such as letters.
>
> (D) The number of customers of both the companies has been gradually increasing.
>
> (E) Pinnacle's e-mail ID is not more widely publicized than Acme's e-mail ID.

Only one option must fit as necessary and unstated assumption and make the argument complete.

3.1.2 Beware of new information

Read the following statement.

Acme has three times the number of laptop customers that Pinnacle has.

The statement certainly makes the conclusion more believable, but the information given is additional information, and hence cannot be counted as assumption. For assumption questions, you have to extract the information hidden in the argument.

if any answer choices contain NEW INFO, it is wrong.

3.2 The process of solving CR questions

You know that there are 41 questions asked in the Verbal section of CR that need to be attempted in 75 minutes, averaging 1 minute and 50 seconds (so, less than 2 minutes). It is important to apply strategy to solve these questions correctly.

An untrained student will go back and forth between the argument, question stem, and options a few times. The student will reread the argument each time he/she reads the options. This will eat up precious time and put a lot of pressure on the test-taker. We recommend a 4-step approach to attempt a CR question.

The 4-step approach

(1) Recognize the question type

(2) Understand the argument construction

(3) Predict the qualifier

(4) Process of elimination

(1) **Recognize the question type**

FIRST As soon as you see CR questions after hitting the "Next" button on your GMAT exam, look at the "Question Stem" rather than the "Argument". Since there are around 10 types of CR questions, it is necessary that, as you read the argument, you keep in mind that you wish to seek out information from a specific point of view. Once you have seen all 10 question types, your mind will be trained to read the argument with a specific objective.

It is critically important to read the question stem fully. Many times students read only qualifying and selective words or phrases in the question stem and suffer greatly. Read the following question stem partially, and then read it fully, and notice the difference.

Questions stem: Which of the following most strengthens the position of the critics against the claim of the US government?

If you hurriedly read the stem and stopped at the word "Strengthen" and decided that is a question on "Strengthen the argument", you are in trouble. When you read fully, you realize that you have to strengthen the claim of critics. If the conclusion of the argument is written from the US government's perspective, then you are supposed to weaken the conclusion. The same question may be a "Weaken the argument" question type.

Invariably GMAT test-makers draft strengthen as well as weaken the argument options for each of the question types of "Strengthen the argument" and "Weaken the argument". So, be careful!

The step of recognizing the question type should not take more than 5 seconds.

(2) **Understand the argument construction**

After identifying the question type, we must understand and analyze the argument. How to analyze the argument? It requires an understanding of the logical structure of the argument: identifying background information, premises, and the conclusion. We have covered these in the previous chapter.

To understand the argument in bits and pieces, many students write notes on scratch-paper. Some write only the conclusion. Some don't, but most students do take some sort of notes. If you are a beginner, do start writing a brief summary for a week and gradually start taking notes in short-hand. The more questions you solve, the less you write; and later you will write notes only on the long-winded arguments.

I will show you my way of taking notes – rather, how I used to take notes! I will recall the 'Pinnacle and Acme' argument once again.

> Companies Pinnacle and Acme provide round-the-clock email assistance to any customer who uses their laptops. Customers send emails only when they find the laptop difficult to use. Since Pinnacle receives four times as many emails as Acme receives, Pinnacle's laptops must be more difficult to use than Acme's.
>
> Which of the following is a necessary assumption required by the argument above?

After reading the question stem, we identified that the question type is the "Assumption" question type. Look at the image below.

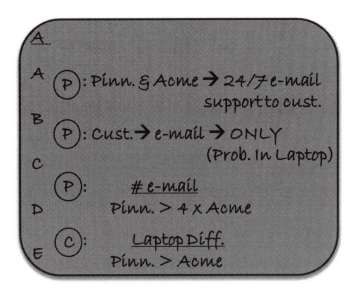

On the scratch-paper, write the question type in abbreviated form: here it is Assumption, so write A; write the 5 options A, B, C, D and E vertically. The first premise reads: *Companies Pinnacle and Acme provide round-the-clock email assistance to any customer who uses their laptops.* You can write in short hand: Pinn. for Pinnacle, Cust. for customer, arrows to show relation between two objects or events. It is totally up to you how you write notes in shorthand. You have to keep it alive for 2 minutes only. It is clear from the image that encircled C stands for conclusion: Laptop Difficult (Pinn. > Acme).

At this stage you will fully understand premises, the conclusion, and logical structure. Now your job is to find out the 4th premise—assumption.

You must not spend more than 60 to 70 seconds on this.

(3) **Predicting the qualifier**

Before jumping directly to the options, predict the qualifier. What is a qualifier? In this example, it is the predictive assumption you can think of. If a question is a strengthen the argument type, you have to predict what the strengthener for the conclusion could be. Similarly, for a weaken the argument type, you have to predict what the weakener for the conclusion could be.

We have done this exercise for this question. I have simply reproduced predictive assumptions for your ready reference. You may refer to the "Predicting Assumptions" section for details.

> **Predictive Assumption 1:** Acme does not receive more complaints than Pinnacle does through other means such as letters and phone calls.
> See the the image below for how you can write predictive assumption 1 in short form.
> **Predictive Assumption 2:** Acme does not sell significantly fewer laptops than Pinnacle.
> See the the image below for how you can write predictive assumption 2 in short form.
> **Predictive Assumption 3:** Both company's laptops must be comparable in terms of configuration and features.
> **Predictive Assumption 4:** Pinnacle does not sell significantly more laptops to customers who are new to computers than Acme.

Predicting qualifiers may not be feasible for some question types, but is always good practice to think of probable correct answer(s) from the test-maker's point of view.

You must not spend more than 30 seconds on this.

(4) **Process of Elimination**

The best approach to reach the correct answer is by going through the options one by one and eliminate what cannot be the answer or hold it as probable with a *?* mark. See the complete argument.

> Companies Pinnacle and Acme provide round-the-clock email assistance to any customer who uses their laptops. Customers send emails only when they find the laptop difficult to use. Since Pinnacle receives four times as many emails as Acme receives, Pinnacle's laptops must be more difficult to use than Acme's.
>
> Which of the following is a necessary assumption required by the argument above?
>
> (A) Acme and Pinnacle have been in business for a sufficiently long period of time.
> (B) Emails to Acme are more or less the same length, on average, as those to Pinnacle.
> (C) Acme does not receive more complaints than Pinnacle receives through other means such as letters and phone calls.
> (D) The number of emails received by each of the two companies has been gradually increasing.
> (E) Pinnacle's email address is not more widely publicized than Acme's email address.

Please see the image below.

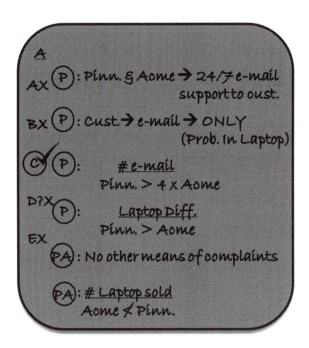

The advantage of predicting a qualifier is that, first, you may find a similarly worded option, and second, you will not be carried away by cleverly crafted incorrect options.

You must not think that your predicted qualifier must be present in the options; it may or may not be present. For the "Pinnacle and Acme" question, we predicted four assumptions; but in the actual test, you will not be able to think of more than two assumptions due to lack of time.

3.2.1 The Negation Test

You may come across a situation where you have trouble choosing between two options. It may seem that both options are correct. First, to choose between the two, ask yourself—Is this option a necessary option? In most questions, you can zero in on one option. If you still cannot decide on one option, apply the negation test.

Let's say that in the "Pinnacle and Acme" argument, you are torn between options C and E. The process for selecting one option is as follows.

(1) Negate the first option

(2) If the option shatters the conclusion, then it is the correct answer.

(3) Negate the second option

(4) If the option shatters the conclusion, then it is the correct answer.

(5) On all assumption questions, this test works. If you are still not able to decide, then revisit the argument and check your understanding of the conclusion.

Option C: Acme does not receive more complaints than Pinnacle receives through other means such as letters and phone calls.

Negation of C: Acme receives more complaints than Pinnacle receives through other means such as letters and phone calls.

Impact on the conclusion: The conclusion: **Pinnacle's laptops must be more difficult to use than Acme's** is derived from the premise: *Pinnacle receives four times as many emails as Acme receives* will be shattered. If Pinnacle receives more complaints through emails, whereas Acme receives it through letters and phone calls, the author cannot conclude that *Pinnacle's laptops must be more difficult to use than Acme's*. Hence option C seems to be the correct answer!

Let us try this test on option E.

Option E: Pinnacle's email address is not more widely publicized than Acme's e-mail address.

Negation of E: Pinnacle's email address is more widely publicized than Acme's e-mail address.

Impact on the conclusion: *If Pinnacle's email address is more widely publicized than Acme's email address,* then the conclusion: *Pinnacle's laptops must be more difficult to use than Acme's* does not get impacted. We cannot assume that a more widely publicized email address will make customers send more emails concerning complaints. Option C is the correct answer!

3.2.2 Quantity Words and Their Negation

Sometime you come across quantity words like Some, All, None, Few, Not All, Most, Many, Always, Never, and Significant. When you negate these quantity words, the knowledge of the real world and the GMAT perspective clash.

Refer to the following table with the quantitative range of these quantity words and their opposites.

Quantity Words	Quantitative Range (In a sample of 100 people)	Opposite
Some	(1-100); 0 excluded	None
No/None	0	Some
All	100	Not All
Not All	0-99; 100 excluded	All
Never	0	Sometimes
Most/Many	Majority; Sizable; More than 50; 51-100	Minority; Not sizable; Less than 50; 0-50
Always	100	Not Always
Significant	Sizable; Considerable	Insignificant

Example Questions

3.3 Examples

Example 1

Since motorbikes less than 150 cc are worthless to speedsters, the State Transport Officer plans to reduce the number of accidents committed by the 18-21 age group by restricting them to drive motorbikes less than 150 cc.

The State Transport Officer (STO) assumes that ....

(A) Some experts find motorbikes less than 150 cc are not less prone to causing accidents than motorbikes more than 150 cc.

(B) Speedsters drive all types of motorbikes—less than 150 cc and more than 150 cc.

(C) All motorbikes more than 150 cc have disk-brakes that come standard, inducing speedsters to drive fast.

(D) Imposing fixed penalty tickets on speedsters will decrease the number of accidents they commit.

(E) Speedsters do not drive motorbikes that are worthless to them.

Argument construction

The State Transport Officer plans to reduce the number of accidents committed by the 18-21 age group by restricting them to drive motorbikes less than 150 cc.

Premise: Motorbikes less than 150 cc are worthless to speedsters.

Conclusion: Restricting the 18-21 age group to drive motorbikes less than 150 cc will reduce the number of accidents they commit.

Predict an assumption

We can predict the following assumptions based on the premise and the conclusion.

Based on the premise—motorbikes less than 150 cc are worthless to speedsters, the STO plans to restrict the 18-21 age group to drive motorbikes less than 150 cc so that the number of accidents they cause will be reduced. It implies that the STO assumes that speedsters find motorbikes more than 150 cc worth driving.

Predictive Assumption 1: Speedsters find motorbikes more than 150 cc worth driving.

Another assumption may be that the STO targets the 18-21 age group. It implies that the STO assumes that most speedsters fall in the 18-21 age group.

Predictive Assumption 2: Most speedsters fall in the 18-21 age group.

The STO also assumes that by imposing a restriction on the 18-21 age group, the youth will comply with it.

Predictive Assumption 3: Speedsters will obey the restriction imposed on them.

Last but not least—the STO assumes that motorbikes less than 150 cc are less prone to causing accidents than motorbikes more than 150 cc.

Predictive Assumption 4: Motorbikes less than 150 cc are less prone to causing accidents than motorbikes more than 150 cc .

Answer choice explanation

(A) This option is **inconclusive**. 'Some' is a tricky quantity word. In the real world, we may equate 'Some' to a significant number, but in the GMAT, 'Some' may range from anything between 0% to 100%; 0 is excluded, hence it is inconclusive. Had 'some' been replaced with 'many', probably the statement would have qualified to be an assumption.

(B) This option is **inconsistent**. It goes against the premise. No one can challenge the premise, even if in the real world, the opposite may seem true. The premise already states that motorbikes less than 150 cc are worthless to speedsters, hence option C is against the premise, as it states that speedsters drive all types of motorbikes including those less than 150 cc (worthless).

(C) This option is **irrelevant**. Why speedsters drive fast is not relevant.

(D) This option is out of scope. The penalty aspect is outside the scope of the argument.

(E) This is the **correct** answer. It is aligned with predictive assumption 1.

The correct answer is option E.

Example 2

Edward Snowden was considered an up-and-coming Julian Assange, the infamous yet upright whistleblower, till the US declared him a spy and issued a warrant against him. It is clear that if the warrant was justified, then Snowden was either an amateur or else a traitor. Soon after the issue of the warrant, however, it was clear that he had never been amateurish. Thus, one can conclude that Snowden must be a traitor.

Which one of the following states an assumption upon which the argument depends?

(A) Snowden was a low-profile intelligence officer.

(B) A warrant for anyone who is a traitor would be justified.

(C) Anyone whose warrant is justified is a traitor.

(D) If someone is a traitor or amateurish, then his warrant is justified.

(E) Snowden's warrant was justified.

Argument construction

Snowden was considered a whistleblower until the US declared him a spy and issued a warrant. If the warrant is justified, then Snowden is either amateurish or a traitor. After the issue of the warrant, it was clear that he had never been amateurish.

Conclusion: Snowden must be a traitor.

Predict an assumption

This is a causal relationship type question.

If X occurs, then either Y or Z occurs. We can conclude that if Z has occurred, then X must have occurred.

The premise is if the warrant (**X**) is justified, then Snowden is either amateurish (**Y**) or a traitor (**Z**). Since he is not amateurish (Y), it is concluded that he is a traitor (Z), which means that his warrant (X) was justified.

Predictive Assumption: Snowden's warrant is justified.

Answer choices explanation

(A) This option is **irrelevant.**

(B) This option is **out of scope**. The statement "A warrant for anyone who is traitor would be justified" is tricky. This option is wrong because it talks about anyone, and not specifically about Snowden. The argument states the conditional declaration about Edward only.

(C) This option is **out of scope**. Like option B, it focuses on anyone.

(D) This option is **inconclusive**. It is a reverse statement of premise. We cannot conclude that if someone is a traitor or amateurish, then his warrant is justified. The premise does not state this. It states that if the warrant is justified, then Edward is either amateurish or a traitor.

"If A, then B" is not equivalent to "If B, then A"

(E) This is the **correct** answer. It is aligned with our predictive assumption.

The correct answer is option E.

Example 3

Because of the soaring number of fatalities incurred in accidents on major interstate highways, the Interstate Highways Commission has put forward a proposal to be considered by the state government that only vehicles less than ten years old be allowed to use major interstate highways. Under the terms of the proposal, older vehicles would be confined to using minor interstate highways. Despite vocal opposition from classic car clubs in particular, the Commission has stated that such a reform would dramatically reduce the number of highway fatalities.

The conclusion drawn in the passage above depends on which of the following assumptions?

(A) The Interstate Highway Commission cannot pass laws without government approval.

(B) Vehicles older than ten years are less reliable than newer vehicles.

(C) Minor interstate highways are overused.

(D) Minor interstate highways are favored by high performance older vehicles.

(E) Major interstate highways have a design flaw.

Argument construction

The number of fatal accidents occurring on major interstate highways is high. To reduce them significantly, the Interstate Highways Commission (IHC) has proposed to state government that only vehicles less than ten years old be allowed to use major interstate highways (major highways), and older vehicles would be confined to using minor interstate highways (minor highways).

Conclusion: The IHC claims that such a reform (that only vehicles less than ten years old be allowed to use major interstate highways) would dramatically reduce the number of highway fatalities.

Predict an assumption

The conclusion for which an assumption has to be found is that vehicles more than ten years old should be banned from major highways to reduce fatal accidents. This leads to our predictive assumption.

Predictive Assumption 1: Vehicles older than ten years are less prone to accidents than newer vehicles.

What if the number of newer vehicles is significantly more than older vehicles? The move to restrict newer vehicles to major highways will not help reduce accidents dramatically.

Predictive Assumption 2: The number of newer vehicles is not significantly more than older vehicles.

Answer choices explanation

(A) This option is **irrelevant**.

(B) This is the **correct** answer. It is aligned with our predictive assumption 1.

(C) This option focuses on minor highways rather major highways. This option is **out of scope**.

(D) Same as option C, this option focuses on minor highways rather major highways. This option is **out of scope**.

(E) This option is **out of scope**.

The correct answer is option B.

Example 4

The State Transport Authority (STA) has voted to strengthen their bid to transform the commuting habits of citizens regardless of the fact that both inner city roads and access highways have become so clogged that some leading city officials have said that a radically new transport policy is necessary. Despite the high toll and purchase taxes levied on car owners by the STA, research has shown that the public transport system would have to be greatly improved and the price fixed at a nominal sum if more people are to be enticed out of their cars.

What assumption is the argument based on?

(A) Road and vehicle purchase taxes will be raised even higher.

(B) Taxpayers will rebel against more investment in public transport.

(C) Private transport is generally considered more convenient than public transport.

(D) The current public transport system is overused and therefore requires improvement.

(E) A new transport policy has been agreed upon.

Argument construction

Both inner city roads and access highways have become clogged. City officials have said that a radically new transport policy is necessary. The STA believes in the need to transform the commuting habits of citizens. Despite the high toll and purchase taxes levied on car owners by the STA, most prefer to use private cars. Research has shown that the public transport system would have to be greatly improved and the price be nominal if more people are to be convinced to avoid their cars.

Conclusion: A greatly improved public transport system and price fixation at a nominal sum will make people use it and thus avoid cars.

Predict an assumption

Predictive Assumption: A greatly improved public transport system and a nominal price will make people use the public transport system.

Answer choices explanation

(A) This option is **irrelevant**. It does not relate to the conclusion and public transport system.

(B) This option is **irrelevant**. It does not relate to the conclusion and public transport system.

(C) This is the **correct** answer. From the premise—despite the high toll and purchase taxes levied on car owners by the STA — it can be inferred that people still use cars. The obvious reason could be that private transport is generally considered more convenient than public transport.

(D) We cannot assume from the argument that the public transport system is overused. The argument states that it needs improvement, but that does not mean that it is overused. Moreover, it does not impact the conclusion.

(E) This option is **out of scope**. The policy agreement aspect is not considered in the argument.

The correct answer is option C.

Example 5

Derrango has come up with a central heating system that industry analysts predict will have to be adopted by other heating equipment manufacturers in order to successfully compete. Prior to this invention, gas burning central heating furnaces employed a system similar to the carburetors in automobiles, mixing air and gas, which is then fed into the burner. However, the Derrango engineers have invented a gas injection method that heats the air before it mixes with gas and thus raises volatility. The system reduces fuel consumption by almost 40% and should lead to an equivalent reduction in utility bills.

Which of the following represents a necessary assumption for the preceding argument?

(A) Homeowners have voiced concern over rising utility bills.

(B) Gas suppliers have warned of possible interruptions to services.

(C) Central heating systems using conventional mechanisms are cheaper.

(D) The new system creates a less humid environment than that created by conventional systems.

(E) The Derrango system is as efficient as a conventional heating system.

Argument construction

The information given in the argument is about conventional systems and a new heating system.

Conclusion: The new heating system should lead to an almost 40% reduction in utility bills.

Predict an assumption

Predictive Assumption: Heating the air before it mixes with gas, and thus raising the volatility, will reduce the fuel consumption by almost 40%.

Answer choices explanation

(A)   This option is **out of scope.** It does not impact the conclusion.

(B)   This option is **out of scope.**

(C)   This option is **inconsistent.** Central heating systems do not use conventional mechanisms. It is against the premise—Derrango engineers have **invented** a gas injection method that heats the air before it mixes with gas and thus raises volatility. The two systems have different mechanisms.

(D)   This option is **out of scope.** The humidity aspect is not under consideration.

(E)   This is the **correct** answer. It compares the two systems. The Derrango system must be as efficient as a conventional heating system to make the conclusion valid.

If in doubt, apply the negation test.

Negation of E: The Derrango system is not as efficient as a conventional heating system.

The negation of E noticeably shatters the conclusion—The new heating system will reduce fuel consumption by almost 40% and should lead to an equivalent reduction in utility bills. Option E is the correct answer.

The correct answer is option E.

Example 6

Icarus Airline Manufacturing Corporation has continuously made greater profits by supplying airlines with quality airplanes which are equipped with increased seating capacity. In an effort to continue this financial trend, the company is set to launch a double-decker jumbo jet.

The plan of the company as described above assumes all of the following EXCEPT:

(A)   The demand for air travel will increase in the future.

(B)   Increased production expenses for the new jumbo jet will be offset by increased revenues.

(C)   Passengers have no preference between the new double-decker jumbo jet and the previous models in the market.

(D)   The new jumbo jet will be technologically reliable once in operation, yet will result in unexpected costs or unrealized revenues.

(E) The new jumbo jet will not require substantial new training of the pilots or building new parking space at airports.

Argument construction

Icarus Airline Manufacturing Corporation (IAMC) has been making greater profits with single-decker planes. It wishes to introduce double-decker jumbo jets so that it can serve more passengers and see more profits.

Conclusion: Double-decker jumbo jets will continue to make greater profits like single-decker jets have been doing.

Predict an assumption

The question is an EXCEPT kind of question. You must be careful while reading the qualifier word in the question stem. The difference between a regular assumption question and an EXCEPT question is that in the case of the latter, there would be four statements that can be assumed from the argument, while only one option cannot be assumed. You have to mark that as the correct answer.

Predictive Assumption 1: IAMC will be able to sell the increased number of seats such that it makes more profits.

Predictive Assumption 2: IAMC is technically competent to manufacture double-decker jets.

Predictive Assumption 3: The cost to manufacture double-decker jets will be overcome by increased revenue in a stipulated time frame.

Answer choices explanation

(A) This is a correct assumption. It is almost aligned with our predictive assumption 1.

(B) This is also a correct assumption. It is aligned with our predictive assumption 3.

(C) This is also a correct assumption. Passengers must not have a preference between the new double-decker jumbo jet and the previous models on the market so that both the models should have optimum sales.

(D) This is the **correct** answer. It cannot be assumed that the new jumbo jet would incur unexpected costs or impede more revenue.

(E) This is also a correct assumption. Training of pilots and new parking space are the cost that will eat up profit, hence it is necessary that no substantial new training of pilots or building new parking space at the airports is required.

The correct answer is option D.

Example 7

Recent research into obesity suggests that although certain amphetamines are capable of quelling physical hunger pangs, they also have a mood-altering affect that frequently leads to food binging. Of the 63 patients that took part in tests carried out by Hopkins Institute scientists, 43 admitted to periodically binging to assuage depression, and at the conclusion of the eight week trial were found to have gained weight. From these results, scientists have concluded that appetite-quelling amphetamines are often counter-productive and should be prescribed to patients only in controlled environments.

The conclusion drawn by scientists is based on which of the following assumption?

- **(A)** Amphetamines induce food binging.
- **(B)** Controlled environments discourage secret binging.
- **(C)** Food binging causes depression.
- **(D)** Obesity is worse than depression.
- **(E)** Food binging is not always coupled with depression.

Argument construction

Research into obesity suggests that although certain amphetamines are capable of suppressing physical hunger pains, they also have a mood-altering affect that frequently leads to food binging. Of the 63 patients that took part in tests carried out by Hopkins Institute scientists, 43 admitted to periodically binging to ease depression, and at the conclusion of the eight week trial were found to have gained weight.

Conclusion: Appetite-quelling amphetamines are often counter-productive and should be prescribed only to patients in controlled environments.

Predict an assumption

Predictive Assumption: Patients will not be allowed to binge on food in controlled environments.

Answer choices explanation

- **(A)** This option is **inconsistent.** The argument states that certain amphetamines, not all, have a mood altering affect that frequently leads to food binging.
- **(B)** This is the **correct** answer. It is aligned with the predictive assumption.
- **(C)** This option is **inconsistent**. It is other way around, as 43 patients admitted to periodically binging to assuage depression. Depression causes food binging.

(D) This option is **irrelevant**.

(E) This option is **irrelevant**.

The correct answer is option B.

Example 8

The government of Akhlazia should stop permitting mafia-run opium companies to subtract shipping expenses from their revenues in calculating the amount of kickbacks that go to the central government. These opium companies would have to pay a higher kickback. As a consequence they would have to raise the price of opium and this price would then discourage buyers on the world market from purchasing Akhlazian opium.

Which of the following is an additional premise required by the argument above?

(A) Opium companies would not be able to offset the payment of extra kickbacks by reducing other operating expenses.

(B) Opium companies would need governmental approval before they can change the price of opium.

(C) Buyers on the world market have no other suppliers of opium other than Akhlazia.

(D) The money the government would earn as a result of increased kickbacks would be used to educate the public about the dangers of drug addiction.

(E) The increase in kickbacks would be equal to the additional income generated by the rise in prices.

Argument construction

The government of Akhlazia should not allow mafia-run opium companies to subtract shipping expenses from their revenues while calculating the amount of payments that go to the central government. Since these opium companies would have to pay a higher kickback, as a consequence they would have to raise the price of opium and this high price would then discourage buyers on the world market from purchasing Akhlazian opium.

Conclusion: Akhlazia opium companies will have to raise the price of opium and the price rise would discourage buyers on the world market from purchasing Akhlazian opium.

Predict an assumption

As stated earlier, assumption is a hidden premise. GMAT may indirectly ask you an assumption question with a twist.

Predictive Assumption 1: the world market can buy the same quality opium from other markets at a reduced price.

Predictive Assumption 2: The government of Akhlazia will not pass on any benefit to opium companies that can offset reduced profits.

Answer choices explanation

- **(A)** This is the **correct** answer. Since opium companies would not be able to offset the payment of extra kickbacks by reducing other operating expenses, they would be compelled to raise the price of opium, resulting in an anticipated loss of business.

- **(B)** This option is **out of scope.**

- **(C)** This option is **opposite.** It implies that the world market has no choice but to buy opium from Akhlazia. It weakens the conclusion.

- **(D)** This option is **out of scope**.

- **(E)** This option is **opposite.** It implies that opium companies can garner more revenue despite an increase in price.

The correct answer is option A.

Practice Questions

3.4 Practice Questions

3.4.1 Questions

Question 1

Although superstars are hailed as great actors, the truth is that superstar movies showcase action and drama. Therefore, superstars should not be considered great actors.

Which of the following is an assumption on which the argument depends?

- (A) Some great actors have acted in superstar movies.
- (B) Few superstars have degrees from a film institute.
- (C) Movies that showcase only action and drama are not the only kind of movies to portray acting prowess of great actors.
- (D) Many have started respecting radio voice-over artists as actors.
- (E) Some superstars have acted in meaningful cinema.

Question 2

Among those automobile mechanics who own their own garages and have completed a qualifying course at Main Street Technical School, 35 percent earn above $80,000 a year. Among those who own their own garages but did not complete the qualifying course at Main Street Technical School, only 10 percent earn above $80,000 a year. These figures indicate the importance of technical education in getting a higher salary.

The argument above depends on which of the following assumptions about the people mentioned in the statistics?

- (A) At least one-third of the group of people who did not complete the qualifying course would today be earning more than $80,000 a year if they had completed the course.
- (B) The group of people who did not complete the qualifying course and the group who did are comparable in terms of factors that determine how much people are paid.
- (C) Most of those people who did not complete the course did so entirely because of the cost of the course.
- (D) As a group, those persons who completed the course are more competent as mechanics than the group that did not.
- (E) The group of people who did not complete the qualifying course and today earn more than $80,000 a year are more capable than the group that completed the course.

Question 3

Mitchell Motor Company recently had a big jump in pick-up truck sales after hiring a new design team to give their pick-up trucks a more upscale look designed to appeal to a more affluent clientele. The company is now planning to launch a new line of sub-compact cars using the same concept.

The company's plan assumes that

- (A) other sub-compact cars with an upscale look do not yet exist in the market

- (B) an upscale clientele would be interested in a sub-compact car

- (C) the same design team could be employed for both projects

- (D) giving sub-compacts an up-scale look requires a design team

- (E) customers who bought older pick-up trucks would be just as likely to buy the new upscale looking pick-up trucks

Question 4

Instead of blaming an automobile accident on driver error, insurance companies should first try to figure out why the error was made by analyzing flaws in road design, automobile designs and in criteria to determine eligibility for a driver's license. Only then will the insurance companies be able to effectively issue guidelines to prevent future accidents, instead of merely punishing the incidental driver.

Which of the following is a presupposition of the argument above?

- (A) Driver error is not a significant factor in most automobile accidents.

- (B) Automobile manufacturers should be the agents who investigate automobile accidents, and not insurance companies.

- (C) Stricter government regulation of the automobile and highway construction industries would make automobile travel safer.

- (D) The investigation of automobile accidents should contribute to the prevention of future accidents.

- (E) Most drivers who make errors in driving repeat those errors unless they are retrained.

Question 5

Two different cages of rabbits were given injections of mild toxins. In addition, the first cage was also exposed to a cold temperature; three-fourths of the rabbits in this cage became sick. Only one-fifth of the rabbits in the normal temperature cage became sick. The lab technicians concluded that cold temperature increases the likelihood of illness in rabbits.

The technicians' conclusion logically depends on which of the following assumptions?

- (A) The exposure to the cold temperature acted as a catalyst for the toxins which made more rabbits in the first cage sick.

- (B) The toxins given to the rabbits in the two cages were of the same strength and the same amount.

- (C) Injecting the rabbits with toxins does not make them sick.

- (D) Even without the exposure to cold temperature, the rabbits in the first cage would have probably gotten sick.

- (E) Even exposing rabbits to slight variances in temperature is likely to induce illness irrespective of which cage the rabbits belong to.

Question 6

Now that the babies of the post-war baby boom have reached retirement age, there is a burgeoning population of elderly people. However, despite a chronic lack of workers throughout the US, employers are still reluctant to take on elderly workers. Age Concern, an elder citizens' rights protection organization, campaigns for greater employment of those past the age of retirement. The Elder citizens' rights protection organization cites numerous examples of successful companies that have an active policy of employing elder citizens and therefore claims that employing older people is good for business.

The claim made by Age Concern is based on which of the following assumptions?

- (A) Since Company A adopted a policy of employing elder citizens, minor thefts by staff have decreased by 45%.

- (B) Certain companies that employ elder citizens have a policy of supporting charitable causes.

- (C) Some companies employing elder citizens report that their elder workers are more punctual than the younger workers are.

- (D) All the companies employing elder citizens accept that output has declined but say this has been more than compensated for by the improvement in public image.

- (E) Most elderly citizens in employment are willing to accept lower wages than those acceptable to young workers.

Question 7

This year, pollution levels, particularly in downtown areas, reached such alarming levels that city councils in several states established temporary exhaust control points on the highways feeding inner city areas. This led to an immediate drop in the number of people suffering from asthma. As a result, several councils have decided to make the exhaust control points a permanent feature.

The decision to make the exhaust control points a permanent feature on highways is based on which of the following assumptions?

(A) All highways pass through the outskirts of downtown areas, which are uninhabitable areas.

(B) Prolonged exposure to pollution causes asthma.

(C) A variation of Asian Flu prevalent in downtown areas has the same symptoms as acute asthma.

(D) A newly available mask does not reduce the risk of acquiring asthma from pollution.

(E) The company running the exhaust checks is paid according to the number of defective vehicles detected.

3.4.2 Answer-Key

(1) C
(2) B
(3) B
(4) D
(5) A
(6) E
(7) B

Solutions

3.4.3 Solutions

Question 1

Argument construction

Although superstars are hailed as great actors, the truth is that superstar movies showcase action and drama.

Conclusion: Superstars should not be considered great actors.

Predict an assumption

Let's look at the conclusion: Superstars should not be considered great actors.

Why does the author think that superstars should not be considered great actors? There must be a qualification that superstars lack, yet great actors possess. What is that qualification? Well, it is not mentioned in the argument. All that is mentioned in the argument is that the superstars focus on the action and drama aspects of movies. It implies that great actors focus on more aspects of the movie than just action and drama.

Predictive assumption: Movies that focus only on action and drama are not the only domain of great actors.

Answer choice explanation

(A) This option is **irrelevant**. This option tells us more about great actors, but does not answer why superstars should not be considered great actors.

(B) This option is **out of scope**. Only a few superstars having a film degree does not explain why superstars should not be considered great actors.

(C) This is the **correct** answer. This option is aligned to our predictive assumption that movies that focus only on action and drama are not the only domain of great actors.

(D) This option is **irrelevant**. The aspect of radio voice-over artists is not relevant.

(E) This option is **inconclusive**. As discussed in a previous question, we cannot conclude anything based on the quantity word some.

The correct answer is option C.

Question 2

Argument construction

There are two groups of automobile mechanics who own their own garages: the first with a qualifying course at Main Street Technical School, and the second without such a course.

Of group one, 35 percent of mechanics earn above $80,000 a year, and of group two, only 10 percent of mechanics earn above that.

Conclusion: Getting technical education helps in getting a higher salary.

Predict an assumption

In order for the comparison of mechanics to imply something about the importance of technical education, the subject groups being compared need to be relatively homogenous in terms of factors which will affect their income as auto mechanics, otherwise the results we see do not clearly reflect how the course increases the ability of auto mechanics to earn a better income.

Predictive Assumption 1: Both groups are homogenous in terms of comparison of income.

What if the remaining 90% of group two mechanics, who earn less than $80000, earn significantly more than the remaining 65% of group one mechanics, who earn less than $80000? The conclusion will be shattered. We cannot conclude that technical education helps get more salary.

Predictive Assumption 2: The remaining 90% of group two mechanics, who earn less than $80000, do not earn significantly more than the remaining 65% of group one mechanics, who earn less than $80000.

Answer choice explanation

(A) Statistically, it looks logical that 33.33% < 35%, but we cannot necessarily state this, as both groups can be heterogeneous in terms of comparison of income.

(B) This is the **correct** answer. It is aligned with predictive assumption 1.

(C) This option is **out of scope.** Cost is out of scope.

(D) This option is **inconclusive.** It focuses on competence, and not on salary.

(E) This option works against the conclusion. It states that the top 10% of group two mechanics earn more than group one mechanics.

The correct answer is option B.

Question 3

Argument construction

The argument is easy to comprehend. The conclusion is missing from the argument, but we can infer the implied conclusion.

Implied Conclusion: By hiring the same design team, and using the same concept, Mitchell Motor Company plans to launch sub-compact cars, and aspires to make good sales.

Predict an assumption

Predictive Assumption 1: Prospective clients will buy the car designed by the new design team.

Predictive Assumption 2: Mitchell Motor Company is competent to manufacture sub-compact cars.

Answer choice explanation

(A) It is not a necessary assumption. Even if there are sub-compact cars on the market, Mitchell Motor Company can still plan to manufacture them. It does not impact the conclusion.

(B) This is the **correct** answer. It is somewhat aligned with predictive assumption 1. Since Mitchell Motor Company has a loyal base of upscale clientele, they would be interested in a sub-compact car manufactured by their truck company—Mitchell Motor Co.

(C) This option is a **rephrase of the premise**. It is already stated.

(D) This option is a **rephrase of premise**. It is already stated.

(E) This option is **out of scope**. It does not focus on cars.

The correct answer is option B.

Question 4

Argument construction

Usually insurance companies blame drivers for accidents. They must analyze the reasons for accidents by studying flaws in road design, automobile designs and criteria to determine eligibility for a driver's license. Only then will the insurance companies be able to effectively issue guidelines to prevent future accidents.

Conclusion: To effectively issue guidelines to prevent future accidents, insurance companies must analyze the reasons for accidents by studying flaws in road design, automobile designs and in criteria to determine eligibility for a driver's license.

Predict an assumption

Predictive Assumption: Flaws in road design, automobile designs and criteria to determine the eligibility for a driver's license are also significant factors in causing accidents.

Answer choice explanation

(A) The argument need not assume this. It does not say so. Driver error is certainly a factor apart from other factors in accidents.

(B) This option is **out of scope**. It talks about who should investigate accidents rather than the causes of accidents.

(C) This option is **out of scope**. It focuses on government regulation of the automobile and highway construction industries, and not on the three factors mentioned in the argument.

(D) This is the **correct** answer. It is a natural hidden premise in the argument.

(E) This option is doesn't hit a bull's eye. It pretends to address the criteria to issue a driver's license, but the argument talks about the eligibility aspect and not about the training aspect.

The correct answer is option D.

Question 5

Argument construction

The argument is easy to understand. In cage one, rabbits were given injections of mild toxins, and were exposed to a cold temperature simultaneously; because of this, three-quarters of the rabbits got sick.

In cage two, rabbits were given injections of mild toxins, but were not exposed to a cold temperature, so only one-fifth of the rabbits got sick.

Conclusion: Cold temperature increases the likelihood of illness in rabbits.

Predict an assumption

If more rabbits became sick in the cage where they were exposed to a colder temperature, as opposed to the warmer cage where fewer rabbits became sick after being injected with the same toxins, it can be assumed that the combination of cold temperature and the toxin makes more rabbits sick.

Predictive Assumption: The combination of cold temperature and the toxin makes more rabbits sick.

Answer choice explanation

(A) This is the **correct** answer. It is aligned with the predictive assumption.

(B) This option does not focus on cold temperature. It does not impact the conclusion.

(C) Like option B, this option too does not focus on cold temperature. It does not impact the conclusion.

(D) This option is **irrelevant**. Like option B & C, this option too does not focus on cold temperature. It does not impact the conclusion.

(E) This option is **inconclusive.** It talks about the impact of slight variances in temperature, which may be hotter than normal temperature too. The argument is concerned about the impact of cold temperature only.

The correct answer is option A.

Question 6

Argument construction

Though there is a growing population of elderly people, despite a chronic lack of workers throughout the US, employers are still reluctant to employ elderly workers. The organization Age Concern campaigns for greater employment for elder citizens. Age Concern cites numerous examples of successful companies that have an active policy of employing elder citizens.

Conclusion: Employing older people is good for business.

Predict an assumption

The definition of good for business is somewhat vague. It can be interpreted as profit, revenue, output, or cost. We will have to go through the options to pin-point the correct assumption. However, we can still predict a couple of assumptions.

Predictive Assumption 1: Elder citizens have broad experience that employers can capitalize on.

Predictive Assumption 2: Elder citizens can be employed at significantly lower wages, yet their output is not significantly lower than that of young workers.

Answer choice explanation

(A) This option is **inconclusive.** It cites a case from company A. It cannot be generalized.

(B) This option is **opposite.** It goes against the conclusion. It states that the motive behind employing elder citizens is not because they can contribute, but that organizations do so because they wish to do some charity, implying that elder citizens are a cost to the organizations.

(C) This option is **inconclusive.** It cites the experiences of some companies. The number of companies may range from few to many. It cannot be generalized.

(D) This option is **inconclusive.** While decline in output is a loss, image building is a gain. We cannot conclude what weighs more.

(E) This is the **correct** answer. It is aligned with predictive assumption 2.

The correct answer is option E.

Question 7

Argument construction

Because of pollution reaching alarming levels, particularly in downtown areas, city councils in several states established temporary exhaust control points on the highways joining inner city areas. This move led to an immediate drop in the number of people living in downtown areas suffering from asthma.

Conclusion: By making the exhaust control points a permanent feature on highways, asthma can be controlled significantly in downtown areas.

Predict an assumption

Predictive Assumption 1: Only pollution causes asthma in downtown areas.

Predictive Assumption 2: There is no other factor that led to an immediate drop in the number of people suffering from asthma.

Answer choice explanation

(A) This option is **out of scope.** The option looks tempting, but it tries to establish that people do not live in highway areas, hence, there are no ill effects due to exhaust in those areas, whereas the argument is concerned with pollution and asthma in downtown areas.

(B) This is the **correct** answer. It is aligned with predictive assumption 1.

(C) This option is **opposite.** It tries to establish that the acute asthma may be due to Asian Flu, and not due to pollution.

(D) This option is **irrelevant.**

(E) This option is **irrelevant.**

The correct answer is option B.

3.5 References for Official Guide Questions

The Official Guide for GMAT Review, 13th Edition: Question # 21, 41, 46, 48, 75, 77, 83, 93, 96, 106, 109, 113;
Diagnostic test question # 28

The Official Guide for GMAT Verbal Review, 2nd Edition: Question # 7, 34, 44, 52, 56, 63, 67, 76

Chapter 4

Strengthen the Argument

4.1 Strengthen the Argument Question type

Strengthen the argument questions are one of the frequently asked question types in Critical Reasoning.

Strengthen the argument questions also belong to the assumption-based family. A strengthener is an additional piece of information that supports the conclusion. Do not get confused between assumption and strengthener, as even though both make the conclusion more believable, they are different. In the last chapter, we saw that an assumption is an unstated hidden premise that the author chooses not to state, but that is necessary to make the conclusion more believable. However, a strengthener is new information provided in the option that supports the conclusion and makes it more believable. The new piece of information will act as evidence that the assumption is valid. Both – assumption and strengthener – make the conclusion more believable, but the strengthener is always NEW INFORMATION.

A strengthener, as additional support, has a wide range. The options could strengthen the argument simply to some extent, or go even further to a great extent. You have to select the option that supports the argument to the greatest extent. You will find the usage of the word 'most' or an equivalent word in question stems so that there is no ambiguity while selecting the correct option.

Look at the image below. There is a dialogue taking place between two people. What do you think could be the strengthener here?

Let us examine this argument: **Steve will get 700+ on his GMAT.**

Assumption	Strengthener
Steve will appear for his GMAT exam.	Steve has consistently been getting 700+ in his mocks.
Steve has prepared well for the GMAT exam.	Steve has studied for over 100 hours for the GMAT exam.
The maximum score for the GMAT is more than 700.	Steve has scored well in similar high-pressure competitive exams.

The following illustration depicts your job for strengthen the argument questions.

Companies Pinnacle and Acme provide round-the-clock e-mail assistance to any customer who uses their laptops. Customers send e-mails only when they find the laptops difficult to use. Since Pinnacle gets four times as many e-mails as Acme does, Pinnacle's laptops must be more difficult to use than Acme's.

Which of the following, if true, most strengthens the argument above?

A. Acme and Pinnacle have been in business for the same period of time.
B. E-mails to Acme are shorter than e-mails to Pinnacle.
C. Acme does not receive customer assistance through other means such as letters.
D. The number of customers of both companies has been gradually increasing.
E. Pinnacle's e-mail ID is not more widely publicized than Acme's e-mail ID.

Only one option supports the conclusion the most, and strengthens it.

The Question Stem

All strengthen question stems include *'if true'* or equivalent words in the question stem. This means that you have to attempt the question keeping in mind that the information given in the options is unquestionable and to be taken as fact. Never judge the validity of the options, or their truth; only judge whether they most strengthen the given argument.

Typical 'strengthen the argument' question stems looks like this.

- Which of the following, *if true,* would most *strengthen* the argument against the automobile manufacturer's claim?

- Which of the following would most likely *support* the data's implication?

Strengthen the argument questions may sometimes skip the exact phrase 'if true', but in some way or another the question stem will convey a similar meaning. In either case, do not get hung up on the phrase, because it is there only to imply that you should not doubt the options.

- Which of the following, *if feasible,* provides the *best basis* for the conclusion?

- Which of the following, *if effectively achieved,* provides *the best reason* for the conclusion?

- Which of the following, *if true,* provides *justification* for the conclusion?

4.2 The Process Of Solving Strengthen The Argument Questions

The 4-step approach is the same as mentioned in chapter 2.

The 4-step approach

(1) Recognize the question type

(2) Understand the argument construction

(3) Predict the qualifier

(4) Eliminate incorrect options

The first 2 steps are the same for strengthen the argument questions. Let us jump to predicting the qualifier.

4.2.1 Predicting the qualifier

We already know what 'predict the qualifier' means. Let us see this from strengthener's point of view.

Take a look once more at the 'Pinnacle and Acme' argument.

> Companies Pinnacle and Acme provide round-the-clock email assistance to any customer who uses their laptops. Customers send emails only when they find the laptop difficult to use. Since Pinnacle receives four times as many emails as Acme receives, Pinnacle's laptops must be more difficult to use than Acme's.

Conclusion: *Pinnacle's laptops must be more difficult to use than Acme's.*

4.2.2 Predicting the Strengthener

Our job is to strengthen the argument by providing new information.

Please read the following statement.

Acme has three times as many laptop customers as Pinnacle.

The statement certainly supports, or strengthens, the conclusion, and the information given is additional information, and hence not an assumption, but a strengthener. It strengthens the argument because it most clearly shows that even though Acme has more laptop customers than Pinnacle does, Pinnacle is the one getting more complaints. So, Pinnacle's laptops must really be more difficult to use.

Predictive Strengthener 1: Desktop computer users also find Pinnacle's desktops more difficult to use than Acme's.

Predictive Strengthener 2: Pinnacle's laptops are not based on a widely used OS (operating system).

Predictive Strengthener 3: Pinnacle also receives more complaints via letters and phone calls.

Example Questions

4.3 Examples

Example 1

Bio-chemists at Perck Pharma Corporation have discovered a new type of allergy. Their research confirms that it is not just caused by the pollen of a certain flower, as was once thought. In fact, they discovered that the flower has to be pollinated by a certain kind of bee to cause the allergy.

Which of the following, if true, would most likely support the data's implication?

(A) In the absence of that particular kind of bee, pollination by other bees does not cause allergic reactions.

(B) The bee has been shown to be a critical element in the reproduction of that particular flower.

(C) Many cases of the allergy have been observed only in the presence of that bee.

(D) In cases in which the allergy does not develop, the flower will grow without the presence of that bee.

(E) The onset of the allergy is usually caused by the flower even if the pollen is not present.

Argument construction

Bio-chemists have discovered a new type of allergy. The allergy is not just caused by pollen of a certain flower. The flower has to be pollinated by a certain kind of bee to cause the allergy.

Conclusion: The flower pollinated only by a certain kind of bee causes the allergy.

Predict a strengthener

We have to strengthen the conclusion that not the flower itself, but the pollination by a certain kind of bee causes the allergy.

Predictive Strengthener 1: Pollination by other kinds of bees does not cause the allergy.

Predictive Strengthener 2: The flower itself does not cause the allergy.

Answer choices explanation

(A) This is the **correct** answer. It is aligned with both predictive assumptions 1 & 2. This option rules out that the flower itself causes the allergy when pollinated, implying that the bee causes the allergy.

(B) This option is **irrelevant**. It does not address the source of the allergy— whether the flower or the bee is responsible.

(C) This option is a close contender. It is certainly a strengthener, but the question stem asks for the option that would support the data's implication the MOST. Also, if you critically analyze this option you cannot rule out that the allergy is not caused by the flower itself.

Imagine this: In an orchard, there is a specific kind of flowers—X; it was pollinated by certain kind of bee—Y. Many cases of the allergy were observed in the orchard. Which can you rightly blame? It may be that the flower itself is the source of allergy, not the bee.

The best way to conclude what is responsible for the allergy is by removing the bee and studying the pollination : exactly what option A does—the **correct** answer.

(D) This option is **inconclusive**. It is a conditional statement. It cites a scenario in which the allergy does not develop. We, however, are not concerned about the growth of the flower, but only about its allergenic effect.

(E) This option is an **opposite** answer. It weakens the conclusion. It blames the flower for the allergy.

The correct answer is option A.

Example 2

Automobile manufacturers defend their substitution of steel frames in cars with cheaper plastic components by claiming that consumer demand for light cars with crumple zones, rather than corporate profit motives, led to the substitution. However, if this trend were true, carbon reinforced tubing, which is lighter than steel but stronger, would be available as an option. It is not.

Which of the following, if true, would most strengthen the argument against the automobile manufacturer's claim?

(A) When carbon tubing was introduced in the market place, it was not yet commercially viable to produce it in large volumes.

(B) Automobile companies are reluctant to invest in high volume industrial technology to produce carbon tubing until profits from the sale of small scale commercial carbon products, such as bicycle frames, have stabilized.

(C) Some types of carbon tubing for sports equipment are in such high demand that there is a back log of several weeks for orders.

(D) Because carbon tubing has completely different chemical properties from plastic frame components, new construction techniques will be required for automobiles.

(E) Any valid comparison among steel, plastic, and carbon frames must be based on identical performance measures.

Argument construction

Automobile manufacturers substituted steel frames in cars with cheaper plastic components. They claim that because of consumers' desire for light cars with crumple zones, they chose plastic and did not do so because of profit motives. The counter view is that, if this trend were true, carbon reinforced tubing, which is lighter than steel but stronger, would be available as an option. However, it is not.

Conclusion: Substitution of steel frames in cars with cheaper plastic components is driven by a profit motive.

Predict a strengthener

This question basically belongs to the weaken the argument category. STRENGTHEN and WEAKEN are opposites. We are asked to strengthen the argument against the automobile manufacturer's claim. Alternatively, we can look at this question as:

Which of the following, if true, would most weaken the claim made by the automobile manufacturers?

Predictive Strengthener 1: The cheaper plastic used is not as strong as steel.

Predictive Strengthener 2: There are expensive materials other than steel available on the market, materials that are lighter than steel yet stronger.

Answer choice explanation

(A) This option is a **weakener**. It provides a reason manufacturers were not able to use carbon tubing instead of cheaper plastic or costlier steel—because it was not commercially viable to produce the carbon tubing in large volumes.

(B) This is the **correct** answer. Automobile companies are unwilling to invest in high volume industrial technology to produce carbon tubing till their profit motives from other operations have steadied. This weakens the claim made by the automobile manufacturers or, in other words, strengthens the argument against the automobile manufacturer's claim. It proves very emphatically that manufacturers are motivated entirely by profits in using the cheaper plastic in car frames.

(C) This option is a **weakener**. It presents another reason the manufacturers could not use carbon tubing – short supply. The manufacturers are not at fault then.

(D) This option is a **weakener**. Another reason for manufacturers being unable to use carbon tubing is that new construction techniques will be required to produce parts for automobiles.

(E) This option is **inconclusive**. It does not conclusively state the merits and demerits of the three materials or provide reasons for the use of any one of three materials.

The correct answer is option B.

Example 3

John, an expert in game theory, predicts that negotiations cannot be resolved unless one party is willing to concede a symbolic step. He also believes that when such a symbolic step of concession is taken, negotiations will be resolved. Other game theory experts, however, believe that these results do not take other variables into account.

Which of the following, if true, best supports the contention in the last sentence?

- (A) Predicting the success of a particular negotiation requires specifying the goal of the negotiation.
- (B) Judging the outcome of a particular negotiation requires knowing about other negotiations that have taken place in the past.
- (C) Learning whether a certain negotiation strategy is good requires observing how that strategy works through several negotiating sessions.
- (D) Parties who are willing to take a symbolic step are more likely to complete negotiations successfully for other reasons.
- (E) Making a negotiation successful requires knowing the symbolic steps that a party in the negotiations might desire.

Argument construction

John, an expert in game theory, predicts that negotiations cannot be resolved unless one party is willing to concede a symbolic step. He also believes that when a symbolic step of concession is taken, negotiations will be resolved. However, other game theory experts believe that this theory does not take other factors into consideration. Thus, these other experts believe that John is not taking other factors that might have led to the resolution into consideration, and is focusing only on the concession.

Conclusion: For a negotiation to be resolved, apart from a symbolic step, other factors also play roles in the resolution.

Predict a strengthener

This is truly a tough one. Let us simplify more.

John: Negotiations can be resolved when a symbolic step is taken.

Other Experts: Apart from the concession as a symbolic step, other factors also play important roles in the resolution.

It is tough to predict strengtheners in this question. We have to strengthen the other experts' claim—*other factors also play roles*, so focus on other factors and any options that talk about other factors leading to the resolution of the negotiation.

Answer choice explanation

(A) Is 'specifying the goal' a part of other factors? Maybe, maybe not...However, we are not concerned with "predicting the success" of negotiations. We are concerned with the "concession of a symbolic step" and its part in the resolution of negotiations. Our goal is not success prediction of negotiation, but its resolution.

(B) Is 'knowing about other negotiations that have taken place in the past'—a part of other factors? Maybe, maybe not. Again, "judging the outcome" is not our goal. Hence, even if "knowing about other negotiations" is a factor for "judging the outcome", we're not concerned with it because our goal is the "resolution of the negotiation, not "judging" whether the negotiation will get resolved.

(C) This option talks about the process of negotiation. It is not relevant to the resolution of negotiations.

(D) This option seems to hit the bull's eye. Out of the 3 options seen so far, this one is the best. It clearly mentions "other reasons" as a driving force in the resolution of the negotiations.

(E) This option tells more about the symbolic step rather than the other factors. It is not a strengthener for other factors. It may strengthen John's case.

The correct answer is option D.

Example 4

A statement by the Finance Minister: Last year was disastrous for our manufacturing sector, which has traditionally made up about 75 percent of our national budget. It is therefore encouraging that there is evidence that the IT sector is growing stronger. Taxes from the IT sector accounted for 15 percent of our national budget, up from 8 percent last year.

On the basis of the statements above, which of the following best supports the above conclusion?

(A) The increase in taxes from the IT sector could have merely been the result of new laws imposed on the IT sector.

(B) The profits of the IT sector remained at a steady level despite the fact that it paid more taxes to the national government.

(C) The rise in the percentage of taxes that the IT sector contributed to the national government was insignificant in actual dollar terms.

(D) It is difficult to determine whether the jump from a 8 to a 15 percent tax contribution by the IT sector will be ongoing.

(E) The information given above does not fairly compare the contribution of taxes paid by different industries to the national government.

Argument construction

The Finance Minister states that last year was disastrous for the manufacturing sector. The manufacturing sector had traditionally contributed to about 75 percent of the national budget, thus his statement implies that it is significantly lower than 75% now.

The minister further states that it is therefore encouraging that the IT sector is growing stronger. Taxes from the IT sector accounted for 15 percent of the national budget, up from 8 percent last year.

Conclusion: The IT sector is growing stronger.

Predict a strengthener

Basically, we need to support the conclusion by proving that either the IT sector will grow even more or at least grow steadily at the current pace. We can do that by proving that the demand for the nation's IT services is increasing. We can also achieve the same effect by demonstrating that the IT sector growth is based on a solid foundation and will remain unaffected.

Predictive Strengthener 1: The IT sector has been making greater profits consistently for the last few years.

Predictive Strengthener 2: The world market sees the nation as one of the most competent IT services providers.

Answer choice explanation

(A) This option is a **weakener.** It rules out the conclusion that the IT sector is going strong, and suggests the increased percentage of tax from 8 to 15% is due to another factor—a new law.

(B) This option is the **correct** answer. Despite paying more taxes, the profits of the IT sector remained at a steady level—clear evidence that the sector is growing increasingly stronger and will continue to add to the national budget and income.

(C) This option is **inconclusive**. It implies that the tax in dollars is nearly the same as before, but we are clueless as to whether the IT sector is growing and whether it will continue to grow.

(D) This option is **inconclusive**. This option implies that one cannot conclude whether the rise in contribution of the IT sector from 8 to 15% is sustainable. The statement has a bipolar nature; the swing to either side will strengthen the argument on one end, and weaken it on the other.

(E) This option is **irrelevant**. Comparing the contribution of taxes from different industries does not impact the conclusion because regardless of the taxes paid by other industries, the contribution of the IT industry will remain what it is.

The correct answer is option B.

Example 5

The fact that many large women's rights organizations consist almost entirely of white middle-class women has led many black feminist critics to question the seriousness of those organizations in speaking out on behalf of the needs of all women in general.

Which of the following generalizations, if justified, would support the criticism implied in the statement?

- **(A)** The ideology of an organization tends to supersede the particular desires of its members.
- **(B)** The needs of black women are substantially similar to the needs of white middle-class women.
- **(C)** Organizations are more capable of resolving issues that individuals alone cannot.
- **(D)** White middle-class women are more likely to join feminist groups than black women are.
- **(E)** The interest of individuals in an organization tends to supersede the objective of organization.

Argument construction

Many black feminist critics question the seriousness of many large women's rights organizations consisting almost entirely of white middle-class women. They doubt whether these organizations will speak out on behalf of the needs of all women (white and black) in general. They feel that since not all ethnic groups and economic classes are represented in these groups, the rights of those missing segments of the population will be ignored.

Conclusion: Many large women's rights organizations consisting almost entirely of white middle-class women will not be able to address the rights and the issues of black women in general.

Predict a strengthener

Predictive Strengthener 1: The needs and issues of white women and black women are different.

Predictive Strengthener 2: The organization is biased toward whites.

Answer choice explanation

- **(A)** This option is a **weakener**. The ideology of the organization is to speak for the rights of all women in general and not to differentiate between black and white women. If the ideology of an organization tends to supersede the particular desires of its members, it means that the organization is upright and unbiased and will help blacks as much as it will help whites.

(B) This option is a **weakener**. It is the opposite of predictive strengthener 1.

(C) This option is **irrelevant**. It does not discuss the "black/white" debate at all.

(D) This option is **inconclusive**. It does not impact the conclusion. Just because white women tend to join such groups more does not mean the rights of all get focused on in the organization.

(E) This option is the **correct** answer. If people tend to join organizations that serve their interests, then the fact that many large women's rights groups consist almost entirely of white middle class women indicates that these groups do not serve the interests of people with other ethnic backgrounds or economic positions. This would mean that the groups will focus on the needs of the white middle-class women and not any other group.

The correct answer is option E.

Example 6

After losing the 5-set final of the Open Tennis Tournament, the runner-up, James Maddy, blamed the partisanship of the spectators for his loss. Against the advice of his trainer, he appealed to the Tennis Association for the result to be annulled and the final to be restaged. As evidence to support his case, Maddy explained he had already won the first two sets, 6-1 and 6-2, when the audience began to loudly support his opponent, Alex Hogan. Maddy claimed that the deafening noise had hampered his concentration, causing him to lose the match.

Which of the following, if true, would provide justification for Maddy's case?

(A) Maddy's unforced errors, losing shots due to his own blunders rather than the opponent's brilliance, were far more in set 3 than in sets 1 & 2.

(B) A pre-match TV report had predicted that Maddy would win.

(C) Hogan's ace serve average over the whole match was 50% more than Maddy's was.

(D) The highest serve speed of the match was achieved by Maddy.

(E) Maddy's standing in the international tennis rankings was above Alex's.

Argument construction

The argument is easy to comprehend. Maddy claims that he would have won the match if the audience had not started loudly supporting his opponent Hogan from the third set onwards.

Conclusion: Due to the deafening noise, Maddy lost his concentration, causing him to lose the match.

Predict a strengthener

The case requiring strengthening is that Maddy lost not through his own mistakes, but because of circumstances set against him, making the match unfair. Perhaps the quickest way to solve such questions is to sort the options into positive and negative categories, in that the correct option, as a strengthener for Maddy's case, must show bias towards Hogan or against Maddy.

Predictive Strengthener: Evidence proving that Maddy lost concentration in the third set onwards, and not before.

Answer choice explanation

- **(A)** Compared to sets 1 and 2, Maddy made more unforced errors in set 3. This makes the case that he lost concentration from set 3 onwards fairly strong. This presents the possibility that it was not Hogan's skill but something else that made Maddy lose set 3 onwards. This option is a contender. We will hold onto this till we find a better one.

- **(B)** This option is **inconclusive**. A TV report, without further qualification, is not a case-builder.

- **(C)** This option is a **weakener**. This supports Hogan.

- **(D)** This option is **irrelevant**. This does not support Hogan or Maddy.

- **(E)** This option is **inconclusive**. Just because Maddy has a higher ranking does not mean he must win whenever he plays against a player of lower ranking.

The correct answer is option A.

Practice Questions

4.4 Practice Questions

4.4.1 Questions

Question 1

Despite many innovative features, the speed of the new Suzuki, like that of all bikes, is still dictated by a delicate ratio involving weight, power, air resistance, and height. Whatever speed increase has been achieved has been made possible by the fine-tuning of these variables to such an extent that one is forced to wonder whether the optimum ratio has finally been reached and any further increase would require a brand new frame and engine.

Which of the following, if unquestionable, would most validate the conclusion drawn above?

(A) A reduction of all the variable factors increases speed.

(B) The ratio governing speed consists of four factors only.

(C) The speed could be increased by increasing the weight while decreasing wind resistance.

(D) The speed could be increased by retaining the current ratio but strengthening the engine and frame.

(E) Many new innovations would make an increase in speed possible.

Question 2

Nearly 1,000 coronary patients at a Utah hospital were subjects in a trial that judged the power of prayer on recovery. Half were chosen to receive remote, intercessory prayers for 28 days from community volunteers given only the first names of the chosen people. Progress or decline of all the patients was charted daily and, at discharge or death, each was given a summed numerical score. It was found that the patients for whom intercession had been requested had a 10% higher score, a fact used by certain doctors now to claim as evidence of the existence of God.

Which of the following, if true, provides the best basis for the claim of the doctors?

(A) Coronary disease is frequently fatal.

(B) The community volunteers imparting intercessory prayers were noble souls.

(C) 62% of all the patients were over age sixty.

(D) National medical authorities accept that the results of the trial were statistically significant.

(E) The intercessory prayers were supervised by representatives from three different religions.

Question 3

The cheetah, the fastest animal on land, uses its incredible maneuvering and acceleration capability when it hunts its prey. It gets the acceleration by exerting approximately five times more power than does the famous sprinter Usain Bolt. In a study of 368 chases that were predominantly for hunting, scientists found that in most hunting chases cheetahs attained about 30 to 35 mph, a speed close to half of their peak speed. Therefore, cheetahs rely more on maneuvering than on their speed to hunt.

Which of the following, if true, would most support the conclusion?

(A) For cheetahs, speed has never been an issue and it is the result of some special physical characteristics that enable it to survive as a predator.

(B) Alan Wilson, a veterinarian, followed five cheetahs in the wild for a year and found that the cheetahs accelerated and changed direction rapidly, and that they ran very fast occasionally—close to a peak speed of 60mph.

(C) The study found that cheetahs can increase their speed by nearly 7 miles per hour in a single stride.

(D) Cheetahs have a very strong grip and can even rip the ground as they run.

(E) It is the use of the animals' claws that enable them to accelerate and decelerate very quickly, according to the study.

Question 4

The incessant monsoon rains are adding to the misery of urban dwellers. As the water level of Yamuna River continues to rise, panic in low-lying areas is growing. More water was released from Hathnikund Barrage on Monday, and it will reach the Yamuna by Tuesday evening. The district administration is contemplating evacuation of over 50,000 people from low-lying areas.

Which of the following, if true, would most support the decision being contemplated by the district administration?

(A) By crossing the 205 meter mark, Yamuna River surpassed the highest water level mark it had ever crossed in the last decade.

(B) The district administration of a neighboring state was late in evacuating over 20,000 people, causing 44 deaths.

(C) Over 50 boats, 68 divers, and a unit of the Disaster Management Force have been deployed to deal with any eventuality.

(D) The city government plans to set up over 160 relief camps to tackle the threat of the aftermath of flooding.

(E) Yamuna River crossed the danger level mark.

Critical Reasoning Guide – Strengthen the Argument

Question 5

Medicare has announced the introduction of a computer system to streamline the registration of new applicants throughout the US. The system will eliminate the possibility of fraudulent claims by cross-checking the names of applicants against past work records and birth certificates. Government officials claim that, once it is up and running, the new system will be able to save more than $500M every year currently paid for assorted medication that is then sold to individuals ineligible to receive Medicare assistance.

Which of the following, if true, most strengthens the claim of the government officials?

(A) The computer system will take approximately $900M to set up and another $100M to implement and run smoothly.

(B) The way the computerization of services is catching on in the US, medical services cannot be left behind.

(C) The computerized registration system will not stop all fraudulent claims.

(D) Many doctors have expressed concern that Medicare staff cannot be fully trained in the handling of the new system.

(E) Critics claim that the new system will prevent many impoverished patients from receiving vital medication.

Question 6

Advertisement: The Adosis tennis racket will revolutionize the entire game. Due to its unique hyper-strengthened lightweight fiberglass frame and super-tension strings, even an amateur player can strike a ball so that it attains speeds of over 100 mph. Amaze your friends and improve your game overnight. Buy the Adosis racket today.

Which of the following, if true, most supports the message of the advertisement?

(A) The material from which the frame is made is also used to strengthen bathroom fittings.

(B) The strings of the racket can be adjusted manually.

(C) Many players would find the weight of the frame optimum.

(D) The tension of the strings and strength of the racket are the only factors dictating speed.

(E) All sports shops stock the Adosis racket.

4.4.2 Answer-Key

(1) B (3) B (5) A
(2) D (4) E (6) D

Solutions

4.4.3 Solutions

Question 1

Argument construction

In short, the argument is: the speed of the new Suzuki, like that of all bikes, is a function of weight, power, air resistance, and height for the same frame and the engine. To further increase the speed, one would require a brand new frame and engine.

Conclusion: Maximum possible speed of bikes has been achieved by fine-tuning a delicate ratio involving weight, power, air resistance, and height.

Predict A Strengthener

Read the variation in the question stem. You may find differently expressed phrases, but they will be similar in meaning to "if true" and "strengthen".

Predictive Strengthener: Variation in any 5th factor will not increase the speed for the given frame and the engine.

Answer choices explanation

(A) This option is **inconsistent.** The premise states that the delicate ratio of four variables has been exploited to the maximum. Stating that reduction of all the variable factors increases speed is against the premise.

(B) This option is the **correct** answer. If there are only 4 factors governing speed, the conclusion is strengthened. It rules out the possibility that any other factor may increase the speed for the given bike frames and engines.

(C) This option is **inconsistent.** As stated earlier, the delicate ratio of these 4 variables has been exploited to the maximum. Stating that the speed could be increased by increasing the weight and decreasing wind (air) resistance is against the premise.

(D) This option is **out of scope.** The argument is concerned with increasing speed with the same frame and engine. This option alters the frame and engine and thus becomes pointless towards this argument.

(E) This option is **out of scope.**

The correct answer is option B.

Question 2

Argument construction

Nearly 1,000 coronary patients were subjects in a trial that judged the power of prayer on recovery. Nearly 500 were chosen to receive remote, intercessory prayers for 28 days from community volunteers. The volunteers were given only the first names of the chosen subjects.

Progress or decline of all the subjects was monitored daily and, at discharge or death, each subject was given a total numerical score. It was found that the subjects for whom intercession had been requested had a 10% higher score. Based on this, certain doctors now claim that there is evidence of the existence of God.

Conclusion: God exists.

Predict A Strengthener

Predictive Strengthener 1: 10% is a significant number to act as proof of the existence of God.

Predictive Strengthener 2: The 500 patients who received prayers were not given any special medical treatment by doctors, and prayer was not received by the other 500 patients.

Answer choice explanation

(A) This option is **irrelevant.** The argument is concerned with the summed numerical score and the finding that those who received prayers got a higher score *whether the subject died or recovered.* Hence, whether the disease is mostly fatal is irrelevant since the argument is not regarding whether prayers saved the subjects from death.

(B) This option is **inconclusive.** *Noble soul* is an ambiguous qualification. This neither strengthens nor weakens the argument.

(C) This option is **irrelevant.** Again, since patients were judged on the basis of their final numerical scores, their age is irrelevant to the "power of prayer".

(D) This option is the **correct** answer. It is aligned with the predictive strengthener. This option lends support to the trial by negating the possibility that the trial is an oddity and affirms that the trial is possibly representative.

(E) This option is **irrelevant.** The argument does not discuss the religion of the god or of the patients. It deals with prayer and its effect on coronary patients, regardless of the religion.

The correct answer is option D.

Question 3

Argument construction

The argument is about the cheetah's ability to maneuver and accelerate when it hunts its prey. The argument states that cheetahs accelerate with approximately five times the power of sprinter Usain Bolt. It is noteworthy that in most of the chases that were predominantly for hunting, cheetahs attained only 30-35 mph, and did not reach their peak speed.

Conclusion: - Cheetahs rely more on maneuvering than on their speed to hunt.

The conclusion is based on the fact that despite having the capability to increase speed—acceleration—to their advantage, cheetahs do not exploit that capability to the fullest, yet they are very successful predators. The contributing factor must be their tactical maneuvering since the argument mentions that a cheetah *uses its incredible maneuvering and acceleration when it hunts its prey,* implying that there are only two factors under consideration.

Predict A Strengthener

Predictive Strengthener: Evidence proving that cheetahs rely more on maneuvering than on their speed to hunt.

Answer choice explanation

(A) This option is **irrelevant.** It focuses on speed and the cheetah's capability of attaining more speed. The option does not focus on why the cheetah does not use its maximum possible speed when it hunts.

(B) This is the **correct** answer. This option is evidence that states that cheetahs accelerate and change direction rapidly, but that they run very fast only occasionally. This provides further proof for the study by talking about specific acceleration and changing direction—a possible maneuvering tactic. If the cheetahs succeeded at hunting without exploiting their capability of speed to the fullest, they must have maneuvered successfully. In other words, they relied more on maneuvering than on speed.

(C) Like option A, this option is **irrelevant.** It also focuses on speed.

(D) This option is **out of scope.** There's no discussion of the effect of their speed on the ground.

(E) Like option A, this option is **irrelevant.** It also focuses on speed.

The correct answer is option B.

Question 4

Argument construction

This is a pretty simple argument to understand. The argument is about panic created in low-lying areas because of the rising level of Yamuna River.

Conclusion: Over 50000 people from low-lying areas should be evacuated.

Answer choice explanation

(A) This option is **inconclusive.** While we are told that the river crossed the 205-meter mark, the highest in the last decade, we do not know whether this mark is dangerous to begin with. It may be quite an ordinary level. This would mean that Yamuna River was not ever, and is not now, a threat to life.

(B) This option is **out of scope.** The situation in the neighboring state cannot mirror the situation in this state. The argument does not state that the two states are similar or that both face danger from Yamuna's rising water levels.

(C) This option tells us about the preparedness of the Disaster Management Force to address any eventuality. This option does strengthen the conclusion to some extent; however, being prepared to encounter any eventuality does not provide concrete proof that over 50,000 people should be evacuated. Any state, regardless of existing danger, should be prepared with a disaster management unit prepared to help in eventualities. We can keep this option in the reckoning till we get the best answer.

(D) This option tells us how the city government will temporarily accommodate the flood-hit people. Like option C, this option also strengthens the conclusion to some extent; however, planning for setting up relief camps to tackle the threat of the flood's aftermath does not provide support for a decision that involves over 50,000 people and their evacuation. We can keep this option in the reckoning till we get the best answer.

(E) This is the **correct** answer. A danger-level mark is a qualifying mark to execute some anticipatory action. Although the preventive action may not necessarily be evacuation, among the three probable options, this one most supports the reason that the evacuation exercise should be carried out.

The correct answer is option E.

Question 5

Argument construction

The argument is easy to understand.

Conclusion: Once the computer system is up and running, the system will be able to save more than $500M a year.

Predict A Strengthener

The claim that needs to be strengthened is that the new system will save money by reducing fraud.

Predictive Strengthener 1: The cost of the new system is not disproportionately high.

Predictive Strengthener 2: It is possible to implement the system and train the staff to use the system to prevent frauds.

Predictive Strengthener 3: The new system is competent enough to stop most fraudulent claims.

Answer choice explanation

(A) While the new system set-up and execution is costly, the new system will pay for itself and start saving millions within two years. This is a close contender. If nothing better than this option is found, this is the **correct** answer.

(B) This option is **irrelevant.** Medical services or computerization in general is not part of the argument.

(C) This option is a **weakener.** This is against predictive strengthener 3.

(D) This option is a **weakener.** This is against predictive strengthener 2.

(E) This option is a **weakener.** This is against the objective of the new system.

The correct answer is option A.

Question 6

Argument construction

Conclusion: The new Adosis tennis racket has a unique hyper-strengthened, lightweight fiber-glass frame and super-tension strings that can enable a player to strike a ball to raise the ball's speed to over 100 mph.

Predict A Strengthener

The racket has three qualities—strength, light weight and strings with super-tension. Based on these qualities, the advertisement claims that a player can raise the ball's speeds to over 100 mph.

Predictive Strengthener: Many veteran players have tested the racket and they endorse the claim.

Answer choice explanation

(A) This option is **inconclusive.** We do not have any clue about the strength of bathroom fittings. Even if we infer that the material is of high strength, it is not new information. The argument already mentions this. We need to test the validity of the racket's qualities influencing the ball's speed.

(B) That the tension of the strings can be adjusted manually is good information, but it does not help support the conclusion—that the racket can make the ball attain go 100 mph.

(C) This option is **inconclusive.** If many players find the weight of the frame optimum, they may prefer to use it, but it does not help support the conclusion—that the racket can make the struck ball attain 100 mph of speed.

(D) This option is the **correct** answer. If the tension of the strings and strength of the racket are the only factors dictating velocity, the Adosis racket is qualified to make the struck ball attain 100 mph.

(E) This option is **out of scope.** It does not address the speed issue.

The correct answer is option D.

4.5 References for Official Guide Questions

The Official Guide for GMAT Review, 13th Edition: Question # 1, 5, 11, 14, 16, 19, 23, 29, 30, 31, 35, 40, 45, 50, 52, 56, 64, 67, 95, 101, 102, 108, 111, 118, 120, 121;
Diagnostic test question # 25, 27, and 32

The Official Guide for GMAT Verbal Review, 2nd Edition: Question # 1, 2, 6, 9, 13, 17, 21, 23, 25, 29, 30, 32, 33, 35, 37, 45, 51, 55, 58, 62, 65, 68, 69, 77, 78, 82

Chapter 5

Weaken the Argument

5.1 Weaken the Argument Question type

Like strengthen the argument questions, weaken the argument questions are one of the frequently-asked question types in Critical Reasoning.

Weaken the argument questions also belong to the assumption-based family. A weakener is an additional piece of information that shatters the conclusion, making the conclusion illogical. The new piece of information will work against the evidence and make the assumption invalid.

Look at the image below. There is a dialogue taking place between two people. What could be a weakener here?

Let us examine this argument: **Steve will get 700+ in his GMAT.**

Assumption	Weakener
Steve will appear for his GMAT exam.	Steve has been inconsistent in getting 700+ in his mocks.
Steve has prepared well for the GMAT exam.	Steve has prepared poorly for the GMAT exam.
The maximum score for the GMAT is more than 700.	Steve has scored poorly in similar high-pressure competitive exams.

The following illustration depicts your job for weaken the argument questions.

> Companies Pinnacle and Acme provide round-the-clock e-mail assistance to any customer who uses their laptops. Customers send e-mails only when they find the laptops difficult to use. Since Pinnacle gets four times as many e-mails as Acme does, Pinnacle's laptops must [be more difficult to use] than Acme's.
>
> Which of the following, if true, [most] weaken the argument above?
>
> A. Acme and Pin[nacle ...] period of time.
> B. E-mails to Ac[me ...] as to Pinnacle.
> C. Acme does no[t ...] receive through other means such as [...]
> D. The number o[f ...] companies has been gradually incr[easing ...]
> E. Pinnacle's e-m[ail ID is similar to Ac]me's e-mail ID.

Only one option weakens the conclusion most, and makes it illogical.

Question Stem

All weaken question stems include 'if true' or an equivalent phrase in the stem. This means that you have to attempt the question keeping in mind that the information given in the options is unquestionable and to be taken as fact.

A typical 'weaken the argument' question stem looks like one of the following.

- Which of the following, if true, would most seriously weaken the argument against the automobile manufacturer's claim?

- Which of the following, if true, would cast the most serious doubt on the validity of the argument?

Weaken the argument questions may sometimes skip the phrase 'if true', but the question stem will still convey a similar meaning.

- Which of the following, if true, most strongly calls the conclusion into question?

- Which of the following, if true, most seriously undermines the claim?

- Which of the following, if true, makes the conclusion flawed?
- Which of the following, if true, is most damaging to the conclusion?
- Which of the following, if true, is ill-suited to the plan?
- Which of the following, if true, makes the argument most vulnerable to criticism?
- Which of the following, if true, most criticizes the conclusion?

5.2 The Process Of Solving Weaken The Argument Questions

The 4-step approach is the same as in chapter 2.

The 4-step approach

   (1) Recognize the question type

   (2) Understand the argument construction

   (3) Predict the qualifier

   (4) Eliminate incorrect options

The first 2 steps are the same for weaken the argument questions. Let us jump directly to the predict the qualifier step.

Predicting the qualifier

We are already familiar with this step. Let us see how this applies to "weakeners".

Take another look at the 'Pinnacle and Acme' argument.

> Companies Pinnacle and Acme provide round-the-clock email assistance to any customer who uses their laptops. Customers send emails only when they find the laptop difficult to use. Since Pinnacle receives four times as many emails as Acme receives, Pinnacle's laptops must be more difficult to use than Acme's.

Conclusion: *Pinnacle's laptops must be more difficult to use than Acme's.*

5.2.1 Predicting the Weakener

Our job is to weaken the argument by providing new information. The optimum approach in predicting weakeners is to shatter assumptions. If you are able to predict assumptions, just work against those assumptions.

Let's see how.

Pinnacle has four times the number of laptop customers of Acme.

Since Pinnacle has four times the number of laptops customers of Acme, it is obvious that there would be significantly more emails sent to Pinnacle. The statement certainly weakens the conclusion. The information given is additional information that weakens the conclusion – a weakener.

Predictive Weakener 1: Desktop computer users find Pinnacle's desktop more user-friendly than Acme's.

We already discussed the following predictive weakeners in chapter 2, so we reproduce them here. What if a significant number of Pinnacle's customers are new to computers? Then obviously Pinnacle will receive more emails regarding how to use the laptop than Acme. This information will make the conclusion illogical.

Predictive Weakener 2: Pinnacle sells a significantly higher number of laptops to people who are new to computers than Acme does.

What if Acme receives more queries for help through letters than Pinnacle does? The conclusion would seem less believable.

Predictive Weakener 3: Acme receives more complaints through letters and phone calls.

5.2.2 Weaken Vs. Flaw Questions

We know that 'weaken the argument' and 'find the flaw in the argument' questions are two different question types, but the key word 'flaw' may appear in the question stem of both question types. Read the following two question stems and identify which one belongs to the 'weaken the argument' category.

Question stem 1: Which of the following, if true, reveals a flaw in the argument?

Question stem 2: Which of the following reveals a flaw in the reasoning in the argument?

Question stem 1 belongs to the 'weaken the argument' category while question stem 2 belongs to the 'find the flaw in the argument' question type. The key to differentiate the two is to look for 'if true' or similar meaning words in the question stem. If that phrase or one like it is present, the question belongs to 'weaken the argument', otherwise it falls under the category of 'find the flaw in the argument'.

Example Questions

5.3 Examples

Example 1

The new subway line, opened barely a year ago to alleviate traffic congestion, has already been deemed insufficient for satisfying demand. The State Transport Authority (STA), commissioned by the Mayor's office to come up with solutions, has admitted that even if more trains and carriages are added, the demand is such that only a 23% reduction in congestion would be feasible. For this reason, the city council is now considering building a new highway linking the downtown business district with the East Canton suburbs.

Which of the following, if true, would most weaken the conclusion of the above passage?

- **(A)** A year is insufficient time to judge the viability of the subway.
- **(B)** A ride-sharing scheme has been successfully operating for more than a year.
- **(C)** The business district suffers from a chronic shortage of parking spaces.
- **(D)** Some residents in the business district are opposed to the scheme.
- **(E)** The cost of the proposed highway would severely strain the city's budget.

Argument construction

The new subway line was opened hardly a year ago to reduce traffic congestion, but it has been deemed insufficient for handling the traffic load. The STA has admitted that even if more trains and carriages are added, the traffic load can only be reduced by up to 23%. For this reason, the city council is now contemplating building a new road linking the downtown business district with the East Canton suburbs.

Premise 1 - The new subway line, opened barely a year ago to reduce traffic congestion, has been deemed insufficient for handling the traffic load.

Premise 2 - More trains and carriages will reduce the traffic load by only up to 23%.

Conclusion: Local government must consider whether to build a highway because of current traffic congestion and the inadequacy of the subway system.

Predict a Weakener

We have to weaken the argument. Let us predict some statements that will weaken the conclusion.

Predictive weakener 1: The proposed new highway will reduce the traffic load by less than 23%.

Predictive weakener 2: The proposed new highway will pose unfathomable and insurmountable challenges.

Predictive weakener 3: Another alternative to address the problem at hand will fare better than the proposed solution of the new road.

Answer choice explanation

(A) This option is **inconsistent**. The statement is not consistent with premise 1. It is evident from premise 1 that the present system is inadequate. You cannot **ever** challenge a premise, but the conclusion can be challenged.

(B) This option is **irrelevant**. Even though a ride-sharing scheme has been operating for a year, it hasn't eased congestion.

(C) This is the **correct** answer. This option is aligned with predicted weakener 2. A problem that cannot be easily overcome is encountered with the proposed plan – the business district suffers from a chronic shortage of parking spaces. It weakens the conclusion that we should build a highway.

(D) This option is **inconclusive**. We have discussed in chapter 1 that the quantity word "some" ranges from 1-99%. We tried to measure quantity words- all, many, some, few, and none. Had the option said, "Most residents in the business district are opposed to the scheme" it would have made a little sense. However, despite using the quantity word 'most', this option lacks a solid reasoning on why residents are opposed to the highway. Opposed to this, option C clearly cites the problem and effectively weakens the conclusion.

(E) This option is **out of scope**. The cost factor is beyond the scope of this argument.

The correct answer is option C.

Example2

Acme University receives 2,000 applications a year from high school students who wish to attend college. The university's admission committee would like to ensure constant standards of quality in the incoming class each year. The admissions committee has decided, therefore, to accept for admission each year only the best 200 students, selected on the basis of the quality of their personal statements.

Of the following, if unquestionable, the best criticism of the admission committee's plan is that:

(A) The universities cannot accept all of the students who seek admission in a given year.

(B) The total number of applications will remain at approximately 2,000 in the coming years.

(C) Each applicant deserves to be considered seriously for admission.

(D) The best 200 personal statements will be difficult to assess.

(E) It is difficult to judge the quality of an applicant based on personal statements alone.

Argument construction

The argument is easy to understand. To standardize quality of the classes, the university will select the 200 best candidates, judged so by the quality of their personal statements.

Conclusion: Selecting the best 200 students on the basis of the quality of their personal statements (SoP) will ensure constant standards of quality.

Predict a Weakener

Predictive Weakener 1: Accessing the quality of students on the basis of only the SoP is flawed.

Predictive Weakener 2: Students have mastered the art of writing great SoPs regardless of their personal qualities.

Answer choices explanation

(A) This option is **irrelevant**. The university only wants to accept 200 students.

(B) This option is **irrelevant**. It implies nothing relevant towards the conclusion.

(C) This option is **inconclusive**. It does not impact the conclusion because the argument does not state that in judging the applicant the university won't consider each applicant seriously.

(D) This option is a possible **weakener**. This option is tricky. It focuses on the difficulty in assessing SoPs, whereas the argument is concerned with the difficulty in assessing the quality of students. It does weaken the conclusion, but compared to option E – the best criticism – we must eliminate this option.

(E) This is the **correct** answer. This option challenges the authenticity of selecting the best 200 on the basis of the SoP alone. If some average students with great SoPs got selected, the quality of the university would be in question. It is aligned with predictive weakener 1.

The correct answer is option E.

Example 3

Companies that launch asteroid mining robots from the moon have a distinct advantage over earth-based asteroid-mining robotic systems because of the moon's lower gravity. The higher the gravity of the object from which the company launches its systems, the more money it has to spend on fuel and on rocket systems that can carry the extra fuel required to enter orbit. In order to be as competitive as lunar-based Apollo Mining Company (AMC), Terra Now Mining Corporation (TNMC), located near the equator in South America, has decided to build a space elevator that will connect an orbiting artificial satellite with the ground base via a super-thin, super-strong cable.

Which of the following, if true, makes the argument most vulnerable to criticism?

(A) The cable is composed of a carbon-based material that has yet to be tested against the effect of thermal changes.

(B) The high cost of building the cable will negate any cost-savings in launching mining robotic systems into orbit for the foreseeable future.

(C) Over its expected lifetime, the cable will cut the cost of placing robots in orbit by 95%.

(D) Mining robots are flexible enough to be sent up and down via thin cable.

(E) The market for elements mined from asteroids is expected to decrease over the next fifty years.

Argument construction

Compared to Earth, the moon has lower gravity; hence companies that launch asteroid mining robots from the moon have a distinct advantage over Earth-based robotic systems. The higher the gravitational force on the object, the more money the company has to spend on fuel and on rocket systems that can carry the extra fuel required to enter orbit.

TNMC is located near the equator in South America. In order to be as competitive as the moon-based AMC, TNMC has decided to build a space elevator that will connect an orbiting artificial satellite with the ground via a super-thin, super-strong cable.

Conclusion: TNMC's plan to launch robots from Earth by building a space elevator will be as competitive as AMC's operation, making a level-playing field for both in the market.

Predict a Weakener

Predictive Weakener 1: The cost of building the space elevator will be so disproportionately high that TNMC cannot compete with AMC.

Predictive Weakener 2: TNMC will encounter insurmountable technical challenges in building the space elevator.

Answer choices explanation

(A) This option is **inconclusive**. Carbon-based material may or may not withstand the effect of thermal changes. We cannot conclude from this option that thermal changes will definitely hamper the space elevator.

(B) This is the **correct** answer. It is aligned with predictive weakener 1. It shows a definitive reason for TMNC not to build a space elevator.

(C) This option is a **strengthener**. We do not know the current cost of production. The option states a scenario which focuses on future.

(D) This option is a **strengthener**. This adds information that shows a reason the space elevator will be helpful.

(E) This option is **out of scope**, but is a tricky option. It does seem to discourage the company from investing in robotic systems because if the markets were to decline, spending stupendous sums on such a project does not make sense. However, it has two issues. One is that we cannot assume that the markets will decline to such an extent that the project is unviable, and two is that a fifty year period is a long-term one. The money invested in the project could be recovered in this period. On the whole, compared to option B, we can eliminate this option.

The correct answer is option B.

Example 4

Investing in Jones & Weston Munitions Company would be a great way to increase the value of one's stock portfolio at the current time. Clock and Roll, a gun enthusiasts' magazine, conducted a survey which indicated that 75 percent of its readers want to buy a second gun within a year. This is a great time for the gun industry. The new study also shows that the gun industry is only able to provide 55 percent of the total population with a new gun a year.

Which of the following, if true, reveals a weakness in the evidence cited above?

(A) The manufacturing of guns requires very precise industrial processes.

(B) Gun manufacturers are not evenly distributed across the country.

(C) The number of people who want a second gun has been increasing each year for the past ten years.

(D) Readers of Clock and Roll are more likely than most people to want a second gun.

(E) Gun magazines include articles about owning a gun as well as articles about hunting.

Argument construction

The argument states that investing in the stocks of JWM Company would increase an investor's portfolio. Clock and Roll, a gun enthusiasts' magazine, conducted a survey which indicated that 75 % of **its** readers want to buy a **second gun** within a year. The new study also shows that the gun industry can only provide 55 % of the total population with a new gun each year.

Conclusion: This is a great time for the gun industry.

Predict a Weakener

This question deals with biased population samples. While it may be true that the readers of that magazine want to buy a gun within a year, what needs to be established is whether the readers of the magazine are representative of the general population. Say, out of 1M people, there are only 100,000 readers of the magazine. In such a scenario, saying that because 75% of those readers want new guns, we can expect gun sales to increase significantly is not a valid statement. There's also the fact that currently the industry can provide for 55% of the **population** and not just 55% of the readers. A weakener would most likely be an option that points out this inconsistency in the samples used for making the claims.

Predictive Weakener 1: People who read magazines about guns will tend to be more likely to buy or want a second gun than those who don't read such magazines.

Predictive Weakener 2: The government is going to pass a resolution under which no one would be allowed to carry second gun.

Answer choices explanation

- (A) This option is **irrelevant** to the conclusion that gun sales will increase.
- (B) This option is **inconclusive** and implies nothing about gun sales going either up or down.
- (C) This option is **strengthener** for the conclusion.
- (D) This is the **correct** answer. It is aligned with predictive weakener 1. It establishes that the general population will not buy guns as the readers of the magazine would. Thus the expected sales are not going to be as much.
- (E) This option is **irrelevant**.

The correct answer is option D.

Example 5

Which of the following, if true, would undermine the validity of the investment advice in the argument above?

- (A) Some gun owners are satisfied with only one gun.
- (B) About half of the people who buy guns also purchase large cartridge magazines.
- (C) About half of the people who buy guns do so to protect their families.
- (D) Only a quarter of the guns that are made are sold within the first four weeks of the year.
- (E) Only a quarter of those who claim that they want a second gun actually end up purchasing one.

Argument construction

Investment Advice: Invest in the stocks of JWM.

Predict an Invalidator

The investment advice is that investing in Jones & Weston would increase the value of one's stock portfolio. This advice implies that the author expects the company to make a large profit by selling more of its product, namely guns. An option that demonstrates that the demand for guns is not as high as the magazine claims will undermine the validity of this advice.

Predicative invalidators are the same as weakeners in the previous question.

Answer choices explanation

(A) This option is **inconclusive**. "Some" is a quantity word that ranges from 1 to 99%. We cannot come to a conclusion on the basis of the word some.

(B) This option is a **validator**. This option shows that sales will rise and provides reason to buy shares of JWM.

(C) This option is **irrelevant** because the reason people buy guns does not make a difference as to whether they will buy more as predicted.

(D) This option is **inconclusive**. This option is cleverly crafted. The tone of the option suggests negative prospects for the gun industry, but we cannot conclusively state this because we don't know when the remaining 75% of guns are sold or which sales period is miserable.

(E) This is the **correct** answer. It shows that only 25% of those who claim they want a second gun end up buying one. Hence, the predictions are inflated and based on flimsy data, which undermines the validity of the investment advice.

The correct answer is option E.

Example 6

Recently, there was a huge flood in Hunan, China during the rice-growing season. This will lead to the doubling of the price of rice this season, and ultimately lead to the cost of making rice-cakes very expensive. Unfortunately, rice-cake consumers in Hunan will now have to pay more for rice-cakes.

Which of the following, if true, is most damaging to the argument above?

(A) The recent flood was not as severe as scientists had predicted.

(B) Regions other than Hunan also supply rice to rice-cake manufacturers in Hunan.

(C) Ingredients other than rice are used in the production of rice-cakes.

(D) Last year the price of rice was actually lower than the average price over the past ten years.

(E) The price of rice will eventually be too high for most consumers because of inflation.

Argument construction

Due to a huge flood in Hunan during the rice-growing season, the price of rice will double. It will make rice-cakes more expensive.

Conclusion: Due to the doubling of the price of rice, consumers in Hunan will now have to pay more for rice-cakes.

Predict a Weakener

Our task is to weaken the conclusion that the price of rice-cakes will rise. The author concludes that the huge flood in Hunan will cause the price of rice to double. He assumes that the flood will destroy a significant amount of rice crops and that the shortage of rice crops will lead to the price rise. This price rise will mean making rice-cakes becomes more expensive.

The author seems to imply that the rice used in Hunan is supplied entirely by Hunan growers. What if Hunan is not the only source of rice? Hunan could import rice from other parts of the country, and possibly at an almost normal price.

Predictive Weakener 1: Rice produced in Hunan is not the only source of rice for Hunan.

Predictive Weakener 2: Damage to rice crops due to the flood in Hunan is not significant.

Answer choices explanation

(A) This option is **inconsistent**. From this option, we cannot infer whether rice crops were affected significantly. Note that predictive weakener 2 is different from this option. The option states that the flood was not severe (inconsistent with the premise), whereas predictive weakener 2 states that damage to the rice crop is not significant, but the floods are, as the premise claimed, severe.

(B) This is the **correct** answer. It is aligned with predictive weakener 1.

(C) A major proportion of rice-cake has to be rice; hence, the impact due to the prices of other ingredients will not be significant.

(D) This option is **irrelevant**. Last year's price does not impact the conclusion dealing with current and future prices.

(E) This option is **out of scope** and much too general.

The correct answer is option B.

Example 7

Enshrined in the US Constitution, a clause protecting the right of citizens to bear arms remains the most potent argument used by the gun lobby in their resistance to those wishing to ban possession of handguns. Opponents of the gun lobby cite the most recent UN statistics that prove conclusively that globally there exists a clear correlation between the number of violent gunfire incidents and the laxity of gun control legislation.

Which of the following, if true, would LEAST support those wishing to ban the possession of hand guns?

- **(A)** Iceland, with the strongest gun laws, has too small a population to be statistically significant in a comparison to the U.S.

- **(B)** Financial support for the gun lobby has decreased considerably over the last two years.

- **(C)** Since its adoption, the US Constitution has proved extremely resilient to change.

- **(D)** Instances of violence have fractionally increased in at least one country that adopted harsh gun possession legislation.

- **(E)** The UN statistics took more than two years to compile.

Argument construction

Argument of the gun lobby: Every citizen has the right to possess guns to protect oneself. It is written in the US Constitution. Their position is – do not ban gun possession.

Argument of opponents: The most recent UN statistics prove that globally there exists a clear correlation between the number of violent gunfire incidents and the leniency of gun control legislation. Their position is – ban gun possession.

Conclusion: Ban guns.

Predict a Weakener

The language of the question stem is unusual. You have to pick an option that would LEAST support the opponents. Since the conclusion is drawn from the gun opponents' point of view, we have to look for the option that weakens the conclusion – Ban guns!

In GMAT CR questions, you have to read "LEAST supports" as one that weakens, and "LEAST challenges" as one that strengthens.

So, we have to cite a reason that justifies the possession of guns.

Predictive Weakener: There is a sizable number of deaths of people who could not protect themselves from criminals because they did not have guns.

Answer choices explanation

- **(A)** This option is **out of scope**. It neither supports nor challenges.

- **(B)** This option is **irrelevant**. The finances of the gun lobby are irrelevant.

(C) This is the **correct** answer. If the US Constitution has proven extremely resistant to change, then the amendment to ban guns will not take place.

(D) This option also weakens the conclusion, but not to the extent option C does because of the use of the words "fractionally" and "one country".

(E) This option is **inconclusive**. A two-year compilation time infers that the data is outdated, so this option is not useful.

The correct answer is option C.

Example 8

The company QuickBite buys free-holiday coupons from people who earned them from Magic Holidays by holidaying frequently at Magic Holidays' destinations. QuickBite sells these coupons to people who pay less for the coupons than they would by buying holiday packages from Magic Holidays. This reselling of coupons results in loss of revenue to Magic Holidays.

To discourage the buying and selling of free holiday coupons, it would be best for Magic Holidays to restrict the following:

(A) the use of coupons to only those who earned the coupons, and their family members

(B) the number of coupons that a person can earn in a particular year

(C) the seasons in which the coupons can be used

(D) the time period within which the coupons can be used after they are issued

(E) the number of holiday destinations for which people can use the coupons

Argument construction

QuickBite buys free-holiday coupons from frequent vacationers who earned these coupons from Magic Holidays for holidaying at Magic Holidays destinations. QuickBite sells these coupons to people who pay significantly less for the coupons than they would have paid had they bought the full holiday package from Magic Holidays. This sale of coupons is the loss of potential business for Magic Holidays.

Conclusion: This reselling of coupons results in loss of revenue to Magic Holidays.

Predict a Solution

We have to discourage the selling of free-holiday coupons by Magic Holidays patrons. We need to find a solution that will keep the marketing going, but will stop the loss of revenue for MH.

Predictive Solution: Restrict the use of the coupons to the patrons who earn them.

Answer choices explanation

(A) This is the **correct** answer. It is aligned with the predictive solution. By restricting the usage of the coupons to patrons and their family members, the selling of coupons will be stalled.

(B) The move to restrict the number of coupons that a person can earn in a particular year will not address the issue. Even a limited number of coupons can still be sold. Moreover, with this move, the objective of the free-coupon reward to patrons will be defeated. Our problem remains.

(C) Like option B, the move to restrict the seasons in which the coupons can be used will not address the issue. The coupons can still be sold for those restricted seasons. Our problem remains.

(D) Again, like option B, the move to restrict the time period within which the coupons can be used after they are issued will not address the issue. The coupons can still be sold in the restricted time period. Our problem remains.

(E) The move to restrict the number of holiday destinations for which people can use the coupons will not address the issue. The coupons can still be sold for the restricted number of holiday destinations. Our problem remains.

The correct answer is option A.

Example 9

Because of new developments in electric accumulators, the path to the marketing of practical and economically viable electric automobiles has been paved. Citing such developments and the urgent need to encourage environmentally-friendly transport systems, Washington State Senator Brenda Sheperton has proposed the adoption of a new state law. This law would offer state subsidies to encourage auto manufacturers to reduce the prices of their range of electric vehicles, and auto retailers to sell one electric-powered vehicle for each gasoline-powered vehicle sold in the state.

Which of the following, if true, best explains why the author's reasoning is vulnerable to criticism?

(A) Not all environmental groups have welcomed the proposal.

(B) The price of electric-powered vehicles is much higher than that of conventional vehicles.

(C) Only a few gas stations in the state have battery-charging facilities.

(D) Only the top four automobile manufacturers have the capability to manufacture electric cars.

(E) Auto retailers have limited space in their showrooms to accommodate more vehicles.

Argument construction

New developments in electric accumulators have led to the marketing of practical and economically viable electric automobiles. A Washington state senator has proposed a state law that would offer subsidies to the state so that the state can encourage the following: one, auto manufacturers to reduce the prices of their range of electric vehicles, and two, auto retailers to sell one electric-powered vehicle for each gasoline-powered vehicle sold in the state. Basically, the senator is pushing for more electric automobiles sales.

Predict a Weakener

What assumptions does this argument contain?

Predictive assumption 1: Electric vehicles are environmentally friendly because they are better than gasoline-powered vehicles.
Predictive weakener 1: Electric vehicles, though not emitting carbon emissions, have other detrimental effects to the environment.

Predictive assumption 2: Subsidies given for electric vehicles are ample enough to encourage the customers to buy electric vehicles over gasoline-based vehicles.
Predictive weakener 2: Benefits given by electric vehicles are NOT ample enough to encourage the customers to buy electric vehicles over gasoline-based vehicles.

Answer choices explanation

(A) This option is **inconclusive**. Just because some environmental groups haven't welcomed the proposal does not mean the proposal is flawed. They may have other reasons to reject the proposal. This option does not show any inherent vulnerability in the reasoning. It merely shows some groups' response to the proposal, which by itself cannot constitute a weakness in any plan.

(B) This option is **inconclusive.** We cannot conclude whether subsidies given for electric vehicles are ample enough to offset the difference in the price of electric vehicles and conventional vehicles.

(C) This is the **correct** answer. The scarcity of battery-charging facilities would severely cripple the plan to promote electric vehicles because people will not buy electric cars until this problem is resolved, regardless of how affordable the electric cars are.

(D) This option is **inconclusive.** We cannot conclude whether the top four manufacturers can manufacture an ample number of electric vehicles to meet the requirements of the state. If they can, this statement is valid. In the absence of data, this option cannot be pinned down as damaging to the argument.

(E) This option is certainly **relevant**, and is a tricky option, but the argument states that the retailer will have to sell one electric vehicle for every conventional vehicle. It does not necessarily translate to scarcity of space in showrooms. The dealers can replace some conventional cars with electric ones to overcome this problem.

The correct answer is option C.

Practice

Questions

5.4 Practice Questions

5.4.1 Questions

Question 1

Although Milton International School provided competent teachers and revamped course offerings, social science and geography scores for grade 10 students failed to reach the expected level. Therefore, parents suggested to the principal that social science and geography subjects be taught in the native language instead of in English.

Which of the following, if true, would cast a serious doubt on the parents' proposal?

(A) Social science and geography are taught by a teacher whose competence in the native language is profound.

(B) A few students can speak the native language fluently.

(C) Currently final examinations are conducted in English; the status quo is not going to change in the near future.

(D) Many grade 10 students were born and brought up in either a town or culturally similar surrounding areas.

(E) Students of Milton International School are consistently scoring satisfactorily in their native language subject.

Question 2

The city's transport authorities have proposed a new contract to union negotiators that would decrease the number of trains in service and do away with guards, but would increase the salaries of subway car drivers by 16%. However, the proposal is facing stiff opposition from rank and file members. It is not so much the increased pay offer, although this falls well short of the figure agreed upon by the arbitration council, but more the fear that unguarded trains would lead to mass redundancies despite the statutory obligation of the authorities to maintain full employment of all union members.

Which of the following would do the most to relieve the fears of the union members?

(A) All those made redundant would receive 50% of their annual bonus entitlement.

(B) The redundancies would be kept to a minimum.

(C) Competent redundant guards would be trained as drivers.

(D) Management would receive a 16% cut in their salaries.

(E) The authorities would adhere to contractual stipulations.

Question 3

People with modern views feel that a genuine belief in astrology is proof of a naive and unscientific mindset. However, in the past, people with great intellect and scientific wisdom accepted astrology wholeheartedly. Therefore, there is no scientific basis for not accepting astrology.

The argument is most vulnerable to criticism on which one of the following grounds?

(A) Since it has been debated for ages whether astrology has any scientific merit, any evidence to show that it has a method of proof will be fallacious.

(B) There has been a rapid progression of intelligence in modern people.

(C) The implied assumption that everyone with modern views does not believe in astrology is false.

(D) A faith can be consistent with the available proofs and accepted scientific notions at one time but not with the accepted proofs and notions at a later time.

(E) There might be an authentic nonscientific basis for not accepting astrology.

Question 4

Statistics demonstrate that children who are beaten usually grow up believing that it is appropriate to beat their children as well. This cycle is just one instance of violence perpetuating violence. A certain religious sect claims, however, that beating children is a form of discipline, not violence, and that this discipline is necessary to develop certain good habits in children, because children are too emotional and are not capable of responding to situations with reason and logic until they reach adolescence.

Which of the following, if true, make the conclusion flawed?

(A) Young children often, for no apparent reason, burst into fits of tears or laughter, thereby showing mixed emotions at times.

(B) If beaten properly, there should be no permanent marks left on children.

(C) Even at an early age, children are capable of differentiating right from wrong and understanding why things should or should not be done.

(D) Even at an early age, children who are more intelligent are beaten for different reasons than less intelligent children are.

(E) Child-beating is an acceptable social practice in some groups.

Question 5

This year the UK's tax hike on tobacco and alcohol places Britain at the head of what many experts call a worrying global trend. The government has defended the rise, which now makes the UK proportionally the world's leading collector of excise tax. They say it is the only effective deterrent against tobacco and alcohol abuse. However, critics claim that such policies are a sham and are intrinsically flawed because the vast sums gathered annually finance so many governmental activities and expenses that if tobacco and alcohol consumers were really deterred, the government would have collapsed.

Which of the following most challenges the position of critics against the UK government?

- (A) The high taxes fund medical and other services in the country.
- (B) By pretending to be interested in tobacco and alcohol deterrence, the government is increasing the wealth of Britain.
- (C) Extreme tobacco and alcohol use is common in many impoverished countries; hence the high tax is justified.
- (D) Incremental tax rises compensate for the gradual decrease in tobacco and alcohol use and the derived revenues.
- (E) Some of the critics are paid lobbyists for the tobacco and alcohol industries.

Question 6

Country Y has appealed to the United Nations, saying that sanctions against it have severely curtailed vital exports and should be lifted. The sanctions were originally put in place to punish Country Y for repeated use of torture in military prisons and the failure of the ruling military junta to hand power over to democratically-elected civilian leaders. As a basis for the appeal, Country Y has officially announced its intention to return to civilian rule, blaming any continuing instances of torture upon rogue officers.

Which of the following, if true, makes the position of Country Y most vulnerable?

- (A) A precise date for the return to civilian rule has been given.
- (B) The generals who led the coup that deposed the previous democratically-elected government are mostly still in power.
- (C) The tight grip of the junta, controlling everything that takes place in the country, has halted the flight of capital.
- (D) Human rights abuse is common throughout the developing world.
- (E) It is alleged that a crash prison building program, ostensibly to alleviate overcrowding, is in fact in preparation for the mass imprisonment of the regime's critics.

Question 7

To claim that computer industry revenues are declining is overstated. It is a fact that the computer manufacturers' share of industry revenues declined from 75 percent three years ago to 60 percent today, but for the same period companies selling computer parts had their share increase from 15 percent to 25 percent, and service companies such as dealers, resellers, and repairers had their share increase from 10 percent to 15 percent.

Which one of the following, if true, best indicates why the data given above provides no evidence to support the conclusion?

- **(A)** There is no explanation given for why the revenue shares of three sectors of the industry changed.

- **(B)** It is likely that the data for the manufacturers' share of revenues came from a source which is different from the sources of data for computer parts and service companies.

- **(C)** Computer manufacturers and parts companies depend on dealers' success in selling computers for their revenue.

- **(D)** The change in the computer industry's overall revenues does not matter; the total of all shares of these revenues is 100 percent.

- **(E)** Although revenue is an important factor, it is not the only factor in determining profits.

Question 8

The wholesale price of mustard has increased substantially in the last six months, whereas that of groundnut has decreased. Thus, although the retail price of mustard oil at grocery shops has not yet increased, it will predictably increase.

Which of the following, if true, is ill-conceived while drawing the conclusion above?

- **(A)** The operating costs of grocery stores have been constant for the last three quarters.

- **(B)** The wholesale price of mustard is usually less than that of groundnut.

- **(C)** The cost of processing mustard oil has decreased in the last year.

- **(D)** The cost of harvesting mustard has decreased in the last two quarters.

- **(E)** The per capita consumption of mustard oil has not changed significantly over the last two years.

Question 9

Workers of community X raise a question of bias against them in recruitment by a certain company. However, the record shows that nearly 65% of applicants belonging to community X have been employed by the company, as opposed to nearly 55% of applicants not belonging to community X. This, therefore, shows that the company is not biased against community X.

The argument is vulnerable to which of the following criticisms?

- **(A)** Nearly 85% of the applicants belonging to community Y have been employed by the company.

- **(B)** According to experts, only nearly 35% of the applicants not belonging to community X should have been employed.

- **(C)** There are a large number of workers employed by the company not belonging to community X.

- **(D)** The majority of the resumes of workers belonging to community X reach the company through an outside recruitment consultant.

- **(E)** Despite having a large number of resumes from non-recruited applicants belonging to community X, the company invites applications from workers not belonging to community X.

5.4.2 Answer-Key

(1) C

(2) E

(3) D

(4) C

(5) D

(6) B

(7) D

(8) C

(9) B

Solutions

5.4.3 Solutions

Question 1

Argument construction

Milton International School employs competent teachers and teaches a revamped course curriculum. Still, the social science and geography scores for grade 10 students are not satisfactory.

Conclusion: Social science and geography should be taught in the native language.

Predict A Weakener

Predictive Weakener 1: Many students do not understand the native language well.

Predictive Weakener 2: Good text books on social science and geography are not available in the native language.

Predictive Weakener 3: Competent teachers who can teach social science and geography in the native language are not available.

Answer choice explanation

(A) This option **strengthens rather than weakens** the argument. If the teacher's competence in the native language is profound, it supports the parents' suggestion.

(B) From the statement, we cannot infer whether only a few students understand the native language well. This option is relevant, but **inconclusive.**

(C) This is the **correct** answer. If the final examination continues to be conducted in the English language, social science and geography must be taught through the English language to allow the students to score well. This option weakens the conclusion.

(D) This option **strengthens rather than weakens** the argument. If many grade 10 students in Milton International School were born and brought up in a town or culturally similar surrounding areas, it is likely that they must be well-versed in the native language.

(E) The argument is concerned about social science and geography only and not about any other subjects. This option is **outside the scope** of the argument.

The correct answer is option C.

Question 2

Argument construction

The city's transport authorities have proposed the following new contract to union negotiators:

1. Decrease the number of trains in service.
2. Do away with guards.
3. Increase the salaries of subway car drivers by 16%.

The objection to the proposal by union members is:

1. Not so much about the increased pay offer.

2. More the fear that unguarded trains would lead to mass redundancies despite the statutory obligation of the authorities to maintain full employment of all union members.

Note that the union does not voice any objection to accidents that may occur because of trains running without guards.

Conclusion: The new proposal will leave the guards jobless.

Predict A Weakener

The fear of the union members that needs to be relieved is that they will be left unemployed despite the obligation of the transport authorities to maintain full employment. This question asks us to weaken the fears of the union.

Predictive Weakener: Redundant guards will be absorbed at the same scale of pay that they currently receive.

Answer choice explanation

(A) The bonus offer will not get back the jobs. The guards would still be redundant.

(B) Minimum redundancies are not zero redundancies. This will not alleviate the fears of the union. As long as there are redundancies, the union would protest.

(C) This option may seem to address the fear to some extent, but not completely, because only the competent redundant guards would be trained as drivers and retained in the job. This means that some guards who are deemed incompetent will be made redundant and will lose their jobs. This will not pacify the unions.

(D) This option is **irrelevant.** This does not deal with either the unions or the guards.

(E) This is the **correct** answer. That the authorities would adhere to contractual stipulations implies that management will retain the jobs of guards, even though the capacity in which the guards will be retained is not mentioned. This is what union wants.

The correct answer is option E.

Question 3

Argument construction

People with modern views feel that those who have genuine belief in astrology are naive and unscientific in their mindset. But, in the past, people with great intellect and scientific wisdom accepted astrology wholeheartedly. So, this marks a contrast in the thinking of two kinds of people.

Conclusion: There is no scientific basis for not accepting astrology.

Answer choice explanation

(A) Debating for long whether astrology has any scientific base or not does not mean that any evidence that attempts to prove that it has evidence will be fallacious. This option is **inconclusive.** It implies that astrology cannot be proven scientific.

(B) This option is **inconsistent** and **inconclusive.** The premise states that in the past, the intellect of people was good enough to analyze and understand the nuances of astrology from a scientific perspective, so this option does not add any value to the argument.

(C) This option **supports** the conclusion rather than weakens it.

(D) This is the **correct** answer. This option states that with the passage of time, beliefs may change in the light of newer proof and accepted scientific notions. It shows that past people may have had scientific reasons to believe in astrology when they did.

(E) A nonscientific basis aspect is outside the scope of the argument.

The correct answer is option D.

Question 4

Argument construction

Statistics show that children who are beaten usually grow up believing that it is appropriate to beat their children as well. The intermediate conclusion is that *this cycle is just one instance of violence perpetuating violence.*

A certain religious sect claims that beating children is a form of discipline, not violence, and that this discipline is necessary to develop certain good habits in children, because children are too emotional and are not capable of responding to situations with reason and logic until they reach adolescence.

Conclusion: Beating is necessary to develop certain good habits in children until they reach adolescence.

Predict A Weakener

The justification provided by advocates of child-beating in the argument is that children must be beaten because they are not able to make logical conclusions, and are unable to respond appropriately to their surroundings. The correct option must directly contest that assertion, weakening the argument. We have to show that child-beating is unnecessary and that children have the requisite amount of intelligence to grow up to be responsible adults.

Predictive Weakener: Children are capable of responding to situations with reason and logic.

Answer choice explanation

(A) This option is a **strengthener.** It supports the reasoning of the child-beaters, who say that children are too emotional.

(B) This option is **irrelevant.** If anything, it shows that there is an effective way to beat children.

(C) This is the **correct** answer. It is aligned with our predictive weakener. It shows that beating children is not the solution.

(D) This option is **irrelevant.** This just points out different reasons for beating children but does not argue against beating them.

(E) This option is **rephrasing** of the argument. We already know this. It does not weaken the argument.

The correct answer is option C.

Question 5

Argument construction

The UK has hiked taxes on tobacco and alcohol, making it proportionally the world's leading collector of excise tax. The UK has defended the tax rise as being the only effective deterrent against tobacco and alcohol abuse.

However, critics claim that such policies are flawed as the vast money gathered annually funds so many governmental activities and expenses. They state that if tobacco and alcohol consumers were really discouraged, the government would have collapsed.

Conclusion: Hiking taxes on tobacco and alcohol to deter against tobacco and alcohol abuse is a pretense and is meant to gather money.

Predict A Weakener

The justification provided by the critics is that the government runs most of its activities using the money collected as taxes. They claim that if the taxes had deterred the users of alcohol and tobacco, the government would have run out of money. We need to contest these assertions by proving that the government does not have a selfish motive in raising and collecting higher taxes. We can do this by either providing a valid use for the collected money or by showing that the high taxes do act as a deterrent for smokers and drinkers.

Predictive Weakener 1: The sum needed to treat tobacco and alcohol-related ailments is rising extremely.

Predictive Weakener 2: The world over, similar countries to the UK have effectively controlled tobacco and alcohol abuse by hiking taxes on them.

Answer choice explanation

(A) This option is **inconclusive.** The statement is tricky. At first sight it seems to be aligned with predictive weakener 1, but reading the statement carefully, we find that the sum gathered is not used for the medical care of tobacco and alcohol abusers. Instead, it is used for all. Secondly, the sum is used for other services apart from medical services. This implies that the government does indeed need the tax money to run its various agencies and that it does not really want to hike taxes to reduce smoking and drinking. This would strengthen the critics' arguments.

(B) This option is **strengthener.**

(C) This option is **out of scope.** The aspect of other countries is not within the scope of the argument.

(D) This is the **correct** answer. It says that the consumption of tobacco and alcohol is gradually decreasing, so the incremental tax rises will compensate for the diminished revenues. It clearly advocates that the vested motive behind the tax hike is not to gather money from tobacco and alcohol users. It proves that the tax revenue from smokers and drinkers will go down, implying that smoking and drinking will be controlled, and that the government won't collapse because it will find other sources of money.

(E) This option is **inconclusive.** "**Some**" is a quantity word that ranges from 1 to 99%. We cannot make a conclusion on the basis of the word some.

The correct answer is option D.

Question 6

Argument construction

Country Y wants sanctions against it lifted. Earlier, the sanctions were imposed for repeated use of torture in military prisons and the failure of the ruling military junta to hand power over to democratically-elected civilian leaders.

Country Y intends to return to civilian rule. It blames any continuing instances of torture on its corrupt officers.

What is the conclusion here?

Is it "sanctions should be lifted" or "country Y will return to civilian rule"?

Both of them are conclusions, but only one of them is the main conclusion and the other is the intermediate conclusion. To identify which of the two is the main conclusion, we shall refer to our discussion in chapter 1. One must ask what the author truly wants to advocate. If still confused, apply the **conclusion test** discussed in chapter 1.

Which one makes better sense?

1. Sanctions should be lifted, because country Y will return to civilian rule

   or

2. Country Y will return to civilian rule, because sanctions should be lifted.

Obviously, the first one makes better sense, hence the main conclusion is— Sanctions should be lifted.

Conclusion: Sanctions should be lifted.

Predict A Weakener

The position of country Y that needs to be weakened is the implication that the country is now in the process of being reformed and therefore doesn't deserve further sanctions. We need to predict something that will show that sanctions shouldn't be lifted.

Predictive Weakener 1: On previous occasions, country Y's military rulers breached commitments to return to civilian rule.

Predictive Weakener 2: Many rogue officers are still in powerful positions.

Answer choice explanation

(A) This option is a **strengthener.** It reflects the commitments of the rulers. It strengthens the position of country Y rather than weakening it.

(B) This is the **correct** answer. It is aligned with predictive weakener 2.

(C) This option is **inconclusive.** The objective of halting the flight of capital is not clear.

(D) This option is **irrelevant.** This proves no point regarding return to civilian rule or the trade sanctions.

(E) This option definitely weakens it, but it is just an allegation. It does not prove anything conclusively.

Another contrary viewpoint is: since the question stem states that all the options *'if true'* are to be judged so, how can we disqualify option E on the basis of the word *allegation*? If option E is true, should *allegation be replaced with truth?* No - what option E means is that it is true that *the allegation has been made.*

The correct answer is option B.

Question 7

Argument construction

The computer manufacturers' share of industry revenues has declined from 75 percent three years ago to 60 percent today. However, for the same period the revenue share of companies selling computer parts increased from 15 percent to 25 percent, while that of service companies increased from 10 percent to 15 percent.

Conclusion: The claim that the computer industry's revenues are declining is overstated.

In other words, we can say that the conclusion means that computer industry revenues are not declining.

Predict A Weakener

Let us examine the question stem. It states that the data given in the argument does not provide any evidence to support the conclusion.

Why does the author state this? The total revenue for the computer industry is made up of revenues from manufacturers, computer parts, and service companies. It should be noted that all the data points given are in percentages. Let us list the scenario for today and for three years ago.

Scenario	Today	Three Years Ago
Computer Manufacturers	60	75
Computer parts companies	25	15
Service companies	15	10
Total Revenue (%)	**100%**	**100%**

From the table, we cannot infer the absolute value of revenues three years ago and today. We can only infer that the percentage revenue share of computer manufacturers is declining, while that for computer parts and service companies is rising. For all we know, the computer industry's revenues may have declined or may have gone up. Simple percentage shares imply no absolute information.

Answer choice explanation

(A) The question is concerned with whether data given provides evidence to support the conclusion. The explanation for why the revenue shares of three sectors of the industry changed is **not relevant**. We have to concern ourselves with whether industry revenues are declining.

(B) This option is **inconclusive.** There is no reason to doubt the veracity or the consistency of data. We have to concern ourselves with whether industry revenues are declining.

(C) This option is **inconclusive** and **irrelevant** because it does not deal with industry revenues.

(D) This is the **correct** answer. The argument lacks the information about the computer industry's overall revenue today and three years ago. It only provides information on the percentage shares of the various industry companies.

(E) This information is **irrelevant**.

The correct answer is option D.

Question 8

Argument construction

The wholesale price of mustard has increased substantially in the last six months, whereas that of groundnut has decreased.

Conclusion: The retail price of mustard oil at grocery shops will increase.

Predict A Weakener

Predictive Weakener: For mustard oil, the successive elements of the costs of mustard and oil, from after the wholesaler sells mustard till it reaches grocery stores, decreased significantly.

We need to show that, for some reason, the cost of mustard oil will not increase.

Answer choice explanation

(A) If the operating costs of grocery stores have been constant for the last three quarters, it will strengthen the conclusion rather than weaken it.

(B) This option is **not relevant.** It compares the wholesale prices of mustard and groundnut.

(C) This is the **correct** answer. If the cost of processing mustard oil has decreased during the last year, it is likely that the distributor may have offset the increase in price, thereby not making the grocery store pay more to distributors. Therefore, it is probable that the oil price will not increase.

(D) This option is **irrelevant.** Harvesting mustard is an activity prior to wholesale trading. We are concerned about the effect on the prices of mustard oil after the mustard was harvested.

(E) This statement means that per capita consumption of mustard oil is almost constant. This information does not help weaken the conclusion.

The correct answer is option C.

Question 9

Argument construction

The allegation of workers from community X: The company is biased against them in recruitment.

Counter-evidence by the company: 65% of the applicants belonging to community X have been employed by he company, as opposed to 55% of applicants not belonging to community X. (Read: more are employed from community X)

Conclusion: The company is not biased against community X.

Predict A Weakener

Your job is to argue against the counter-evidence. What could be the flaw in the counter-evidence: *65% of applicants belonging to community X have been employed by the company, compared to 55% of applicants not belonging to community X.*

There could be two predictable flaws; one, the 65% figure should be significantly more, and/or second, the 55% figure should be significantly less.

Predictive Weakener 1: Significantly more than 65% of applicants belonging to community X should have been employed by the company.

Predictive Weakener 2: Significantly less than 55% of applicants not belonging to community X should have been employed by the company.

Answer choice explanation

(A) This is **out of scope.** The argument focusing on community Y is beyond the scope of the argument.

(B) This is the **correct** answer. It is in line with predictive weakener 2.

(C) This is **inconclusive.** Stating that there are a large number of workers employed by the company not belonging to community X does not mean that there are few workers employed by the company belonging to community X.

(D) This is **irrelevant.** It tries to distract you by alluding that possibly due to an outside consultant's fault, this situation has persisted.

(E) A large number of resumes from non-recruited applicants belonging to community X may not be a good fit for the job. The company has every right to invite new applications from workers from any community, including those not belonging to community X.

The correct answer is option B.

5.5 References for Official Guide Questions

The Official Guide for GMAT Review, 13th Edition: Question # 2, 4, 20, 25, 32, 37, 43, 51, 58, 62, 71, 73, 79, 80, 82, 87, 88, 90, 97, 107, 112, 115, 117, 119, 122;
Diagnostic test question # 18, 20, 23, 26, 30, and 34

The Official Guide for GMAT Verbal Review, 2nd Edition: Question # 4, 5, 11, 15, 16, 18, 20, 22, 24, 26, 27, 31, 36, 39, 41, 46, 47, 49, 50, 71, 80, 81, 83

Chapter 6

Evaluate the Argument

6.1 Evaluate the Argument Question type

An evaluate the argument question asks you to select a question, some data, or a piece of information from among five options that would best help to establish the validity of the argument. In other words, you have to choose the option that confirms whether the argument is valid.

Evaluate the argument questions also belong to the assumption-based family. There may be a logical gap in the argument. We recognize this gap by posing a question which, when answered, either increases or decreases the validity of the argument. So, we can say that *evaluate the argument questions are a combination of strengthen the argument and weaken the argument.*

Look at the image below. There is a dialogue taking place between two people. What could be an evaluating question here?

Following illustration depicts your job for evaluate the argument question type.

> Companies Pinnacle and Acme provide round-the-clock e-mail assistance to any customer who uses their laptops. Customers send e-mails only when they find the laptops difficult to use. Since Pinnacle [...] times as many e-mails as Acme does, Pinnacle's laptops must be mor[e ... than] Acme's.
>
> Which of the following must be j[udged in order to eva]luate the argument?
>
> A. Acme and Pinna[...] of time.
> B. E-mails to Acme [...] Pinnacle.
> C. Acme does not r[eceive complaints] through other means such as letters, a[nd ...]
> D. The number of e[-mails ...] has been gradually increasing. (B)
> E. Pinnacle's e-mai[l ...] e-mail ID.
>
> *Only one option weakens and strengthens the conclusion the most, and makes it valid and invalid.*

Question Stem

Most evaluate the argument **question stems will contain one of the following:**

-evaluate/determine/investigate/judge whether...
-Asking what would be useful to know/important to know/necessary to establish in order to determine the validity of the conclusion
-Asking what would help most to access the argument

Evaluate the argument question stems may look like the following.

- Which of the following must be judged in order to evaluate the argument?

- Which of the following would it be most important to know in establishing whether Pinnacle's laptops are more difficult to use than Acme's?

- The answer to which of the following questions would help most to access the argument?

Evaluate the argument questions may use different phrases/words from the above, but the objective will be the same – **what is significant to study, access, understand, or validate the argument?**

6.2 The Process Of Solving Evaluate The Argument Questions

The 4-step approach is the same as mentioned in chapter 2.

The 4-step approach

(1) Recognize the question type

(2) Understand the argument construction

(3) Predict the qualifier

(4) Eliminate incorrect options

We have seen the 4-step approach to solve a CR question. It is applicable to "Evaluate the Argument" type also. There is some additional work to be done at step 3.

Predicting the qualifier

As we do in assumption questions, the third step is still to predict the assumption(s), but in the next step you have to predict the evaluator(s) too in the question form. Basically, we have to answer what additional information would help us establish the validity of the assumption.

Let us take a look at the 'Pinnacle and Acme' argument. Say the question stem is—"Which of the following must be judged in order to evaluate the argument?"

> Companies Pinnacle and Acme provide round-the-clock email assistance to any customer who uses their laptops. Customers send emails only when they find the laptop difficult to use. Since Pinnacle receives four times as many emails as Acme receives, Pinnacle's laptops must be more difficult to use than Acme's.

6.2.1 Predicting the Evaluator

We will predict a few evaluators to validate the argument. As per the 3rd step, we need to first predict the assumption(s). As we have already done this exercise in chapter 1, we will simply reproduce the same here.

Predictive Assumption 1: Acme does not receive more complaints than Pinnacle does through other means such as letters or phone calls. An evaluating question framed from this assumption would be as follows:

Predictive Evaluator 1: Does Acme receive more complaints than Pinnacle through other means such as letters or phone calls?

If the above question is answered correctly, it will validate the argument. Let us see how.

If Acme receives more complaints than Pinnacle receives through other means such as letters and phone calls, then the conclusion that Pinnacle's laptops are difficult to use is <u>invalidated</u>.

Conversely, if Acme does not receive more complaints than Pinnacle does through other means such as letters or phone calls, the conclusion that Pinnacle's laptops are difficult to use is <u>validated</u>.

This establishes that the above question is the correct question to raise to check the validity of the conclusion/argument.

One assumption may lead to multiple evaluating answer choices.

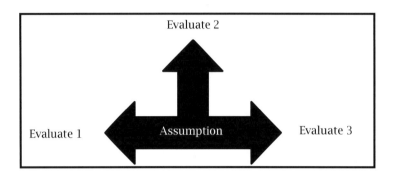

Let us see how.

Predictive Assumption 2: Acme does not sell significantly fewer laptops than Pinnacle.

Predictive Evaluator 2.1: Does Acme sell significantly fewer laptops than Pinnacle?

If Acme sells significantly fewer laptops than Pinnacle, it is logical that Acme will receive fewer emails than Pinnacle, and then the conclusion that Pinnacle's laptops are difficult to use will be <u>invalidated</u>, since the comparison is illogical and size-biased.

Conversely, if Acme does not sell significantly fewer laptops than Pinnacle, it is logical that the number of laptops sold by Acme is comparable to the number sold by Pinnacle, and then the conclusion that Pinnacle's laptops are difficult to use is <u>validated</u>.

This establishes that the above question is the correct question to raise to check the validity of the conclusion/argument.

Predictive Evaluator 2.2: Does Pinnacle sell significantly more laptops to people who are new to computers than Acme?

Predictive Evaluator 2.3: Does Pinnacle sell significantly more high-end configured laptops than Acme?

By now you have gone through the "Pinnacle and Acme" argument a few times. Try answering the above questions once with a "yes" and then with a "no". You will notice that the above questions are the correct questions to raise to check the validity of the conclusion/argument because one answer will strengthen the conclusion and the other one will weaken the conclusion.

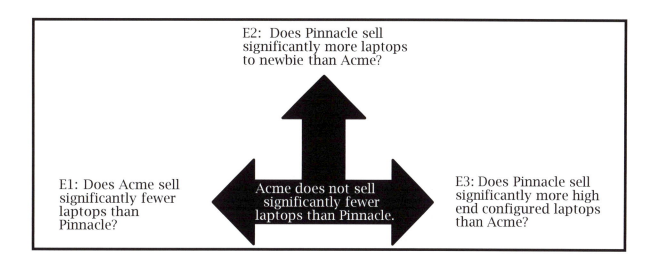

6.2.2 The Evaluation Test

You may come across a couple of close contenders for the correct answer in a particular question. To pick one of those two, apply the evaluation test.

We have so far understood that the correct option is a question which, when answered, will validate the argument.

As per the evaluation test, you have to answer the close contenders once with **yes** and then with **no**. The correct option's answers will strengthen and weaken the conclusion. For example, if the answer "yes" weakens the conclusion, the answer "no" will strengthen the conclusion. This can work vice versa too. However, in wrong options, both answers will either weaken or strengthen, or do nothing. The wrong options can also be irrelevant to the conclusion. Only the correct answer choice will reflect its **bipolar** behavior. Let us see this in action!

We will take two close contenders from the 'Pinnacle and Acme' argument – options A and B.

Option A: *Does Acme receive more complaints than Pinnacle through other means such as letters or phone calls?*

Answer with yes: Yes, Acme receives more complaints than Pinnacle receives through other means such as letters and phone calls.

Since Acme receives more complaints through letters and phones calls, while Pinnacle receives them through emails, the conclusion that Pinnacle's laptops are difficult to use is **weakened** or **invalidated.**

Answer with no: No, Acme does not receive more complaints than Pinnacle receives through other means such as letters and phone calls.

Since Acme does not receive more complaints through letters or phone calls, while Pinnacle receives more complaints through emails, the conclusion that Pinnacle's laptops are difficult to use is **strengthened or validated.**

Option A reflects its **bipolar** behavior, hence it is the correct answer.

Option B: Is the length of emails to Acme, on average, more than that to Pinnacle?

Answer with yes: Yes, the length of emails to Acme, on average, is more than that to Pinnacle.

Does this strengthen or weaken the conclusion?

No. The conclusion is based on the number of emails rather than the length of emails.

Answer with no: No, the length of emails to Acme, on average, is not more than that to Pinnacle.

Does the 'answer with no' strengthen or weaken the conclusion? No; hence this cannot be the correct answer option.

Example Questions

6.3 Examples

Example 1

McDougal's and Deep Fry are two fast food chains locked in a bitter contest to dominate the minimal-pay, yet labor-intensive, fast food business in the north-eastern states. Both chains are eager to expand, but McDougal's lacks capital because it spends almost forty percent of its gross profits on wage costs. To raise funds to finance expansion, McDougal's plans to cut the wages of newly-hired staff by 12%, and the wages of experienced staff by 10%.

The answer to which of the following is most important to know in order to raise funds as per the proposed plan?

- **(A)** Are the areas in which MacDougal's intends to expand already served by a successful fast food chain?
- **(B)** Is wage rate a crucial factor in attracting fast food business staff?
- **(C)** Has McDougal's acquired a reputation for good service and food quality?
- **(D)** Has Deep Fry planned to open two branches for every one opened by McDougal's?
- **(E)** Has the restaurant workers' union protested the proposed wage cut?

Argument construction

The argument is easy to understand.

Conclusion: By cutting the wages of newly-hired staff by 12%, and of experienced staff by 10%,, McDougal's can save money to finance its expansion.

Predict an Evaluator

The question specifically asks us to evaluate only the fundraising plan and its chances of success. So, we have to find an option that will reveal whether McD's fundraising is likely to work. Let's put ourselves into their place and figure out the reasoning and assumptions behind the proposed wage cuts. McD's is assuming that the employees would go along with the wage cuts and not quit. McD's is also assuming that the given amount of wage cuts would be sufficient for its expansion plans.

Predictive Assumption 1: Despite cutting wages, McDougal's can hire new staff, and retain experienced staff.

Predictive Evaluator 1: Can McDougal's hire new staff and retain experienced staff despite cutting staff wages?

Predictive Assumption 2: By cutting the wages of newly hired staff by 12%, and the wages of experienced staff by 10%, McDougal's can save sufficient money to finance expansion.

Predictive Evaluator 2: Is the sum accrued from wage cuts sufficient enough to finance expansion?

Answer choice explanation

(A)   This option is **irrelevant**. It does not answer the question whether McDougal's must cut wages to raise funds. This deals with another scenario.

(B)   This is the **correct** answer. This is aligned with predictive evaluator 1. If wage is a crucial factor in the fast food business, it follows that attrition of a competent workforce may severely affect McDougal's operations. If we answer "yes" to this option, the conclusion is weakened, while "no" strengthens the conclusion.

(C)   This option is **irrelevant** in determining whether McDougal's wage cutting will work in funding its expansion.

(D)   This option is **irrelevant** in determining whether McDougal's wage cutting will work in funding its expansion.

(E)   This option is a tricky one, but is **inconclusive.** Even if the restaurant workers' union protests the proposed wage cut, it does not necessarily mean that the union has **rejected** the wage cut. Option B is more important to know to determine whether McDougal's wage cutting will work in funding its expansion. This option will become operative once the plan is deemed feasible.

The correct answer is option B.

Example 2

The music industry has demanded that the government pass legislation preventing internet-based companies from playing music over the net. Such services invite consumers to illegally download music to CD recorders and thereby damage sales of legally marketed CDs. This, they claim, takes as much as 25% of their potential profits and harms artists struggling to launch their careers.

Which of the following needs to be evaluated to validate the conclusion?

(A)   Are the internet companies willing to pay for the rights to music they play on the net?

(B)   Has the reduction in sales of recorded CDs led to reduced tax bills for music companies?

(C)   Is the quality of pirated CDs more or less equal to that of conventionally recorded CDs?

(D)   Does piracy mainly target world famous groups, singers, and musicians?

(E)   Is the price of pirated CDs fractionally low compared to conventional CDs?

Argument construction

The music industry wants the government to prevent internet-based companies from playing music over the net. Since consumers illegally download music to CD recorders, this eats up the sales of legally marketed CDs. The music industry claims that it eats up as much as 25% of their potential profits and thereby harms artists struggling to launch their careers.

Conclusion: The government must prevent internet-based companies from playing music over the net because it reduces profits and harms struggling artists.

Predict an Evaluator

Based on our understanding of the argument, we can draw some predictive assumptions and their associated evaluators.

Predictive Assumption 1: Most music piracy is being done by internet-based companies.

Predictive Evaluator 1: Is most music piracy being done by internet-based companies?

Predictive Assumption 2: Most people do not wish to spend money on conventional CDs.

Predictive Evaluator 2: Do most people want to avoid spending money on conventional CDs, yet enjoy the music freely available over the internet?

Predictive Assumption 3: There is no way to use technology so that internet companies can continue airing music, while at the same time prevent illegal downloading.

Predictive Evaluator 3: Is there is any way to use technology so that internet companies can continue airing music, while at the same time prevent illegal downloading?

Answer choice explanation

(A) This is the **correct** answer. Answering "yes" to the question will weaken the conclusion by implying that there is no need to prevent internet companies from playing music over the net because music companies can earn money from them. Answering "no" will strengthen the conclusion by implying that internet companies will continue to play pirated music over the net, thereby harming CD sales.

(B) If the reduction in sales of recorded CDs leads to reduced tax bills for music companies, we cannot conclusively infer that the reduction in such sales is due to internet piracy. There may be a number of reasons why sales plummeted. This option does not qualify to be evaluated because "yes" or "no" will be irrelevant to the conclusion.

(C) If the quality of the pirated CDs is more or less equal to that of conventionally recorded CDs, people will be motivated to illegally download music; it validates the conclusion. Conversely, even if the quality not as good as conventional CDs, people may still choose to download from the net. The conclusion is not invalidated. This option does not reflect the requisite bipolar behavior.

(D) Whether piracy mainly targets only world famous performers or newcomers, it will eat up the profits of music companies. This option does not qualify to be evaluated because "yes" or "no" will be irrelevant to the conclusion.

(E) If the price of pirated CDs is significantly lower than that of conventional CDs, people will be motivated to illegally download music; it validates the conclusion. Conversely, even if the price is relatively lower, though not fractionally lower, people may still choose to download from the net. The conclusion is not invalidated. This option does not reflect the requisite bipolar behavior.

The correct answer is option A.

Example 3

Residents of Delta City want to have a cleaner environment in their city and a better quality of life. This means construction of more parks and greenways in the city center. If they build more parks and designate certain areas as greenways, however, housing prices will go up in the long term as less land will remain available for habitation. The rise in housing prices will then have a negative impact on their quality of life as they will have to pay more for the same amount of space.

The answer to which of the following questions would be LEAST relevant to evaluating whether the residents indeed face the choice the author says they do?

(A) Could park and greenway developments be carried out under an alternative plan without increasing the cost of living?

(B) Would development of parks and greenways benefit the residents of other cities?

(C) Would the jobs created to develop the parks and greenways be filled by the residents of Delta City?

(D) Do residents of Delta City support or oppose development of these parks and greenways?

(E) Will the cost of housing remain at current prices without the development of parks and greenways?

Argument construction

The argument is easy to understand. The citizens want better life and environment. However, doing so will raise real estate prices.

Conclusion: Allocating land for parks will negatively affect residents' lives.

Predict an Evaluator

The question is to find the least relevant option that helps to evaluate it. Unlike in standard 'evaluate the argument' type questions, in this question you will find 4 options that qualify as evaluators. The option that is not an evaluator is the answer.

Predictive Assumption 1: The benefit derived from building parks is less than the negative impact of the rise in housing prices.

Predictive Evaluator 1: Is the benefit derived out of building parks less than the negative impact of the rise in housing prices?

Predictive Assumption 2: Housing prices are either not rising, or rising at a slower rate.

Predictive Evaluator 2: Are housing prices either not rising, or rising at a slower rate?

Basically, the author says that building parks would mean less benefit to the residents than we think. Hence, his conclusion is that the parks will have a negative impact. A good evaluator in this question will be anything that shows that parks can have a positive impact too (or negative) as long as it shows both strengthening and weakening. Anything that shows that parks may actually not benefit the residents at all will strengthen the conclusion, but not weaken it. Thus, there's nothing "bipolar" about it. We must orient our thinking towards the option that does not show any benefits for the residents. That option would be the correct answer.

Answer choice explanation

(A) This option qualifies to be **evaluated**. It talks about reduction in cost—a matter of interest to the residents and the "yes/no" answer to this would strengthen and weaken the conclusion.

(B) This is the **correct** answer. This option does not qualify to be evaluated. It talks about benefit to other cities – a matter of no interest to the residents.

(C) This option qualifies to be **evaluated**. It talks about job creation—a matter of interest to the residents and the "yes/no" answer to this would strengthen and weaken the conclusion.

(D) This option qualifies to be **evaluated**. It talks about the apprehensions of residents – a matter of concern to the residents and the "yes/no" answer to this would strengthen and weaken the conclusion.

(E) This option qualifies to be **evaluated**. It talks about the rise in house prices – a matter of interest to the residents and the "yes/no" answer to this would strengthen and weaken the conclusion.

The correct answer is option B.

Example 4

Privatization of utilities has led to higher prices despite promises that it would lower them. The streamlining and paring down of workforces may well have reduced costs, but these savings have been used to pay the dividends of shareholders instead of being passed on to customers. The amount of capital investment made has been recouped, particularly in relation to water supplies. Consumer associations claim that water companies are overcharging consumers. In answer to such accusations, the companies claim that the higher charges are due to the constant need for repairs and maintenance.

Which of the following must be studied in order to validate the conclusion put forth by the water company?

- **(A)** Are companies legally obliged to supply water regardless of cost?
- **(B)** Have unusual weather conditions resulted in a severe water shortage in many states?
- **(C)** Does the number of paying customers far outnumber the number of non-paying customers?
- **(D)** Was service prior to privatization worse than the service currently provided?
- **(E)** Are 'repairs and maintenance costs' a secondary cost in the cost of water supply and management?

Argument construction

Privatization of utilities was done so that bills would go down, but, on the contrary, they went up. The restructuring of workforces in the companies may have reduced costs, but the savings were used to pay the dividends of shareholders, and not passed on to customers. Capital investment has also been recouped, especially in the case of water companies. Consumer associations claim that water companies are overcharging consumers. The companies refute the claim by stating that the higher charges are due to the constant need for repairs and maintenance.

Conclusion: Higher water bills for consumers are due to the constant need for repairs and maintenance.

Predict an Evaluator

We must validate the conclusion that higher bills are due to the constant need for repairs and maintenance. What would justify the frequent need for repairs and maintenance? It may be that machinery and pipelines are old, or maybe the previous company did poor maintenance.

Predictive Assumption 1: Water supply machinery and pipelines have aged.

Predictive Evaluator 1: Have the water supply machinery and pipelines aged?

Predictive Assumption 2: The previous company that supplied the water maintained water supply machinery and pipelines poorly.

Predictive Evaluator 2: Did the previous company that supplied the water maintain water supply machinery and pipelines poorly?

Answer choice explanation

(A) This option is **inconclusive**. We have to judge the conclusion that states that the reason for overcharging is excessive repairs. This option is not related to the reason for overcharging. This option poses a moral question. If we answer **yes,** that companies are **obliged** to supply water regardless of the cost, the conclusion remains that they are overcharging because of repairs. If we answer no, that the companies are **not obliged** to supply water regardless of the cost, the conclusion remains that they are overcharging because of repairs. This option's range does not affect the conclusion at all.

(B) This option is tricky. 'Unusual weather conditions' may be inferred as wear and tear to the equipment and water pipes. However, the option states that the weather causes water shortages. Our conclusion does not deal with a complaint about water shortage, but about overcharging in the current water scenario. If we say yes, the weather has caused a shortage, the conclusion that there is a lot of repair work is unharmed. If we say no, that the weather has not caused a water shortage, the conclusion about extra costs of repairs still remains intact. Hence, this option is not the right answer.

(C) This option is **irrelevant.** It has no relevance to the claim. We are discussing if the company's charging is valid or invalid, and not if the customers are paying those bills or not.

(D) This option is the **correct** answer. If we answer **"yes",** that before privatization the government, too, provided bad service, the conclusion that there is a lot of repair work to be done can be justified **(strengthened)**. If we say **"no",** that before privatization the government did not provide bad service, then the conclusion that there is a lot of repair work to be done is invalid **(weakened)**. Hence, determining the answer to this option will help us judge the validity of the conclusion.

(E) This option is also a tricky one, but is **inconclusive**.

Let us apply the evaluation test.

Yes, 'repairs and maintenance costs' are a secondary cost in the cost of water supply and management. The conclusion that excessive charges are due to repairs remains intact.

No, 'repairs and maintenance costs' are not a secondary cost in the cost of water supply and management. This does not mean that it is a primary cost; it may be tertiary cost too. The conclusion that excessive charges are due to repairs remains intact.

The correct answer is option D.

Practice

Questions

6.4 Practice Questions

6.4.1 Questions

Question 1

Many small children have problems with nightmares. Recent studies done by psychologists show that these nightmares can be reduced by letting the children fall asleep with the lights on. Two groups of children took part in such a study. The group that fell asleep with the lights off indicated that they had more nightmares than the group that fell asleep with the lights on.

Which of the following questions would be most useful for evaluating the conclusion?

- **(A)** Are nightmares more prevalent among children than among adults?
- **(B)** Did teenagers who fell asleep with the lights on have the same number of nightmares as before?
- **(C)** Are children who play violent computer games more likely to have nightmares?
- **(D)** Did children who previously had problems with nightmares show a markedly decreased incidence of nightmares after five months of falling asleep with the lights on?
- **(E)** Do children with a high level of self-esteem have fewer problems with nightmares than children with average levels of self-esteem?

Question 2

You have seen the following question in chapter 1. We present to you its 'evaluate the argument' version.

Recent research into obesity suggests that although certain amphetamines are capable of quelling physical hunger pangs, they also have a mood-altering affect that frequently leads to food binging. Of the 63 patients that took part in tests carried out by Hopkins Institute scientists, 43 admitted to periodically binging to assuage depression, and at the conclusion of the eight-week trial were found to have gained weight. From these results, scientists have concluded that appetite-quelling amphetamines are often counter-productive and should be prescribed to patients only in controlled environments.

Which of the following would help best to access the argument?

- **(A)** Whether all amphetamines cause depression.
- **(B)** Whether patients in controlled environments have been known to binge secretly.
- **(C)** Whether the degree of weight gain varied according to the individual patient.
- **(D)** Whether some of the patients who gained weight were given higher doses of amphetamines than those who lost weight.
- **(E)** Whether the other patients were also reported as suffering from depression.

Question 3

The recent increase in the value of the dollar is worrying US exporters, who see themselves as being undercut by foreign competition. The rise was triggered by an upward interest rate modification declared by the Federal Reserve, but the rise would not have occurred had there not been simultaneously-announced cutbacks in this year's defense-spending budget.

Which of the following would most qualify to be evaluated to test the conclusion?

- **(A)** Whether past increases in defense spending were frequently followed by simultaneous rises in interest and decreased values of the dollar.

- **(B)** Whether the recent decline in export sales is more because US goods are not able to manage a very price-sensitive foreign marketplace.

- **(C)** Whether defense cutbacks are often the result of economic declines coupled with budget deficits.

- **(D)** Whether a rise in the percentage of export trade captured by foreign competitors often results in increased defense spending to emphasize US military superiority.

- **(E)** Whether an overvalued dollar is sometimes accompanied by a rise in US exports of IT goods.

6.4.2 Answer-Key

(1) D | (2) B | (3) A

Solutions

6.4.3 Solutions

Question 1

Argument construction

The argument is easy to understand.

Conclusion: Children sleeping with the lights on will have significantly fewer nightmares than those sleeping with the lights off.

Predict An Evaluator

Predictive Assumption 1: Both groups studied had nearly the same number of nightmares before the experiment.

Predictive Evaluator 1: Did both groups have nearly the same number of nightmares before the experiment?

This question is necessary to evaluate because if the group that slept with the lights on already had significantly fewer nightmares before the experiment, the conclusion is invalidated.

Predictive Assumption 2: Repeating the experiment by switching the groups will yield the same result.

Predictive Evaluator 2: Will repeating the experiment by switching the groups yield the same result?

Predictive Assumption 3: Repeating the experiment at later dates will yield the same result.

Predictive Evaluator 3: Will repeating the experiment at later dates yield the same result?

Answer choice explanation

(A) This option is **out of scope.** Adults are beyond the scope of the argument.

(B) This option is tricky. If teenagers who fall asleep with the lights on had the same number of nightmares as before, the conclusion is invalidated. Conversely, if teenagers who fall asleep with the lights on did not have the same number of nightmares as before, then we cannot conclude whether they had fewer nightmares now than before. So, the option only weakens the conclusion but does not strengthen it.

Similarly, note that the argument compares the number of nightmares between two groups – those who slept with lights on vs. those who slept with them off, but option B compares the number of nightmares before and after within the group that slept with the lights on.

Also, this option is ruled out on the basis of its focus on 'teenagers' only, which is a sub-set of the group "children". 'Teenagers' cannot be representative of the entire group.

(C) This option is **out of scope**. Video games are beyond the scope of the argument.

(D) This is the **correct** answer. If children who previously had problems with nightmares showed a markedly decreased incidence of nightmares after five months of falling asleep with the lights on, the conclusion is **validated.** Conversely, if children who previously had problems with nightmares did not show a markedly decreased incidence of nightmares after five months of falling asleep with the lights on, then conclusion is **invalidated.** It shows the bipolar nature of the option. It strengthens and weakens the conclusion in its two possibilities.

Also, it is aligned with predictive evaluator 3.

(E) This option is **out of scope.** The argument deals solely with the effect of lights on the reduction of nightmares in children, and not with self-esteem.

The correct answer is option D.

Question 2

Argument construction

A research into obesity suggests that although certain amphetamines are capable of suppressing physical hunger pains, they also have a mood-altering affect that frequently leads to food binging. Of the 63 patients that took part in tests carried out by Hopkins Institute scientists, 43 admitted to periodically binging to ease depression, and at the conclusion of the eight-week trial were found to have gained weight.

Conclusion: Appetite-quelling amphetamines are often counter-productive and should be prescribed to patients only in controlled environments.

Predict An Evaluator

Concluding that amphetamines should be prescribed to patients only in controlled environments implies that there is an underlying assumption here – food binging will not be allowed in controlled environments.

Predictive Assumption: Patients will not be allowed to binge on food in controlled environments.

Predictive Evaluator: Will patients be allowed to binge on food secretly in controlled environments?

Answer choice explanation

(A) This option is **irrelevant.** It is not related to food binging. The conclusion remains intact whether you answer "yes" or "no", because the argument specified certain amphetamines.

(B) This is the **correct** answer. It is aligned with the predictive evaluator. Answering "yes" will weaken the conclusion, while "no" will strengthen it.

(C) This option is **out of scope.** Degree of weight is beyond the scope of the argument. The conclusion remains intact whether you answer "yes" or "no".

(D) This option is **out of scope.** The degree of doses of amphetamines is beyond the scope of the argument. The conclusion remains intact whether you answer "yes" or "no". Note that when you answer "yes", the answer is not that **all** patients who gained weight were given a higher dose of amphetamines, but the answer is that yes, **some** patients who gained weight were given more amphetamines. The "yes" answer does not impact the conclusion because only some of those who gained weight were given more amphetamines.

(E) This option is **irrelevant.** The conclusion remains intact whether you answer "yes" or "no". The answer "yes" does not change the fact that 43 gained weight, and neither does the answer "no".

The correct answer is option B.

Question 3

Argument construction

US exporters are worried about the recent increase in the value of the dollar. They claim that because of the high price of the dollar, they will lose business to foreign competition.

The rise in the dollar was triggered by the simultaneous occurrences of an upward interest rate modification declared by the Federal Reserve, and cutbacks in this year's defense-spending budget.

Conclusion: The rise in the dollar was triggered by the simultaneous occurrence of an upward interest rate and cutbacks in this year's defense-spending budget.

Predict An Evaluator

From the argument, we can infer that the effect – the rise in the dollar – was triggered by the *cause – an upward interest rate modification + simultaneously-announced cutbacks in the defense spending budget.*

Predictive Assumption 1: An upward interest rate modification with cutbacks in the defense-spending budget mostly triggers a rise in the dollar.

Predictive Evaluator 1: Does an upward interest rate modification with cutbacks in the defense-spending budget mostly trigger a rise in the dollar?

Predictive Assumption 2: The rise in the dollar is not due to other reasons.

Predictive Evaluator 2: Is the rise in the dollar not due to other reasons?

Answer choice explanation

(A) This is the **correct** answer. This option is the inverse of our predictive evaluator 1. The answer to this question will prove whether a cause and effect relationship of the type mentioned in the conclusion of the argument exists. If we answer "yes" to this, the conclusion is strengthened, and "no" will weaken the conclusion because 'no' will prove that the argument is making a flimsy connection for the three events (rise in the price of the dollar, upward interest rate modifications, and cutbacks in defense spending).

(B) This option is a **rephrase.** We already know this from the premise: *The recent increase in the value of the dollar is worrying US exporters who are seeing themselves undercut by foreign competition.* Thus we need not determine this information to evaluate the validity of the conclusion.

(C) This option is **tricky but incorrect.** It sounds like this option is also discussing the three events that are mentioned in the cause and effect relationship in the argument's conclusion, but this option is incorrect because it does not specifically discuss those three events. It discusses the three events generally , and requires us to make a lot of assumptions not sanctioned by the argument before we can accept it as correct. To say economic decline is linked to the dollar price, we will need to assume that economic decline always affects the dollar price. Similar assumptions need to be made about budget cuts and upward interest rate modifications. Hence, this option is incorrect because by itself it proves nothing. If we say "yes" or "no", the conclusion remains intact.

(D) This option is **irrelevant** too. It suffers from the same flaws as option C.

(E) This option is **irrelevant** too. It establishes the relationship between the dollar and exports of IT goods alone and is out of scope.

The correct answer is option A.

6.5 References for Official Guide Questions

The Official Guide for GMAT Review, 13th Edition: Question # 7, 10, 15, 27, 36, 42, 47, 53, 68, 70, 72, 110, 114, 124;
Diagnostic test question # 21, 22, and 29

The Official Guide for GMAT Verbal Review, 2nd Edition: Question # 3, 28, 40, 42, 54, 66, and 70

Chapter 7

Find the Flaw in the Argument

7.1 Find the Flaw Question type

Unlike strengthen or weaken the argument questions, find the flaw in the argument questions are infrequently asked in Critical Reasoning. These types of questions will appear when you are doing well in the verbal section.

Find the flaw in the argument and weaken the argument questions are similar in nature, but quite different in concept. Though both types of questions weaken the argument, each type of question focuses on a different aspect of the argument. Find the Flaw questions also belong to the assumption- based family.

Find the flaw questions reveal the flaw or the weakness in the reasoning used to draw the conclusion. While drawing the conclusion, the author makes a few assumptions without proper justification and these become flaws in his thinking, or reasoning. So, a flaw in reasoning exposes the dangerous assumptions that the author makes, those assumptions that can eventually weaken his argument. Unlike the options of weaken questions, the options of find the flaw questions are presented in abstract language.

7.1.1 Differences between flaw and weaken question types

The following table will help you better differentiate between the two types.

	Flaw	Weakener
Role	Find the flaw or the weakness in the reasoning to reach the conclusion.	Make the argument flawed or weakened by introducing new information to the argument.
Focus	It focuses on the assumption. It advocates that if the unstated assumption falls flat, the argument is flawed.	It focuses on the conclusion. By introducing new information to the argument, it makes the argument flawed.

Question stem	Occasionally, the question stem may **not** contain the word 'flaw', but it will also **not** contain the words 'if true' or similar-meaning words or phrases.	Occasionally, the question stem may contain the word 'flaw', but it will also contain the words **'if true'** or similar phrases.
Options	Options are written in an abstract manner, highlighting the reason for the flaw.	Options are true, new pieces of information.
Why vs. What	The correct option illustrates **why** the reasoning is flawed.	The correct option illustrates **what** new information can make the argument flawed.

Look at the image below. There is a dialogue taking place between two people. What could be a flaw here?

Critical Reasoning Guide – Find the Flaw

7.1.2 Assumption vs. Flaw vs. Weaken question types

Let us see an argument: **Steve will get 700+ in his GMAT**.

Assumption	Flaw (dealing with assumption reasoning)	Weakener (adding information that weakens the conclusion)
Steve will appear for his GMAT exam.	The reasoning is flawed as it fails to consider whether Steve will appear for his GMAT exam.	Steve has been inconsistent in getting 700+ in his mocks.
Steve has prepared well for the GMAT exam.	The reasoning is flawed as it fails to consider whether Steve has prepared well for the GMAT exam.	Steve has prepared poorly for the GMAT exam.
Steve is an intelligent student.	The reasoning is flawed as it fails to consider whether Steve is a fairly intelligent student.	Steve has scored poorly in similar high-pressure competitive exams.

The following illustration depicts your job for find the find the flaw question type.

> Companies Pinnacle and Acme provide round-the-clock e-mail assistance to any customer who uses their laptops. Customers send e-mails only when they find the laptops difficult to u_____ e-mails as Acme does, Pinnacle's lapt_____.
>
> The reasoning in the_____
>
> *Only one option will rightly expose the flaw in the reasoning used to draw the conclusion.*
>
> A. consider whethe_____ently long period of time.
> B. establish if e-mails to Acme a_____ length, on average, as to Pinnacle.
> C. identify any other alterna_____ may have receive more complaints than Pinnacle recei_____ means.
> D. supply information on the number o_____ ils received by each of the two companies has been gradually increasing.
> E. consider that Pinnacle's e-mail ID could be more widely publicized than Acme's e-mail ID.

Question Stem

When specifying that the reasoning in the argument is flawed, the test makers may use 'vulnerable to criticism' or phrases with a similar meaning.

Here are a few possible question stems:

- The *reasoning* above is flawed because it fails to consider that...

- Which of the following most accurately describes a flaw in the argument's *reasoning*?
- The *reasoning* above is most vulnerable to criticism due to...
- A questionable aspect of the *reasoning* above is that it...

7.2 The Process Of Solving Find The Flaw Argument Questions

The 4-step approach is the same as in chapter 2.

The 4-step approach

(1) Recognize the question type

(2) Understand the argument construction

(3) Predict the qualifier

(4) Eliminate incorrect options

The first 2 steps are the same for find the flaw questions. Let us jump directly to the predict the qualifier step.

7.2.1 Predicting the qualifier

Let us examine the "predict the qualifier" step from 'Find the Flaw' perspective.

We will try it on the 'Pinnacle and Acme' argument.

> Companies Pinnacle and Acme provide round-the-clock email assistance to any customer who uses their laptops. Customers send emails only when they find the laptop difficult to use. Since Pinnacle receives four times as many emails as Acme receives, Pinnacle's laptops must be more difficult to use than Acme's.

Conclusion: *Pinnacle's laptops must be more difficult to use than Acme's.*

Our job is to find the flaw in the reasoning used to draw the conclusion. The optimum approach is to predict assumptions. After predicting assumptions, reverse them. It may seem like the methodology used for solving weaken the argument questions, but in find the flaw questions, you have to attack the reasoning used to make the argument. **The focus is on the reasoning.**

7.2.2 Predicting the Flaw

Let's look at the predictive assumptions derived in chapter 2.

Predictive Assumption 1: Acme does not receive more complaints than Pinnacle does through other means such as letters or phone calls.
Predictive Flaw 1: The reasoning above is flawed because it fails to consider that Acme could receive more complaints than Pinnacle does through other means such as letters or phone calls.

Predictive Assumption 2: Acme does not sell significantly fewer laptops than Pinnacle.
Predictive Flaw 2: The reasoning above is flawed because it fails to consider that Acme might

sell significantly fewer laptops than Pinnacle.

Predictive Assumption 3: Both company's laptops must be comparable.
Predictive Flaw 3: The reasoning is questionable because it fails to consider whether the laptops of both companies are comparable.

Predictive Assumption 4: Pinnacle does not sell significantly more laptops to people who are new to computers than Acme does.
Predictive Flaw 4: The reasoning above is most vulnerable to criticism because it fails to supply information as to whether Pinnacle sells significantly more laptops to people who are new to computers than Acme does.

Example Questions

7.3 Examples

Example 1

Newly appointed worker: "How would I benefit from joining the union?"

Union Recruiter: "By joining the union, your future is secure. The union has a legally binding deal with the company. You only contribute 5% of your monthly paycheck and the union will protect you from arbitrary dismissal. As long as you stick with the job you've been hired to do, we'll stick with you, and after 20 years you'll be eligible to get all your dues back with interest."

The reasoning above is flawed because it fails to consider whether:

(A) the interest earned by the union is significantly more than what the union pays back.

(B) unions in other companies charge less than 5% dues to keep the job secure.

(C) the company has diversification plans.

(D) the worker will get pro-rata dues back with interest in case he chooses to change jobs during the 20 year period.

(E) the union will loan the proportional accrued sum to the worker in case any emergency arises.

Argument construction

This is a question about a proposal from a union to a worker. The benefits offered by the union are life-time job security with the company, and all dues returned with interest after 20 years.

Predict a Flaw

What assumptions does this argument contain?

Predictive assumption 1: The union will not breach the commitment.
Predictive flaw 1: Whether the union has a reputation of honoring the commitments it makes.

Predictive assumption 2: The union will not raise dues disproportionately in the future.
Predictive flaw 2: Whether the union will raise dues disproportionately in the future.

Predictive assumption 3: The worker wants to be with the company for twenty years.
Predictive flaw 3: Whether the union will return dues with interest if the worker wishes to change jobs for a new opportunity.

Answer choice explanation

(A) This option is **irrelevant**. The worker may be concerned with the rate of interest he will receive from the union on his dues, but the union earning a significantly higher interest rate is irrelevant to him.

Critical Reasoning Guide – Find the Flaw

(B) This option is **out of scope.** In the real world, this situation may be of interest to us, but we must focus on the proposal given by the union for the company under discussion. Better proposals by unions of other companies are out of scope. If there were two unions in the same company and one union charged less than 5%, that knowledge would be useful to the worker. However, unions in other companies hardly benefit the worker in this company.

(C) This option is **out of scope**. The worker or the union is not concerned with diversification unless it involves changes in the specific dues being charged.

(D) This is the **correct** answer. It is in line with predictive flaw 3. The unions assume that the worker will remain with the company for twenty years, and if he doesn't remain for that long, he wouldn't be concerned about his dues being returned to him when he quits.

(E) This option is certainly a **relevant** and tricky option, but compared to option D, it is definitely not a preferred one. Compared to getting back dues with interest, getting a loan on the accrued sum is less important. Such a situation is based on a further assumption that the worker will necessarily need a loan. If the worker has no such plans, he would not be at all concerned with loan possibilities. So, the loan aspect if **out of scope.**

The correct answer is option D.

Example 2

The average output of workers in company X per month ranges from 150-170 pieces in the fourth month of joining the company. Therefore, if the output of a worker is below 120 pieces in the fourth month of joining, his average output gain has been below company X average.

Which of the following indicates a flaw in the reasoning above?

(A) Output is only one measure of company X's growth.

(B) The output of some workers reaches up to 190 in the fourth month of joining.

(C) Quality is ignored for output.

(D) The phrase 'below average' does not necessarily mean incompetent.

(E) Average output gain does not imply average output.

Argument construction

Average output per month per worker = 150-170 pieces in the fourth month
Output of a worker < 120 pieces in the fourth month

Conclusion: Average output gain < average output of company X.

Predict a Flaw

Read the conclusion precisely and you will predict the flaw. The flaw is that the author erroneously compares the **average output gain** and the **average.**

Predictive Flaw: Erroneously comparing 'average output gain' and 'average'.

Answer choice explanation

(A) This is **out of scope.** Other factors are beyond the scope of the argument.

(B) This is not a flaw. It is consistent with the premise.

(C) This is **out of scope.** Other factors are beyond the scope of the argument.

(D) This is **out of scope.** The phrase "below average" does not mean incompetent.

(E) This is the **correct** answer. It is in line with the predictive flaw.

The correct answer is option E.

Example 3

When students do not find their projects challenging, they become disinterested and so accomplish less than their abilities would have otherwise allowed. On the other hand, when students find their projects too challenging, they give up and so again accomplish less than what they are capable of accomplishing. It is therefore clear that no student's full potential will ever be realized.

Which one of the following is a flaw of reasoning contained in the argument?

(A) Erroneously equating what is actual and what is merely possible.

(B) Assuming without merit that a circumstance allows only two outcomes.

(C) Relying on subjective rather than objective proof.

(D) Confusing the coincidence of two episodes with a causal relation between the two.

(E) Depending on the vague use of a key term.

Argument construction

When students do not find their projects challenging, they become less interested and in turn they achieve less than their abilities. On the contrary, when students find their projects very challenging, they give up and so again achieve less than what they are capable of achieving.

Conclusion: No student's full potential can ever be realized.

Predict a Flaw

The argument cites two extreme scenarios. One, when projects are not challenging; and two, when projects are too challenging. It completely misses out an intermediate possibility – when projects are moderately challenging, which can help students reach their full potential. Learning processes are not either black or white. They can be any shade of gray in between as well. The author implies that because the teaching system fails at two poles, it fails across every longitude and latitude.

Predictive Flaw: Missing out an intermediate possibility that can invalidate the conclusion.

Answer choice explanation

(A) The argument does not mistakenly equate the actual and the possible; it merely cites two extreme possibilities which can actually occur. It misses out on intermediate possibilities.

(B) This is the **correct** answer. This option is in keeping with our predictive flaw. The argument misses out a third possibility, when the projects are moderately challenging.

(C) The argument does not provide any proof; it merely cites facts which are objective, but extreme.

(D) The two episodes are not coincidences. These are two separate incidences (less challenging and much too challenging projects) that lead to the same outcome (poor accomplishment).

(E) The argument is comprehensible; there is no vague key term used at all.

The correct answer is option B.

Example 4

Social scientist: Moral policing on the kind of clothes students wear at college is an archaic move for a liberal and the intellectual society. Therefore, those advocating restraint with potentially outrageous clothes are preaching something that is damaging to society.

Politician: You're wrong, because many people are in agreement about what potentially outrageous clothes are.

The politician's rebuttal is flawed because it..........

(A) attempts to define a general rule from a specific case

(B) draws an erroneous norm from a commonly held belief

(C) attacks the social scientist's character instead of the argument

(D) counters with an irrelevant reason to reject the social scientist's argument

(E) attacks the claim with exaggerated inflammatory language that obscures the issue at hand

Argument construction

Social scientist: Exercising checks on the kind of clothes students wear at college is an old-fashioned thought for a liberal and intellectual society. Those who do so regarding possibly disgraceful clothes are doing damage to society.

Politician: It is wrong to claim the above because many people agree on what possibly disgraceful clothes are.

Predict a Flaw

The question stem suggests that the rebuttal (denial) made by the politician is flawed. Your job is to understand the flaw, and phrase it. Let us understand the claims and the reasoning used by the two.

The claim of the social scientist: Those who want a check on possibly disgraceful clothes are damaging society.

Reasoning: Since our society is liberal and intellectual, exercising a check on the kind of clothes one wears is not only old-fashioned, but also damaging to society.

Assumption 1: The society is liberal and intellectual.

Assumption 2: Curbing liberty, be it regarding clothing or something else, is damaging to society.

The claim of the politician: There must be a check on the kind of clothes students wear at college.

Reasoning: Since many people agree on what possibly disgraceful clothes are, there must be a check on the clothes students wear at college.

Assumption: Many people agreeing on what possibly disgraceful clothes are means that they want a check on the clothes students wear at college.

Basically, the politician implies that since many people agree on what XYZ is, those people want to regulate XYZ.

The problem with the politician's argument is that he addresses an entirely different argument and not the social scientist's argument. The social scientists states that a liberal society should not regulate clothing. The politician states that because it is possible to distinguish objectionable clothing, we must regulate clothing. The politician seems to respond to an irrelevant argument – that since we cannot judge what objectionable clothing is, we therefore cannot regulate clothing. So, the flaw in the politician's argument is that he does not counter the scientist's argument, but instead counters some hypothetical one.

The possible replies that the politician should have made are:

Critical Reasoning Guide – Find the Flaw

Predictive reply 1: Society is not liberal to the extent that outrageous clothes are welcome.

Predictive reply 2: Allowing outrageous clothes is not necessarily a sign of an intellectual society.

Predictive reply 3: How can avoiding outrageous clothes damage a society?

However, the politician fails to address the reasoning of the social scientist and instead focuses on an entirely irrelevant argument.

Answer choice explanation

(A) The politician does not attempt to define any rule.

(B) The politician does not draw any norm. He merely states a commonly held belief.

(C) The politician does not attack the social scientist's character.

(D) This is the **correct** answer. It is in keeping with the analysis done above.

(E) The politician neither attacks with exaggerated inflammatory language nor obscures the issue at hand with his statement.

The correct answer is option D.

Practice Questions

7.4 Practice Questions

7.4.1 Questions

Question 1

During harvest season, a farmer collects 45 kilos of apples per week from his orchard. The farmer claims that he sorts his crop and rejects 10 kilos from this quantity to ensure that he gets the same quality of apples every week.

Of the following, the best criticism of the farmer's plan is that the plan assumes that:

(A) Grocery shops cannot accept all the apples that are harvested.

(B) The overall quality of the apples would not be improved if the total number of apples collected was reduced.

(C) Sorting on the basis of a quantity parameter gives better results than on the basis of a quality parameter.

(D) It is difficult to judge the quality of an apple.

(E) The 35 kilos of apples that are accepted will be of good quality from week to week.

Question 2

Opponents of the move to legalize the use of marijuana, while accepting that the drug itself may not be as harmful as other drugs are, have called it a 'stepping stone' drug, pointing out that almost every heroin user begins with marijuana. Proponents of marijuana legalization scorn this stand, saying that, by the same logic, milk should be banned because almost every heroin abuser drank milk as a baby.

Which of the following would reveal most clearly the absurdity of the counter-argument?

(A) Discounting the possibility that any excess is necessarily harmful

(B) Comparing two essentially incomparable things

(C) Not comparing marijuana, which is less harmful, to heroin, which is more harmful

(D) Not considering the fact that milk-drinkers are essentially infants who lack knowledge of proper consumption

(E) Not considering the fact that a baby will consume anything given

Question 3

A methodical study on the declining standard of soccer in a certain country indicates that the most significant improvements have resulted from better training of coaches. Sporting equipment employed to raise the performance of players was not present in most soccer clubs during the period of the study. Therefore, the increased use of such sporting equipment in soccer clubs will not significantly raise the performance of players.

A flaw in the argument is that....

(A) the evidence cited shows that one factor led to a certain result but is not sufficient to show that a second factor will not lead to that same result

(B) the reason given in support of the conclusion presupposes the truth of that conclusion

(C) the evidence cited shows that a certain factor was absent when a certain result occurred but does not show that the absence of that factor caused that result

(D) the evidence cited in support of the conclusion is not consistent with other information provided

(E) the reason given for the claim that one event caused the second more strongly supports the claim that both events were independent effects of another event

Question 4

Ghazal, a form of Urdu language poetry, is a set of two liner couplets which should strictly end with the same word, have the same rhyme, and should be within one of the predefined meters of a ghazal. There has to be a minimum of five couplets to form a ghazal. Hindi language lyricists tend to disregard this fact. Ignoring the parameters, they generally treat any five couplet Hindi poem with a "ghazal feel" as a ghazal. This demonstrates that Hindi lyricists do not respect Urdu traditions, despite the fact that some of their own poetry is derived from it.

The reasoning is flawed because it.......

(A) obscures matters of objective fact with matters of subjective feeling

(B) draws a conclusion that is wider in scope than is justified by the evidence provided

(C) banks on stereotypes instead of advancing evidence

(D) overlooks the possibility that the case it cites is not unique

(E) fails to acknowledge that overlooking an aspect implies an adverse verdict on another aspect

7.4.2 Answer-Key

(1) E | (2) B | (3) A | (4) B

Solutions

7.4.3 Solutions

Question 1

Argument construction

A farmer collects 45 kilos of apples per week from his orchard. He sorts his crop and rejects exactly 10 kilos of apples to ensure that he maintains the same quality of apples every week.

Predict A Flaw

This is a question to find the flaw in the argument.

The farmer is setting a limit on determining good quality apples. For every 9 apples, he will get rid of 2 to ensure quality. (This is the ratio of 45:10 simplified). Read the word 'exactly'.

The farmer's assumption: Every week, for every 9 apples, there are necessarily 2 rotten apples.

The flaw in this assumption is that the farmer is sure that the 7 apples that he chooses will all be of good quality. What if, in a particular week, there are 4 bad apples for every 9 and yet he throws out only 2 apples? 2 bad apples will remain in the chosen lot. The answer we need as the flaw should precisely demonstrate that the percentage of apples remaining will not necessarily be of good quality just because the farmer chooses to throw out 10 kg of every 45 kg he grows.

Predictive Flaw: Fixing the ratio of Good : Bad :: 7 : 2 is flawed.

Answer choice explanation

Only option E is aligned with the predictive flaw. 35 kg of apples accepted as good apples may contain some bad apples, and conversely, 10 kg apples rejected as bad apples may contain some good ones. The farmer should not sort quality on the basis of kilograms of apples rejected or chosen randomly.

The correct answer is option E.

Question 2

Argument construction

Opponents to the legalization of marijuana accept that marijuana may not be as harmful as other drugs, but they claim that its consumption leads to heroin usage. They reason that almost every heroin user starts by using marijuana. However, proponents of marijuana legalization ridicule this stand. They say that by the same logic, milk should be banned because almost every heroin abuser drank milk as a baby.

Conclusion: Marijuana is not a stepping stone to other drugs, as it is made out to be. Marijuana is not harmful.

Predict A Flaw

The question stem uses a different word for flaw, but conveys the desired meaning. This is a question to find the flaw.

Predictive assumption: Milk and marijuana are comparable.

This kind of question requires bearing in mind that only the information provided in the passage has any relevance. The reasoning flaw in the assumption is that milk and marijuana are comparable. The opponents of marijuana legalization link marijuana to heroin, while the proponents of legalization argue that a similar relationship can be thought to exist between milk and heroin, implying that if the opponent's argument were extrapolated, milk would have to be banned. Clearly, the answer must relate directly or indirectly to milk and marijuana. While milk is certainly not harmful, marijuana can be harmful.

Predictive flaw: Comparing two unlike things – one is harmful (marijuana), and the other is not (milk).

Answer choice explanation

(A) The argument discusses the ill-effects of marijuana and heroin. It is implied that that their consumption in excess is harmful. Hence, this is not the inherent flaw in the reasoning.

(B) This is the **correct** answer. It is aligned with the predictive flaw. Milk and marijuana are essentially incomparable, yet the proponents compare these two items to conclude that marijuana consumption should be legalized.

(C) By calling marijuana a "stepping stone" to heroin, the argument **does** compare a less harmful drug with a more harmful drug.

(D) The argument considers that everyone drank milk as a baby. However, the fact that babies lack the knowledge of proper consumption does not reveal the flaw in the argument because the proponents don't imply that babies are comparable to marijuana users. However, the proponents do imply that marijuana is the same as milk!

(E) Even if the argument does not consider the fact that a baby will consume anything given, it does not serve any purpose to reveal the flaw in the reasoning used in the argument because the proponents don't imply that babies are comparable to marijuana consumers..

The correct answer is option B.

Question 3

Argument construction

A study on the quality of soccer indicated that the most significant improvements in the performance of players can be achieved by the better training of coaches. It is to be noted that sporting equipment used to raise the performance of players was not present in most soccer clubs when the study was conducted.

Conclusion: The increased use of such sporting equipment in soccer clubs will not significantly raise the performance of players.

Predict A Flaw

Quickly run through the options to get a glimpse of the key terms used. Do not try to understand the options in detail. Merely scanning them quickly is sufficient. The purpose is to grasp what key words are to be dealt with.

The key terms used are – evidence, result, conclusion, factor, presupposition, cause and effect, and consistency. We will analyze the argument and extract these terms from it.

Conclusion: The increased use of such sporting equipment in soccer clubs will not significantly raise the performance of players.

Experiment: Study the performance of players without added perforance-enhancing equipment.

Result: The most significant improvements in the performance of players can be achieved by better training of coaches.

Evidence: Sporting equipment used to raise the performance of players was not present in most soccer clubs when the study was conducted.

Assumption: The benefit derived from coaching is sufficient and more than that from equipment.

Our task is to find the flaw made in deriving the conclusion.

How can the author conclude that the benefit (the result) derived from coaching (factor 1) cannot be enhanced with the usage of certain equipment (factor 2)?

Predictive Flaw: The author erroneously assumes that the result derived with one factor cannot be achieved with the other factor.

Answer choice explanation

(A) This is the **correct** answer. It is in keeping with the predictive flaw. The absence of certain equipment while studying performance does not mean that, with the usage of equipment, the performance cannot be raised.

(B) The reason given in support of the conclusion does not presuppose the truth of that conclusion; it cites the reason, though flawed, for what it concluded.

(C) This option is a tricky one and may distract you. This is an **opposite** answer. The evidence used in the conclusion shows that a certain factor was absent when the result occurred, but it **does** show that the absence caused the result, although without proving it conclusively. This option states the opposite.

The evidence cited – equipment was not used – shows that a certain factor – equipment – was absent when a certain result – raised performance – occurred, but does not shows that the absence of that factor caused that result.

(D) The evidence cited in support of the conclusion is consistent with other information provided, but the reasoning advanced is flawed.

(E) This statement is written in a convoluted manner. There are references to three events; it is not clear from the option statement which events they refer to. We can eliminate this option on the basis of lack of clarity and the appropriateness of option A.

The correct answer is option A.

Question 4

Argument construction

The argument defines what a ghazal, a form of Urdu language poetry, is. It should be written within predefined meters. It must have a minimum of five couplets. Hindi language lyricists flout these rules. They generally treat any five couplet Hindi poem with a "ghazal feel" as a ghazal. This shows that Hindi lyricists do not respect Urdu tradition, even when some of their own poetry is derived from it.

Conclusion: Hindi lyricists do not respect Urdu tradition.

Predict A Flaw

Quickly run through the options to get a glimpse of the key terms used. Do not try to understand the options in detail. Merely scanning them quickly is sufficient. The purpose is to grasp what key words are to be dealt with. The major flaw in the given argument is that in disregarding one aspect of Urdu tradition (how to make a "ghazal"), Hindi poets are guilty of disregarding Urdu tradition itself. This would be justifiable if Urdu tradition were limited to writing ghazals.The argument extrapolates one happening (disregarding the Urdu tradition of writing ghazals) and makes it representative of something larger (disregarding Urdu tradition as a whole).

The key terms used are – objectivity, subjectivity, conclusion, evidence, stereotype, and aspect. We will analyze the argument and extract these terms from it.

Conclusion: Hindi lyricists do not respect Urdu traditions.

Evidence: Hindi lyricists generally treat any five couplet Hindi poem with a "ghazal feel" as a ghazal while ignoring the parameters of writing ghazals.

Assumption: Treating any five couplets not written as per the guidelines as a ghazal implies disrespect to Urdu tradition in its entirety.

Critical Reasoning Guide – Find the Flaw

The terms objectivity, subjectivity, stereotype, and aspect are difficult to infer at this stage; we will leave them unexplored now and look into them when we discuss the relevant options later.

Predictive Flaw: The reasoning is flawed because it erroneously concludes that not following the parameters of one element is akin to disregarding the whole set.

Answer choice explanation

(A) No particular poem is referred to in the argument, so it is not a matter of objective fact.

(B) This is the **correct** answer. The conclusion drawn – disregarding the entire Urdu tradition – is wider in scope than is justified by the evidence provided – not following the parameters of writing ghazal – one part of Urdu tradition. As discussed above, Urdu tradition represents a set, while ghazal-writing represents just one element.

(C) The argument does provide evidence—Hindi lyricists generally treat any five couplet Hindi poem with a "ghazal feel" as a ghazal while ignoring the parameters on writing ghazals.

(D) Whether the case cited is unique does not change the fact that the author uses one element to define all the elements within a set.

(E) This option is a tricky one. Had you hurriedly read it, you might have chosen it. The correct answer should have been negation of this statement. The argument certainly fails to acknowledge that overlooking an aspect – not following the parameters of writing ghazals – does NOT imply an adverse verdict regarding another aspect – disregarding the entire Urdu tradition. Since NOT is missing in the statement, this option is opposite to the answer.

The correct answer is option B.

7.5 References for Official Guide Questions

The Official Guide for GMAT Review, 13th Edition: Question # 2, 8, and 100

Chapter 8

Method of Reasoning

8.1 Method of Reasoning Question type

Like find the flaw in the argument questions, method of reasoning (MoR) questions are infrequently asked in Critical Reasoning. These types of questions will appear when you are doing well in the verbal section.

As the name suggests, method of reasoning questions focus on the method applied to advocate the reasoning in the argument rather than only on the reasoning or the conclusion. MoR questions belong to the structure-based family. Some test-prep companies also call it dialogue-based or dialogue structure questions.

The answer choices are somewhat abstract in nature and discuss the structure of the argument. The correct answer choice would be the one that best describes the method used by the author to form the argument.

The most common form of MoR questions will present two opposing points of view. The question stem will ask you how the second person responds to the argument made by the first person.

Look at the image below. There is a dialogue taking place between two people. What could the method of reasoning be here?

Question Stem

Method of reasoning questions may use a variety of formats, but in each case the question stem will refer to the method, technique, strategy, or process used by the author while making the argument. Here are several question stem examples:

- Jack responds to Jill's argument by...

- The argument derives its conclusion by...

- Which of the following describes the technique of reasoning used above?

- Which of the following describes the reasoning strategy used in the argument?

- The argument applies which of the following reasoning techniques?

The following illustration depicts your job for the MoR question type.

Critical Reasoning Guide - Method of Reasoning

Imran: The freebie of 667 liters of water per household, announced by the chief minister, must be withdrawn immediately. If quashed, people will respect the value of the limited resource and [obscured]. [obscured] price, almost equivalent to zero, m[obscured] inducing restraint on consumption.

Dorsey: You are missi[obscured] as many as seven states in the country; [obscured]

Which one of the following most a[obscured] Dorsey's response to Imran's statement?

A. Dorsey insincerely blames Imra[obscured]self.
B. Dorsey falsely charges her argumen[obscured]ran personally.
C. Dorsey reveals an unstated assumption e[obscured]aining Imran's position.
D. Dorsey makes the conclusion that is similar to the one Imran has concluded.
E. Dorsey fails to counter the reason Imran mentions in his conclusion.

8.2 The Process Of Solving Method of Reasoning Argument Questions

The 4-step approach is the same as in chapter 2.

The 4-step approach

(1) Recognize the question type

(2) Understand the argument construction

(3) Predict the qualifier

(4) Eliminate incorrect options

The first 2 steps are the same for MoR questions. Let us jump directly to the "predict the qualifier" step.

Predicting the qualifier

Let us examine how to predict the qualifier from a 'method of reasoning' question perspective.

MoR questions contain abstract terms in the options, hence you need practice in order to predict the qualifier. You can:

(1) Understand each person's viewpoint or position

(2) Infer the conclusion of each person. Frequently the second person does not explicitly state the conclusion; however, you must understand the implied conclusion. In the arguments when the second person responds with flawed or irrelevant reasoning, you don't need to infer the conclusion.

(3) Understand the agreement and/or disagreement of both people regarding the discussed issue. It may be that both agree with the conclusion, but disagree with the reasons. Alternatively, the second person may disagree with the conclusion drawn by the first person as well as with the reasoning.

(4) Paraphrase the method applied by the second person in response to the first by using general terms.

(5) Look for that pre-phrased (predictive) answer in the options. The one similar in meaning to the pre-phrased answer is the correct answer.

Example Questions

8.3 Examples

Example 1

Harry: I advocate that subsidies have no place in a developed economy. They are an indirect way of charging tax. All subsidies must be withdrawn immediately.

Jack: I do not agree because of the steep rise in prices.

Jack's response to Harry's statement...

(A) demonstrates that Harry's claim is wrong.

(B) expresses concern over the issue of the consequence of subsidies.

(C) is in line with Harry's with respect to the issue of subsidies.

(D) shows that Harry's statement is self-contradictory regarding the tax issue.

(E) fails to completely understand Harry's viewpoint on the issue of subsidies.

Argument construction

Let us elaborate on the meaning and implications of Harry's and Jack's statements.

Harry: I advocate that subsidies have no place in a developed economy. They are an indirect way of charging tax. All subsidies must be withdrawn immediately.

Meaning: Harry thinks that subsidies – sums of money granted by the government to assist an industry – indirectly charge tax to people. What it means is that people pay taxes to the government and the government in turn allocates the fund to subsidize a particular industry. So, according to Harry, the government charges tax to people in order to provide subsidies. He is of the opinion that the subsidies must be withdrawn immediately.

Jack: I do not agree because of the steep rise in prices.

Meaning: Jack is concerned about the steep rise in the prices of commodities. Jack moves ahead from the subsidy issue and reacts to the repercussions of the complete withdrawal of subsidies.

He reasons that the complete withdrawal of subsidies will lead to a disproportionate rise in the prices of commodities.

Does Jack disagree with Harry about the issue of subsidy withdrawal? Well, we cannot say yes or no for sure. However, we can conclude that Jack is concerned about the consequences of withdrawing subsidies completely.

Predictive reasoning: Jack is concerned about the consequences of withdrawing subsidies completely.

Answer choice explanation

(A) No, we cannot conclude that Jack's statement demonstrates that Harry's claim is wrong. Jack may or may not agree that subsidies must be withdrawn either completely or partially. Jack is worried about the consequences of the action. We cannot say that Jack disapproves of the action per se.

(B) This is the **correct** answer. It is aligned with our predictive reasoning for Jack. This shows that Jack is more worried about the consequences than about the correctness of the action itself.

(C) No, we cannot conclude that Jack's statement is in line with Harry's with regard to the issue of subsidies. Jack may or may not agree that subsidies must be withdrawn either completely or partially.

(D) No, Jack's statement does not show that Harry's statement is self-contradictory over the tax issue. Harry talks about the subsidy, however Jack does not explicitly talk about the subsidy issue, rather about its consequences.

(E) No, Jack's statement does not reveal that he does not understand Harry's viewpoint on the issue of subsidies. It is more likely that he understands the subsidy issue because his response discusses the consequences of the subsidy withdrawal.

The correct answer is option B.

Example 2

Senator A: I propose that we limit welfare payments to those single mothers who give birth to an illegitimate child while receiving payments for an earlier illegitimate child. The current situation isn't just a drain on resources; it also encourages promiscuity and a lack of social responsibility.

Senator B: Such a proposal is absurd! If payments were limited, it would be in breach of our statutory obligations, and could well cost us votes from ethnic minority groups.

Which of the following best describes the attitudes of Senators A and B respectively?

(A) Heartless and compassionate

(B) Pragmatic and romantic

(C) Moralistic and populist

(D) Insulting and populist

(E) Tight-fisted and insulting

Argument construction

We have to analyze the attitudes of both senators. Let us understand their perspectives.

Senator A: He proposes that the welfare payments to single mothers who give birth to an illegitimate child and already receive payments for another such child be restricted. He reasons that otherwise these welfare payments not only waste money, but also incentivize immorality and lack of social responsibility.

Attitude of senator A: He seems to be a rationalist and moralistic person who cares for values in the society. While financially supporting single mothers, he wishes to motivate them against what he construes as an immoral act, by not supporting the second illegitimate child. He wishes to make a statement to society that giving birth to an illegitimate child is an immoral act and an undue financial burden on society.

Senator B: He disregards senator A's proposal, treating it as absurd. He reasons that the proposal must not be accepted because of statutory obligations, which mandate supporting single mothers and their children. However, he has a practical interest in the votes from ethnic minority groups. He fears that such a proposal may cost their party dearly in the election by alienating such groups who might see the proposal as a harsh action.

Attitude of senator B: He seems to be very public-relations oriented – one who wishes to keep everyone happy – a true politician. His morals are not clear to us, but we can say that he sees things from a practical side.

Let us go through the options one by one to choose the correct answer.

Answer choice explanation

(A) Senator A: He is not heartless; that is too extreme a judgment to be made on the basis of the given information. Senator B: He may seem compassionate, but we cannot say that from the exchange shown. Here Senator B comes across as careful about his party and politics.

(B) Senator A: He seems to be pragmatic in his approach. He is trying to deal with moral and resource issues sensibly and realistically, in a way that is based on practical rather than theoretical considerations. Senator B: 'Romantic' does not necessarily mean to do with "romance". The original meaning of "romantic" is "not practical". Senator B is not impractical; if anything, he seems very practical about his party and political career.

(C) Senator A: Senator A is distinctly moralistic. This can be inferred by his thinking, which shows that he expects the government to provide moral guidance to society about what is correct behavior. This attitude reflects that he is a moralistic person.
Senator B: He seems to try to appease minority groups, and wishes to ensure his political standing with the population. This attitude reflects that he is a populist person. This is the **correct** answer.

(D) Senator A: 'Insulting' is an irrelevant characteristic with respect to the argument. Senator B: We discussed this in option C. He is a populist person.

(E) Senator A: By saying that the current situation is a drain on resources, he reflects tight-fisted behavior.
Senator B: 'Insulting' is an irrelevant characteristic with respect to the argument.

The correct answer is option C.

Example 3

Politician A: We must make a strong moral statement against the oppressive government of Qarnak. Only complete military intervention can dethrone the Qarnak government. Therefore, we must go to war.

Politician B: Our aim should be to encourage the government of Qarnak to change its policies and become more open. An embargo, as opposed to full-scale military intervention, is the best way to achieve this. Therefore, we should only buy products from other countries, and do as much as possible to encourage other countries to boycott Qarnak.

Politician A's and Politician B's arguments differ in which of the following ways?

(A) They state the same goal but propose different ways of achieving it.

(B) They state different goals but propose the same way of achieving them.

(C) They state different goals and propose different ways of achieving them.

(D) They disagree about whether the government should do anything at all.

(E) They disagree about whether Qarnak's policies are objectionable.

Argument construction

Looking at the options, we understand that the question wants us to define each politician's goal and his way to achieve that goal. Let us understand the argument.

Politician A: On strong moral grounds, he proposes complete military intervention to topple the oppressive government of Qarnak.
Conclusion: War against the government of Qarnak.

Politician A's goal: Topple the oppressive government.
Politician A's way: Go to war; complete military intervention

Politician B: He is of the opinion that they should encourage the government of Qarnak to change its policies and become more open. He proposes a trade ban against Qarnak instead of going to war.
Conclusion: Boycott Qarnak. Trade with other countries but not Qarnak, and encourage other countries to follow the same embargo.

Politician B's goal: Retain the Qarnak government; make it change its policies and be more open.

Politician B's way: Boycott Qarnak—trade restriction; economic measures

Clearly, both politicians have different goals and different ways of achieving those goals.

Answer choice explanation

The correct answer is option C. That's the only option that matches our deductions.

Practice Questions

8.4 Practice Questions

8.4.1 Questions

Question 1

Imran: The giveaway of 667 liters of water per household, announced by the chief minister, must be withdrawn immediately. If quashed, people will respect the value of this limited resource and will use it wisely. Alternatively, a nominal price, almost equivalent to zero, must be charged to act as a psychological barrier inducing restraint on consumption.

Robert: You are missing something. Free water is prevalent in as many as seven states in the country; hence it should also be free in our state.

Which one of the following most accurately exemplifies Robert's response to Imran's statement?

(A) Robert accuses Imran of contradicting himself.

(B) Robert falsely charges his argument against Imran personally.

(C) Robert reveals an unstated assumption explaining Imran's position.

(D) Robert makes a conclusion that is similar to the one Imran has concluded.

(E) Robert fails to counter the reason Imran mentions in his conclusion.

Question 2

Suzy: It is ironic that people raise their voices against obscene and vulgar content on television, but sadly enough, every morning, read newspapers publishing similar content. Children who might read the newspaper are getting exposed to this obscene and vulgar content. Therefore, the content in newspapers must be regulated too.

John: Your concerns are understandable. Your recommendation, however, should not be accepted because the publishing media represents a responsible corporate citizen in this country. Newspapers, a bridge to the world, without such content would become dull and insipid, thus limiting their reach.

John uses which one of the following techniques in his response to Suzy?

(A) He charges a personal attack against her rather than addressing the argument she puts forth.

(B) He advocates that her recommendation is based on self-interest rather than on real concern for the content.

(C) He justifies why her recommended action is not applicable to the scenario she advocates, though his objective is to help.

(D) He tries to disregard her recommendation by saying that her recommendation in any form is an infringement on the fundamental rights of the concerned parties.

(E) He avoids discussion on her recommendation by raising the issue of whether her concerns about the contents are justified.

8.4.2 Answer-Key

(1) E (2) C

Solutions

8.4.3 Solutions

Question 1

Argument construction

We have to understand the characteristics of the response made by Robert. To achieve this we must understand the argument.

Imran: The Chief Minister announced that 667 liters of free water per household would be granted, but Imran proposes that this free water be withdrawn immediately. He reasons that by charging at least a small sum, people will then respect the value of this limited resource, and in turn they will use water wisely. He believes that charging such a sum will act as a psychological barrier and make people behave more responsibly.

Imran's position: Don't offer water for free; charge at least a little to act as a psychological barrier; induce people to respect this limited resource.

Robert: Robert disagrees with Imran. He reasons that since as many as seven states in the country offer water for free, it should be the same in their state.

Robert's position: Offer free water; if many offer it free, why don't we, too?

Robert's conclusion is the opposite of Imran's. However, his reasoning to counter Imran's argument is irrelevant because his only reason against Imran's position is that certain other states offer the free water that Imran wants retracted. He does not cite any reasons to establish that those 7 states are comparable to the state under discussion. He does not even judge the validity of offering or retracting the offer. He makes a counter-statement only because of what some other states are doing.

Answer choice explanation

The correct answer is option E. As discussed above, Robert fails to address the reason Imran cites in his conclusion and makes an entirely illogical counter to it.

Question 2

Argument construction

We have to understand the technique used by John in responding to Suzy. To achieve this, we must understand the argument.

Suzy: She is against the showing of obscene and vulgar content on television, but is surprised that people do not raise their voice against similar content in newspapers. She further reinforces her point by saying that children are getting exposed to such content.
Suzy's conclusion: The content in newspapers must be regulated too.

John: He understands her concerns. However, he does not agree with her recommendation of regulating the media. He reasons that the publishing media is a responsible entity. Further, he observes that one must read newspapers. If newspapers are regulated, they will become dull and will lose their readers.

John's conclusion: The content in newspapers must not be regulated.

John's conclusion is the opposite of Suzy's conclusion. He cites the negative implications of regulating newspapers. By stating that the publishing media is a responsible party, he implies there is self-regulation on the part of the publishing media.

Answer choice explanation

(A) This option is **irrelevant.** He does not direct a personal attack against Suzy.

(B) By stating that Suzy's concerns are understandable, he means that Suzy's concerns about the content are real.

(C) This is the **correct** answer. As discussed above, he justifies why moral policing should not be exercised for the media, which should be responsible on its own; however his tone, sincerity, and objectivity in response were to help Suzy resolve her doubt.

(D) This option is an extreme one. By stating that the publishing media is a responsible group, he advises self-regulation on the part of the publishing media, suggesting that he does not mean that there should not be any form of censorship.

(E) On the contrary, he does participate in the discussion whole-heartedly, and acknowledges Suzy's concerns.

The correct answer is option C.

8.5 References for Official Guide Questions

The Official Guide for GMAT Review, 13th Edition: Question # 34, 84, 85, 123;

The Official Guide for GMAT Verbal Review, 2nd Edition: Question # 79

Chapter 9

Parallel Reasoning Argument

9.1 Parallel Reasoning Argument Question type

Parallel Reasoning, or Mimic the Argument, questions are quite rare in Critical Reasoning. These kinds of questions will seldom appear on your GMAT exam even if you are doing well in the verbal section. Learning this chapter would be fruitful for understanding "application-based" reading comprehension questions.

Parallel Reasoning questions also belong to the structure-based family. While Method of Reasoning (MoR) questions ask you to select the option that describes the method applied in the reasoning in the argument, Parallel Reasoning questions ask you to select an argument from the given five options that is similar in structure and reasoning to the question argument. In a nutshell, you have to analyze 1+5 = 6 arguments, and select one argument that is similar to the question argument. Some test-prep companies also call this question type 'Mirror the Argument'.

The topic of the arguments may or may not be the same. In fact, they will mostly be different. Say the topic of the question argument is "concern over the fall in production". The topics for the option arguments may vary from "school education" to "anthropology" to "economy" to "astrology". So, it is important that you don't pay attention to the similarity or diversity of topics as one of the factors in selecting the correct option. Instead you must focus only on the structural and reasoning aspects of the arguments, and deduce the parallelism.

Question Stem

Here are several question stem examples:

- Which one of the following is most closely parallel in its reasoning to the reasoning in the argument above?

- Which of the following presents a pattern of thinking that is most closely analogous to the preceding situation?

- In terms of its logical features, the argument above most closely resembles which one of the following?

- Which one of the following arguments is most similar in its pattern of reasoning to the argument above?

- Which of the following is logically the most similar to the argument above?

The following illustration depicts your job for the Parallel Reasoning question type.

The demand for large, family-sized vehicles will slump dramatically over the next ten years; major automobile companies are cutting orders for steel plating usually placed five years in advance of plating to active previous production.

Which of the following arguments is most closely analogous to the passage above?

(A) A newspaper publisher is cutting the order of paper due to reduced circulation.
(B) A State Government is cutting the police budget because of fall in crime rate.
(C) A major political party increases its advertising budget because of decreasing support among the electorate.
(D) Because of a predicted lower demand for housing, building companies cease buying up vacant development plots.
(E) Because of the cyclical nature of a certain strain in flu that appears every five years, pharmacies are stocking up on anti-flu remedies.

Only one option will rightly describes the method used by the author to form the argument.

9.2 The Process Of Solving Parallel Reasoning Argument Questions

Unlike other question types, Parallel Reasoning questions involve a 5-step approach.

The 5-step approach

(1) Recognize the question type

(2) Understand the argument construction

(3) Run through the options

(4) Develop the argument's approach

(5) Eliminate incorrect options

The first 2 steps are the same for Parallel Reasoning questions. Let us jump directly to the "run through the options" step.

Run through the options

After identifying that the question belongs to the Parallel Reasoning question type, we must run through the options quickly. A quick rundown of the options helps to develop the approach to attack the question.

Remember that the topics of the arguments are not important, but the structure and the reasoning are. Do not invest more time than necessary on each option at this stage; just having a fair idea is sufficient as you develop the approach.

Develop the argument's approach

There are many kinds of arguments, and each argument can be mimicked. We have discussed four questions in this chapter that will help you understand the approach aspect. You need to figure out the elements used in the argument to derive the conclusion. The most important aspect in the Parallel Reasoning question type is that you must not look for sequential ordering of the premises, the counter-premises and the conclusion. However, you need to match the essential elements of the question argument to the essential elements of the option arguments.

Look at the following arguments and deduce which of the two given arguments, argument 1 or argument 2, is parallel to the question argument.

Question Argument: "John is an intelligent boy. However, he did not study well for the exam. Therefore, he will not score well on the exam."

Argument 1: "It is clear that the all-terrain vehicle "Potent3250" will break down after 200,000 miles. Chassis-tempering is surprisingly ignored, although the chassis itself is super strong.

Argument 2: "Suzy is an ardent dancer. She did not study well for the exam due to dance practice. Therefore, she will not score well in the exam."

Let us understand each argument.

Question Argument:

Premise: John is an intelligent boy. **Counter-Premise:** He did not study well for the exam. **Conclusion:** Therefore, he will not score well on the exam.

The arrangement of the argument is - **Premise – Counter-Premise – Conclusion**

Meaning: Despite being intelligent, John will not score well on the exam since he did not study well for it.

Argument 1:

Conclusion: It is clear that the all-terrain vehicle "Potent3250" will break down after 200,000 miles.
Premise: Chassis-tempering is surprisingly ignored. **Counter-Premise:** Although the chassis itself is super strong

The arrangement of the argument is –**Conclusion – Premise – Counter-Premise**

Meaning: Despite having a super strong chassis, the vehicle will break down since the tempering aspect of the chassis has been ignored.

Although the arrangement of the argument is not identical to the question argument, the structure and reasoning aspects are parallel. Therefore, Argument 1 is parallel to the question argument.

Argument 2:

Premise: Suzy is an ardent dancer. **Additional Premise:** She did not study well for the exam due to dance practice. **Conclusion:** Therefore, she will not score well on the exam.

The arrangement of the argument is - **Premise – Additional Premise – Conclusion**

Meaning: Since Suzy did not study well for the exam due to dance practice, she will not score well on it.

Note that the conclusion can be derived without the premise. Thus, the premise is not an essential element of the argument. Only the additional-premise is sufficient to conclude anything, hence the argument is not parallel to the question argument in structure and reasoning aspects. It is insignificant that the arrangement of premise, counter-premise, and conclusion is identical to the question argument.

However, since argument 1 contains exactly similar elements to the question argument, i.e. premise, counter-premise, and conclusion, argument 1 contains reasoning that is parallel to that of the question argument.

Another important feature of the Parallel Reasoning argument is that the arguments may or may not contain the conclusion. The argument may have only two premises, or a premise and a counter-premise, or merely one premise. Whichever is the case, you need an approach to solve the question.

Example

Questions

9.3 Examples

Example 1

The recent shut-down of Amco Chemicals proves that a board of directors who is out-of-touch fosters a lack of trust, resulting in decreased morale and, eventually, falling production.

In terms of its logical features, the argument above most closely resembles which one of the following?

- **(A)** When managers stop believing that elephants can dance, costs escalate and revenues fall.

- **(B)** When a kitten and a mouse mutually exchange vibes of hatred, trust is lost and they start hating each other.

- **(C)** When people go to watch a movie with the anticipation that it will be bad, they notice its bad points more than its good points.

- **(D)** When consumers begin to doubt the purity of a city's drinking water, complaints to the authorities soar and water supply administration overheads increase.

- **(E)** When a car acquires a reputation for having design faults, generally it does suffer many breakdowns.

Argument construction

After identifying that this is a question on 'parallel reasoning', we must run through the options quickly. We will notice that all five options are on different topics, and each option has a factor leading to other factor(s). Unlike other question types, a quick rundown on the options helps develop the approach to attack the question.

Let us understand the meaning of the argument and analyze its components.

A phenomenon was observed at Amco Chemicals. The BoD who was out-of-touch, and that fostered a lack of trust between them and employees (factor 1). This led to low morale in employees (factor 2) and that resulted in a drop in production (factor 3).

In a nut shell, we can observe that there are three negative factors – one leads to the other – so, a series of three factors. The option with this pattern of reasoning and structure will be the correct answer.

Answer choice explanation

- **(A)** "When managers stop believing that elephants can dance, costs escalate and revenues fall." –This proverb-style statement has two flaws: One is that the meaning of 'elephant' is not clear. It could refer to a large organization lacking agility; but we cannot infer such a meaning here. The second flaw is that "costs escalates and revenue fall" are two complementary effects of one factor. So this statement consists of two factors only. This option does not mimic the question argument.

(B) "When a kitten and a mouse mutually exchange vibes of hatred, trust is lost and they start hating each other". This statement is written in such a way that it seems possible to identify three factors. Factor 1 - exchange vibes of hatred; factor 2 - trust is lost; factor 3 - start hating. But it is not the most appropriate parallel reasoning argument vis-a-vis the question argument because factors 1 and 3 are, in fact, the same. Factor 1 talks about "hatred" and so does factor 3. It is a case of circular reasoning rather than parallel reasoning.

(C) "When people go to watch a movie with the anticipation that it will be bad, they notice its bad points more than its good points." It has only two factors. Factor 1 - with the anticipation that it will be bad; factor 2 - notice its bad points more than its good points. This option does not mimic the question argument.

(D) This is the **correct** answer. "When consumers begin to doubt the purity of a city's drinking water, complaints to the authorities soar and water supply administration overheads increase". It has three negative factors in order – one leading to other. Factor 1 - begin to doubt the purity of a city's drinking water; factor 2 - complaints to the authorities soar; factor 3 - water supply administration overheads increase. It is to be noted that factors 2 and 3 are negative in meaning, as the meanings of 'soar' in the phrase 'complaints to the authorities soar', and 'increase' in the phrase 'water supply administration overheads increase' are negative.

(E) "When a car acquires a reputation for having design faults, generally it does suffer many breakdowns". It has only two factors. Factor 1 - acquires a reputation for having design faults, and factor 2 - suffer many breakdowns. This option does not mimic the question argument's structure of a phenomenon happening because of three factors.

The correct answer is option D.

Example 2

An important consequence of a hot summer is increased incidence of skin cancer. However, the last three summers have not been hot, so there has not been a high incidence of skin cancer.

Which of the following is logically the most similar in the argument above?

(A) When the police are hailed as the guardians of society's values, they infiltrate and arrest gangs of traffickers, seizing large amounts of narcotics. Recently, no traffickers have been arrested, so society has no values.

(B) When they infiltrate and arrest gangs of traffickers, seizing large amounts of narcotics, the police are hailed as the guardians of society's values. Recently, no traffickers have been arrested, so society has no values.

(C) When they infiltrate and arrest gangs of traffickers, seizing large amounts of narcotics, the police are hailed as the guardians of society's values. Recently, many traffickers have been arrested, so society has many values.

(D) When they infiltrate and arrest gangs of traffickers, seizing large amounts of narcotics, the police are hailed as the guardians of society's values. Recently, no traffickers have been arrested, so the police are not hailed as the guardians of society's values.

Critical Reasoning Guide – Parallel Reasoning

(E) When the police are not hailed as the guardians of society's values, they don't infiltrate and arrest gangs of traffickers, seizing large amounts of narcotics. Recently, many traffickers have been arrested, so society has many values.

Argument construction

After identifying that this is a question on 'parallel reasoning', we run down the options quickly. We notice that all five options are on the same topic, and have four identifiable parts. This question is a typical cause & effect argument.

Let us understand the argument and analyze its components. We will name the cause X and the effect Y.

X: the hotter the summer
Y: the greater the incidence of skin cancer
We can draw its generic version as

Premise: If X, then Y.
Conclusion: Therefore, when no X, no Y.

No X: no hot summer
No Y: no incidence of skin cancer

Basically, the argument structure is "if X happens, Y happens", and therefore, conversely, "when no X happens, no Y can happen". The option parallel to this reasoning and structure is the **correct** answer.

Answer choice explanation

Let us name the cause X and the effect Y.

(A) X: The police are hailed as the guardians of society's values; Y: The police arrest traffickers
Logically, 'No X and No Y' should be:
No X: The police are not hailed as the guardians of society's values; No Y: The police do not arrest traffickers.

However, the converse 'No X' and 'No Y' parts, as per the option statement, are:
No X: no traffickers have been arrested; No Y: society has no values.

Neither 'No X' nor 'No Y' matches. This option does not mimic the question argument.

(B) X: The police arrest traffickers; Y: the police are hailed as the guardians of society's values
Logically, 'No X' and 'No Y' should be
No X: The police do not arrest traffickers; No Y: the police are not hailed as the guardians of society's values

However, the converse 'No X' and 'No Y' parts as per the option statement are:
No X: no traffickers have been arrested; No Y: society has no values.

While 'No X' is parallel to the argument (as infiltration and trafficking are used interchangeably in the argument) 'No Y' is not parallel. This option does not mimic the question argument.

(C) X: The police arrest traffickers; Y: the police are hailed as the guardians of society's values
Logically, the converse 'No X' and 'No Y' parts should be:
No X: The police do not arrest traffickers; No Y: the police are not hailed as the guardians of society's values.

However, the converse 'No X' and 'No Y' parts, as per the option statement, are:
No X: traffickers have been arrested; No Y: society has values
Neither 'No X' nor 'No Y' matches. This option does not mimic the question argument.

(D) X: The police arrest traffickers; Y: the police are hailed as the guardians of society's values
Logically, 'No X' and 'No Y' should be:
No X: The police do not arrest traffickers; No Y: the police are not hailed as the guardians of society's values

'No X' and 'No Y', as per the option statement, are:
No X: The police do not arrest traffickers; No Y: the police are not hailed as the guardians of society's values

Both 'No X' and 'No Y' match rightly parallel. This is the **correct** answer.

(E) X: The police are not hailed as the guardians of society's values; Y: the police do not arrest traffickers
Logically, 'No X' and 'No Y' should be:
No X: The police are hailed as the guardians of society's values; No Y: the police arrest traffickers.

However, the converse 'No X' and 'No Y' parts, as per the option statement, are:

No X: The police arrest traffickers; No Y: society has many values

Neither 'No X' nor 'No Y' matches. This option does not mimic the question argument.

The correct answer is option D.

Practice

Questions

9.4 Practice Questions

9.4.1 Questions

Question 1

The demand for large, family-sized vehicles will slump dramatically over the next ten years. Major automobile companies are cutting orders for steel plating usually placed five years in advance of delivery to obtain maximum price reduction.

Which of the following presents a pattern of thinking that is most closely analogous to the preceding situation?

(A) A newspaper publisher cuts back on orders for printing paper due to reduced circulation.

(B) A state governor reduces the number of police stations because of a fall in the crime rate.

(C) A major political party increases its publicity budget because of decreasing support among the electorate.

(D) Because of a predicted low demand for housing, building companies cease buying up vacant lots.

(E) Because of the cyclical nature of a certain strain of flu that appears every five years, pharmacies are stocking up on anti-flu remedies.

Question 2

Discovered during construction of a new civic library, the now-excavated Roman brothel of Salonika has proved such a lucrative tourist attraction that the city council has decided to abandon the civic library project and preserve the brothel as a permanent museum.

In terms of its logical features, the situation above most closely resembles which of the following?

(A) The site chosen for the John Dillinger Museum, dedicated to the famous gangster, being in one of the Chicago banks he robbed

(B) The donation of valuable books by a once notorious Hollywood madam to a local library

(C) The transforming of an infamous Japanese prison camp in Malaysia into a 5 star tourist hotel and recreation center

(D) The old building intended to become a city church having so many interesting books that it was converted to a library

(E) The preservation of the London Millennium Dome as a permanent exhibition instead of a temporary one as originally planned

9.4.2 Answer-Key

(1) D

(2) D

Solutions

9.4.3 Solutions

Question 1

Argument construction

We notice that all five options are on different topics. This question is a typical cause & effect argument.

Let us understand the argument and analyze its components. The argument can be simplified as:

It is said that in the next decade demand for a certain type of car will go down. Companies generally order their steel plating 5 years in advance to get the maximum discount. It follows that the companies would order steel plating for this car type years in advance if the cars are popular. Now, after they learn that demand will go down, they want to decrease their orders for steel plating for cars they would have made in the future, but now won't because of decreasing demand.

A generic version can be derived:

Due to an expected future slump, an activity planned for the future ceases. The option that matches this pattern of reasoning will be the correct answer.

Answer choice explanation

(A) This option does not mimic the argument, as the newspaper publisher cuts back on orders for printing paper due to the current reduction (slump) in circulation. It is unlike the scenario in the question argument where the activity planned for the future is cut back to guard against an expected future slump.

(B) Like option A, this option also has the same problem. The state governor reduces the number of police stations due to the current fall (slump) in the crime rate.

(C) In this option neither part mimics the argument. One, the party increases its budget rather than decreases it; two, there is a current decrease (slump) in support among the electorate, whereas in the argument the current status is fine, but a future slump is expected.

(D) This is the **correct** answer. "Predicted low demand" is parallel to "an expected slump in demand", and "building companies cease buying up vacant lots" is parallel to "activity planned for the future is stopped". It should be noted that the 'vacant lots' would have been bought in advance to eventually develop into buildings (just as steel plating would be bought in advance to use for cars to be made).

(E) This option implies that because of periodical reoccurrence of an event, pre-orders are executed to obtain leverage on it. It is the opposite of the question argument.

The correct answer is option D.

Question 2

Argument construction

We notice that all five options are on different topics. Let us understand the argument and analyze its components.

The argument: During the construction of a new civic library, an ancient Roman brothel was discovered. This discovery started attracting many tourists and generating good money for the city. The city council, therefore, decided to abandon the civic library project and reserve the brothel as a permanent museum.

The argument can be simplified in a generic version as follows:

An activity was started with a goal in mind, however, due to accidental gain, the planned goal and the activity were cancelled, and the gain from the accidental activity was continued.

We need to find an option that matches this pattern of reasoning.

Answer choice explanation

(A) This option is irrelevant. It says that that the location of the muscum dedicated to the famous gangster John Dillinger is in one of the Chicago banks he robbed. It does not repeat the idea of planning something initially, but discarding those plans to follow through on some accidental but profitable discovery.

(B) This option is irrelevant. It is a plain statement with no attributes of the question argument. It does not contain any plans that are later discarded.

(C) This option means that an infamous Japanese prison camp in Malaysia was transformed into a 5 star tourist hotel and recreation center. However, it does not present the idea of planning something initially, and discarding those plans to follow through on some accidental but profitable discovery.

(D) This is the **correct** answer. This option repeats the idea of planning something initially, and then changing those plans because something different but profitable was accidentally discovered.

(E) Only this option is close to the correct option D. However, 'the preservation as permanent instead of temporary' does not mirror 'original project was shelved and another project was started'. The preservation of the London Millennium Dome (the original project) was still executed.

The correct answer is option D.

Chapter 10

Boldface Argument

10.1 Boldface Argument Question type

Boldface, or Role play, question types are not as common as assumption, strengthen, or weaken question types, but not as rare as find the flaw or MoR question types. You are likely to face at least one boldface question.

Boldface questions also belong to the structure-based family. Usually in the argument of a typical boldface question, two specific portions are written in boldface font. This type of question is easy to recognize because unlike the arguments of other CR question types, it has portions in bold. Very rarely you may encounter an argument with only one boldfaced portion; however, your task, approach, and strategy to answer remains the same as for two portions in bold.

The question stems asks you to identify the roles the boldfaced portions play in the structure of the argument, or in relation to each other.

What is the meaning of "role play"? Simply put, the role is the purpose the boldfaced portions serve in the argument. A typical argument may have a premise, a counter-premise, an intermediate conclusion, or background information. The intermediate conclusion could also be a counter-conclusion. A counter-conclusion is a conclusion against which the author makes his main conclusion.

Look at the following dialogue to get a broader understanding.

By now you must have gone through earlier chapters and understood various elements of the arguments. It may seem that if boldface questions are limited to identifying a premise, a counter-premise, an intermediate conclusion, or background information, they can be easily tamed. However, the scope is not limited to this extent. The arguments of boldface questions are usually complex and lengthy, and use abstract diction and convoluted verbiage. Moreover, identifying the relationship of one boldfaced portion with another boldfaced portion or other non-boldfaced portions, compounded with the usage of abstract non-definitive terms, makes things complicated.

However, there's an approach to deal with these questions.

The following illustration depicts your job for the boldface question type.

Critical Reasoning Guide – Boldface

> CEO: Some of the board members claim that the company's current market undervaluation has been caused by my policies, and that I am responsible for the undervaluation. Although I admit that **the company has encountered market undervaluation during my tenure**, I do not agree that I am at fault for this problem. The busi[ness] [...] [c]urrent undervaluation, an[d] [...] **my administration, th**[e ...] **[b]een even worse.**
>
> In the CEO's argu[ment ...] [which] of the following roles?
>
> *(Only one option will rightly describe the roles both the boldfaced portions play.)*
>
> A) The first is a pre[mise ...] the second supports the board [members ...]
> B) The first is a statement a[...] second is a consequence of the board members' claims.
> C) The first is a fact that [...] [con]tradict his conclusion; the second offers support in co[nclu...]sion.
> D) The first is evidence of uneth[ical ...] [th]e CEO; the second is evidence offered by the CEO to explain that ac[...]
> E) The first is evidence that undermines the CEO's position; the second is a statement that follows from that position.

Question Stem

The boldface question type does not use many formats of question stems. As said earlier, this type of question is easy to recognize because, unlike the arguments of other question types, the argument of this kind of question has some portion in boldface. The two most common question stems are:

- In the argument above, the two portions in boldface play which of the following roles?

- What function do the statements in boldface fulfill with respect to the argument presented above?

Diction

Usage of key terms and their inter-relationship in the context of the argument deserve a lot of attention. So far, we have seen key terms like premise, counter-premise, intermediate conclusion, background information, evidence, fact, position, support, strengthen, weaken, and a couple of others; but there are many more to be studied.

Boldface questions, particularly in the options, may contain terms such as circumstance, finding, data, observation, judgment, stance, prediction, opinion, synopsis, allegation, consideration, explanation, justification, etc. Your job is to understand the nuances of these key terms. Below is a partial list of these terms classified into "Fact", "Claim", or "Fact or Claim". The list is not exhaustive, and the categorization is suggestive; it may change according to the context of the argument.

Fact	Claim	Either—Fact or Claim
Premise	Conclusion	Consideration
Counter-Premise	Intermediate-Conclusion	Explanation
Evidence	Counter-Conclusion	Justification
Finding	Opinion	Support
Circumstance	Position	Reasoning
Data	Belief	Advocacy
Information	Prediction	
Observation	Judgement	
	Stance	
	Synopsis	
	Notion	
	Theory	
	Hypothesis	
	Phenomenon	

Verbiage

Many times the verbiage of the options may cloud your thinking process, and you may get caught in a trap laid by the test makers.

Let us look at a couple of option statements in order to understand their meaning.

Option 1: The first is a prediction that is challenged by the argument; the second is a finding upon which the argument depends.

Meaning: Here "first" means the first boldfaced portion; "prediction" can be substituted with claim as suggested by the table above; "challenged by the argument" means that the author opposes the claim made in the first boldfaced portion; "second" means the second boldfaced portion; "finding" can be substituted with fact as suggested by the table above; "upon which the argument depends" means that the conclusion is drawn based on the fact presented by the second boldfaced portion.

In other words, we can rewrite the option as:

"The first boldfaced portion is a claim that the author opposes; the second boldfaced portion is a fact on which the conclusion is drawn."

The option becomes much more comprehensible than it was before.

Option 2: The first is an opinion put forth to support a conclusion that the argument rejects; the second is a consideration that is introduced to counter the force of the conclusion.

Meaning: "Opinion" can be substituted with claim as suggested by the table above; "put forth to support a conclusion" means that the claim strengthens the conclusion drawn in the argument; "conclusion that the argument rejects" means that the author opposes the claim;

"consideration" can be substituted with <u>claim</u> or <u>fact</u> depending upon the context of the argument; "consideration that is introduced to counter the force of the conclusion" means that the consideration (fact or claim) works against the conclusion.

In other words, we can rewrite the option as:

"The first boldfaced portion is a claim that strengthens the conclusion; the second boldfaced portion is a fact or claim that works against the conclusion."

10.2 The Process Of Solving Boldface Questions

The 4-step approach

(1) Recognize the question type

(2) Understand the argument construction

(3) Analyze each statement

(4) Eliminate incorrect options

The first 2 steps are the same for boldface questions. Let us jump directly to the 'analyze each statement' step.

Analyze each statement

Usually boldface arguments are lengthy and comprise three to four statements. After understanding the argument, you should understand and analyze what role each statement – and not just the boldfaced portion – plays. This step can further be divided into 6 steps.

(1) Understand the conclusion; it may not necessarily be one of the boldfaced portions.

(2) Understand the intermediate/counter-conclusion, if any.

(3) Categorize each statement as conclusion, intermediate/counter-conclusion, premise, counter-premise, fact, claim, or as either fact or claim.

(4) Understand what part each statement and boldface portion mutually play in the argument.

(5) Understand whether both boldfaced portions are on the same side or opposite sides.

(6) Pre-phrase what role each boldfaced portion plays. It is likely that you will encounter different terms used to articulate the roles boldfaced portions play in the options; you should replace the synonymous key terms as suggested in the "Diction" section above, and select the correct option.

Example Questions

10.3 Examples

Example 1

While some people complain that the democratic system of governance is impotent and lackluster, **the same people do not protest when a pseudo-dictator tries to swindle the system.** These people are missing out on a basic proposition: a system is always bigger than an individual. Taken this way, **democracy is de facto the best form of governance.**

The two boldfaced portions play which of the following roles?

- (A) The first is a generalization accepted by the author as true; the second is a consequence that follows from the truth of that generalization.

- (B) The first is evidence that supports one of two contradictory points of view; the second supports the point of view that the first supports.

- (C) The first is a commonly held point of view; the second is the support for that point of view.

- (D) The first is one of two contradictory points of view; the second is the other point of view.

- (E) The first concedes a consideration that weighs against the viewpoint of the author; the second is that viewpoint.

Argument Analysis

Some people gripe about the democratic system of governance. They see it as a powerless and boring form of governance. The author changes the direction here; he blames the same people by arguing that they do not raise their voices when a powerful individual akin to a dictator exploits the system. The author further adds that those people ignore the fact that the system is always bigger than an individual or a dictator. The author concludes that democracy is by default the best form of governance.

Predictive Role Play

Let's dissect this argument.

The easiest part of the question is to find what role the second boldfaced portion plays. While understanding the argument, we find that it is the conclusion of the author, or argument.

Conclusion: (Boldface 2): Democracy is de facto the best form of governance.

Statement 1: (While some.......lackluster.): This statement can be a fact or the author's opinion. The author rejects this fact. Hence, this is not supporting the author.

Statement 2: (Boldface 1): This statement can be a fact or the author's opinion. The author accepts this fact but he accepts it as a fact that goes against the earlier sentence, which states that democracy is bad. How is "Boldface 1" – BF1 related to "Boldface 2" – BF2, the conclusion? We can simply infer that both BF1 and BF2 are on the same side, and BF1 helps BF2 – the conclusion – build its ground. BF1 is the evidence the author provides to prove his point (BF2) that democracy is the best form of government and to prove his opposition's point – that democracy is bad – wrong.

Statement 3: (These people........individual): This statement is also in line with statement 2. It also supports BF2 – the conclusion.

Statement 4: (Boldface 2): As discussed. It is the author's conclusion.

Hence, we can predict that BF1 is the evidence that the author uses to prove himself right and prove his opposition wrong, and that BF2 is the author's position.

Answer choice explanation

(A) **BF1:** What does *generalization accepted by the author as true* mean? It can be inferred that generalization is a word used for opinion. However, we know that BF1 is a fact that the author uses to support his point and goes against the generalization given in the argument.

BF2: What does a *consequence that follows from the truth of that generalization* mean? It means that BF2 – the conclusion – follows from the consequence of BF1. This is not correct. Let us rephrase it—*It is true that some people do not raise their voices against dictators when they exploit the system, but this does not follow that democracy is the best form of governance.*

(B) **BF1:** *evidence can be interchangeably used for fact, so this is fine.* What are the two *contradictory points of view?* They are **point of view 1:** Democracy is bad; **point of view 2:** Democracy is good. The option statement states that BF1 supports one of the points of view. Yes, that is correct. It does support the 2nd point of view. So far it's going well.

BF2: This is also right. In our analysis, we concluded that BF1 and BF2 are on the same side, and this option says so. Hence, option B is the **correct** answer.

(C) **BF1:** This is incorrect. BF1 is the author's evidence against the point of view that democracy is bad.

BF2: This is wrong. BF2 is a conclusion that opposes that point of view.

(D) **BF1:** This is incorrect. As discussed above, BF1 is a fact that the author uses against his opposition and to support himself. This option calls BF1 a conclusion and one that opposes the author.

BF2: This is correct. BF2 is the other (opposing) point of view.

(E) **BF1:** The first part of the option statement means that BF1 provides a consideration that is against the viewpoint of the author. That is wrong. We concluded that BF1 and BF2 are on the same side, but this option says otherwise.

   BF2: This is correct. BF2 is the viewpoint of the author.

The correct answer is option B.

Example 2

Supermarkets frequently offer items with innovative and appealing mega-sale discount schemes comparable to offers from competing stores. **Because such schemes are quickly copied by other stores,** many retail giants charge as little as possible for items to extract as much sales volume as possible. However, sales generated by mega-sale discount schemes give stronger incentive to competitors to copy these schemes. Therefore, **the best strategy to maximize overall sales from mega-sale discount schemes is to charge more than the lowest possible price.**

The two boldface portions play which of the following roles?

- (A) The first is an assumption that supports a described course of action; the second provides a consideration to support a preferred course of action.
- (B) The first is a consideration that helps explain the appeal of a certain strategy; the second presents an alternative strategy endorsed by the argument.
- (C) The first is a phenomenon that justifies a specific strategy; the second is that strategy.
- (D) The first is a conclusion that demonstrates why a particular approach is flawed; the second describes a way to amend that approach.
- (E) The first is a factor used to rationalize a particular strategy; the second is a factor against that strategy.

Argument Analysis

The argument is easy to understand. We will outline the crux.

Supermarkets frequently offer mega-sale discount schemes. Since mega-sale discount schemes are quickly copied by the competition, many retail giants charge as little as possible to sell more. However, this strategy is quickly copied. Therefore, the best strategy to maximize overall sales from the discount schemes is to charge more than the lowest possible price.

Conclusion: The best strategy to maximize overall sales from mega-sale discount schemes is to charge more than the lowest possible price.

Predictive Role Play

There are two strategies discussed here:

Strategy 1: Charge as little as possible.
Strategy 2: Charge more than the lowest possible price.

The easiest part of the question is to find what role the second boldfaced portion plays. While understanding the argument, we find that it is the conclusion of the author, or the argument.

Conclusion:(BF 2): The best strategy to maximize overall sales from mega-sale discount schemes is to charge more than the lowest possible price. This is strategy 2.

Statement 1: (Supermarkets.......stores): It is either a fact or background information or a simple premise.
Statement 2: (BF 1): It is fact or premise that supports strategy 1(many retail giants.......possible).
Statement 3: (However.......scheme): It is a counter-premise that goes against strategy 1. It supports strategy2 – BF2.

Answer choice explanation

(A) **BF1:** An assumption is also a premise, but BF1 is a fact, not an assumption.
 BF2: It is not a consideration to support a preferred course of action implying strategy. BF2 itself is a strategy or the main conclusion.

(B) **BF1:** This is correct. It is a consideration (fact) that helps to explain the appeal of strategy 1.
 BF2: This is correct. It is an alternative strategy (strategy 2) endorsed by the argument. It is the **correct** answer.

(C) **BF1:** This is correct. It can be called a phenomenon that justifies a specific strategy (strategy 1).
 BF2: This is wrong. BF2 is strategy 2 and not strategy 1.

(D) **BF1:** This is wrong. It is not the conclusion. BF2 is the conclusion.
 BF2: This is correct. BF2 does propose an alternate strategy.

(E) **BF1:** This is correct. BF1 does rationalize a strategy.
 BF2: It is not a factor used against strategy 1, but it is the strategy itself.

The correct answer is option B.

Example 3

A biologist claims that **microorganisms have a much larger impact on the complete ecosystem than scientists typically recognize.** Now a team of researchers has gathered and archived the results of hundreds of studies on animal-bacterial interactions and shown clearly that the biologist is right. The combined analysis suggests that the evidence supporting his view has reached a critical point, demanding that scientists re-examine the basic characteristics of life through the lens of the complex interwoven relationships among microorganisms and other very different organisms. **The results will deeply change the way the researchers continue with their own areas of interest.**

In the argument given, the two boldfaced portions play which of the following roles?

(A) The first identifies the content of the conclusion of the argument; the second is the main claim of the argument.

(B) The first provides support for the conclusion of the argument; the second identifies the content of that conclusion.

(C) The first states the conclusion of the argument; the second calls that conclusion into question.

(D) The first provides support for the conclusion of the argument; the second calls that conclusion into question.

(E) Each provides support for the conclusion of the argument.

Argument Construction

A biologist claims that microorganisms are more important that we believe them to be. Recent studies have proven this. This in turn will bring about a rewriting of fundamentals, and change most areas of study.

Predictive Role Play

Statement 1 (BF 1)—(microorganisms....recognize) This is the claim by the biologist. Hence, BF1 is a claim. The portion in boldface is the claim that is proven right in the argument, and supports the argument's intermediate conclusion that the biologist is right.

Statement 2—(Now a team.......the biologist is right) This statement is clearly the evidence that the author uses to state that the biologist is right. However, the part "the biologist is right" is an **intermediate conclusion** of the author.

Statement 3—(The combined......very different organisms.) This sentence consists of additional facts that support the biologist's and the author's claims, and it also contains predictions of what the claim will bring about.

Statement 4 (BF 2)—(The results......of interest) This statement is a claim that will happen because biologist is right. Thus, BF2 is the main conclusion of the author.

Answer choice explanation

(A) This is the **correct** answer. BF1 is the claim part only of the argument. We can consider BF1 as "content of the conclusion"; BF2 is the main conclusion.

(B) While BF1 can be taken as support for the argument, we cannot say that BF2 is the content of the main conclusion. We discussed above that BF1 is the claim, and BF2 is the main conclusion.

(C) While BF1 is the claim, BF2 is not calling the conclusion into question.

(D) While BF1 can be thought of as supporting the conclusion, BF2 is not calling the conclusion into question.

(E) BF1 is not a fact. This option calls both BFs supports, i.e. facts. We discussed above that BF2 is a conclusion.

The correct answer is option A.

Example 4

Many intellectuals feel that **strong copyright and patent laws are necessary to encourage and nurture creativity.** Many argue that competitors are free to steal ideas, create knockoffs, and drain profits from innovators when such protections are not in place. Yet these people fail to consider that a number of major industries such as fashion, cuisine, open-source software, finance, font design, stand-up comedy, and more thrive, compete, and innovate without much legal protection for intellectual property. As a matter of fact, in most of these industries, copying and blatant imitation is widespread. In fact, this imitation sets trends, propels people, and boosts the economy. **The fashion industry is the best representative of the idea that imitation encourages innovation and creativity.**

In the author's argument, the two portions in boldface play which of the following roles?

(A) The first is a claim that has been used to support a conclusion that the argument accepts; the second is that conclusion.

(B) The first is evidence that has been used to support a conclusion for which the argument provides further evidence; the second is the main conclusion of the argument.

(C) The first is a finding whose implications are at issue in the argument; the second is a claim presented in order to argue against deriving certain implications from that finding.

(D) The first is a claim that the argument strongly disputes; the second is evidence put forth to establish the contradictory conclusion that the argument proposes.

(E) The first is a finding whose accuracy is evaluated in the argument; the second is evidence presented to establish that the finding is accurate.

Argument Construction

The above argument claims that while traditional wisdom holds that copyright and patents increase creativity, the opposite is true. The argument states many examples in support of this.

Predictive Role Play

Statement 1 (BF 1)—(strong copyright....creativity) The first portion in boldface is the traditional belief that the argument strongly disputes.

Statement 2—(Many argue......not in place) This is evidence that supports the conventional beliefs and claims.

Statement 3—(Yet these people fail......property) Notice the use of contrast word "yet", which shows a distinctive change in direction. This statement is evidence, but it does not support the conventional beliefs. Thus, it supports the author's beliefs and the author holds beliefs that are contradictory to conventional beliefs.

Statement 4—(In fact,....economy) This seems to be the crux of the author's talk, i.e. his main conclusion.

Statement 5 (BF 2)—(**The fashion industry.......creativity**) The second portion is an example cited as evidence for the main conclusion of the argument that copying sets trends. This main conclusion is contradictory to the traditional belief.

Answer choice explanation

(A) While BF1 is a claim, the argument does not accept this claim. BF2 is not a conclusion, but a fact/example.

(B) BF1 is not evidence/fact that the argument accepts. BF2 is not the main conclusion of the argument, as discussed above.

(C) BF1 is not a finding even though it is at issue in the argument. BF1 is a claim. BF2 is not a claim/conclusion, even though it argues against BF1.

(D) This is the **correct** answer. BF1 is being strongly disputed in the argument and BF2 provides evidence that supports a contradictory (main) conclusion.

(E) BF1 is not a finding even though its accuracy is being evaluated in the argument. BF2 argues against BF1 and does not prove BF1 right.

The correct answer is option D.

Practice Questions

10.4 Practice Questions

10.4.1 Questions

Question 1

CEO: Some board members claim that the company's current market undervaluation has been caused by my policies, and that I am responsible for the undervaluation. Although I admit that **the company has encountered market undervaluation during my tenure,** I do not agree that I am at fault for this problem. The business policies of the prior CEO caused the current undervaluation, and **were it not for the business policies of my administration, the current undervaluation would have been even worse.**

In the CEO's argument, the two boldface portions play which of the following roles?

- (A) The first is a premise that has been used against the CEO; the second supports the board members.

- (B) The first is a statement accepted by the CEO; the second is a consequence of the board members' claims.

- (C) The first is a fact that the CEO believes does not contradict his conclusion; the second offers support in consideration of that conclusion.

- (D) The first is evidence of unethical activity by the CEO; the second is evidence offered by the CEO to explain that activity.

- (E) The first is evidence that undermines the CEO's position; the second is a statement that follows from that position.

Question 2

There is not one good reason for allowing managers to work from home, while there are several good reasons to deny the same. For one, it would be an additional operational challenge to businesses. Businesses are already facing many challenges all over the world, and so adding additional impediment is not an option. If the manager behaves like a manager, he can manage his family as well. **If the manager doesn't behave like a manager, he will not be able to manage his family, regardless of whether he is at home or at work.**

In the argument given, the two portions in boldface play which of the following roles?

- (A) The first is the primary conclusion of the argument, and the second is a secondary conclusion.

- (B) The first is the advocacy of the argument, and the second raises doubts about this advocacy.

- (C) The first provides evidence as to why a certain policy should not be adopted by businesses, and the second further strengthens this evidence.

(D) The first is a conclusion that the argument disagrees with; the second provides the reasoning behind this disagreement.

(E) The first is the primary conclusion of the argument, and the second provides reasoning supporting the primary conclusion.

Question 3

Using graphic simulations and conceptual frames, scientists projected the effects of almost negligible (about a pinch of salt per person per day), steady annual cutback of sodium intake in the U.S. diet, cutting sodium consumption by 40 percent to about 2,200 mg/day over a decade. A gradual cutback in sodium intake by 40 percent to about 2,200 mg/day over a decade is projected to save between 280,000 and 500,000 lives. An even better result is possible, and **about 60 percent more deaths could be averted over this decade** if these same cutbacks could be achieved faster by upping the cutback amount (500,000 to 850,000 lives).

In the argument given above, the two boldface portions play which of the following roles?

(A) The first is a prediction that, if accurate, would provide support for the main conclusion of the argument; the second is that main conclusion.

(B) The first is a prediction that, if accurate, would provide support for the argument; the second is a conclusion drawn in order to support that main conclusion.

(C) The first is an objection that the argument rejects; the second is the main conclusion of the argument.

(D) The first is an objection that the argument rejects; the second presents a conclusion that could be drawn if that objection were allowed to stand.

(E) The first is a claim that has been advanced in support of a position that the argument opposes; the second is a claim advanced in support of the main conclusion of the argument.

10.4.2 Answer-Key

(1) C   (2) E   (3) B

Solutions

10.4.3 Solutions

Question 1

Argument Analysis

Let us understand the argument.

Some board members think that the CEO's business policy is the reason for the company's undervaluation in the market. However, the CEO does not think so. His position is – I am not responsible for it. While he admits that the company's market position became undervalued during his tenure, he reasons that it is because of his predecessor's policies and not his. Further, he strengthens his position by stating that had his policies not been implemented, the situation would have been much worse than it is now.

Conclusion: I am not at fault for this problem of market undervaluation.

Predictive Role Play

By now you have likely followed the detailed approach to attack the boldfaced questions. Let us attack this question with an alternate approach.

Let us dissect the argument and understand the positions of the board and the CEO.

Board Members: The CEO's policies are at fault.

CEO: I am not at fault. I admit the problem occurred during my tenure, but my predecessor is at fault.

BF 1: It is a fact based on which board members make the CEO liable for the problem.

BF 2: It is a possibility used by the CEO (counter-evidence) in which he strengthens his position and supports the conclusion (that he is not at fault).

Answer choice explanation

(A) The first part of the option is correct; however, the second boldface does not support the board members, it in fact contradicts them.

(B) The first part of the option is correct. The CEO admits that the problem exists. The second boldface, however, is not a consequence of the board members' claims. It is CEO's counter-evidence to strengthen his position.

(C) This is the **correct** answer. The first boldface is a fact which cites a problem, but the CEO believes that this fact does not contradict his conclusion. The second bold face supports the CEO's conclusion.

(D) This option is irrelevant. There is no discussion of unethical activity committed by the CEO.

(E) While the first part of the statement is correct, the second boldface does not follow from the CEO's position or the conclusion – *I am not at fault.* In fact, the reverse is true—the CEO's position follows from the second boldface because the second boldface is the evidence he uses for his position.

The correct answer is option C.

Question 2

Argument Analysis

The first statement is against the policy of allowing managers to work from home. This statement can easily be understood as the main position of the argument and the author. The argument cites as a reason that allowing such a thing would be an additional operational challenge to businesses and that working from home would pose more challenges. The argument also ventures a judgment about why a work-from-home policy should not be implemented. It says that if the manager behaved like a manager, he could also manage his family well; and, conversely, if he doesn't behave like a manager, he will not be able to manage his family well, regardless of whether he works from home or the office.

Predictive Role Play

Let us solve this question with the alternate approach.

Let us dissect the argument and understand the role of the boldfaced portions.

Conclusion: There is not one good reason for allowing managers to work from home.

BF 1: It is the conclusion.

BF 2: It is the judgment of the author that supports the main conclusion.

Answer choice explanation

(A) The first boldface is certainly the primary, or main, conclusion, but the second boldface is not a secondary conclusion, it is a judgment advanced in support of the main conclusion.

(B) The first boldface is not is the advocacy or the reasoning of the argument. It is the conclusion. The second boldface is the advocacy of the argument, but it does not raise doubts. Rather, it reasons why the conclusion is justified.

(C) The first boldface is not evidence, it is the main conclusion. The second boldface does strengthen the first boldface, but it is not evidence, it is a judgment.

(D) The first boldface is certainly a conclusion, but the argument agrees rather than disagrees with it. The second boldface provides the reasoning behind this agreement rather than disagreement.

(E) This matches our argument analysis, and so this is the **correct** answer.

The correct answer is option E.

Question 3

Argument construction

The argument discusses the projected effects of a sodium intake cutback on lives and longevity. It provides various figures with different expectancy rates based on the amount of sodium cutback. The first part shows current projections and plans, but the second part shows some further predictions and figures. The author's main reason in furnishing this extra data is to state that "a better result is possible". Thus, "even a better result is possible" is the main conclusion of the argument.

Predictive Role Play

Statement 1 (BF 1)—(Using graphic simulations.....the U.S. diet) The first portion in boldface describes the presentation of a study that might save lives.

Statement 2—(A gradual cutback.....500,000 lives) This statement is another prediction that forms the basis of the claim that lives can be saved by this whole exercise.

Statement 3 (BF 2)—(An even better.....(500,000 to 850,000 lives)) This sentence contains the main conclusion "even a better result is possible". However the main conclusion part is not bold. BF2 is further predictions (or intermediate conclusions) that will prove the main conclusion right.

Main conclusion - An even better result is possible.

Thus BF1 is a prediction supporting the argument, and BF2 is part of the conclusion that supports and contains the main conclusion of the argument.

Answer choice explanation

(A) While the BF1 part of this option is correct, BF2 is not the main conclusion, as discussed above.

(B) This is the **correct** answer. BF1 is a prediction that, if accurate, supports the argument, and BF2 is a conclusion that helps the main conclusion.

(C) The argument does not reject BF1, and BF2 is not the main conclusion, as discussed above.

(D) The argument does not reject BF1, and BF2 is not standing in opposition to BF1.

(E) BF1 is a claim, but the argument does not go against this claim. BF2 is a claim that supports the main conclusion of the argument.

The correct answer is option B.

10.5 References for Official Guide Questions

The Official Guide for GMAT Review, 13th Edition: Question # 18, 28, 63, 76, 78, 89, 98, and 116

The Official Guide for GMAT Verbal Review, 2nd Edition: Question # 48, and 74

Chapter 11

Resolve the Paradox Argument

11.1 Resolve the Paradox Argument Question type

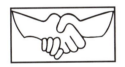
Resolve the Paradox, or Explain the Discrepancy, questions consist only of premises, mostly factual statements, and sometimes claims. Since arguments contain only premises, the conclusion is missing from the arguments. The two premises presented will be contradictory in some way, and will seem almost mutually exclusive, creating confusion. Resolve the Paradox questions belong to the evidence- based family.

Frequently the argument will employ phrases or words denoting contradiction, such as "surprisingly", "yet", "however", "although", "paradoxically", and "but".

Your job is to select one of the five true premises given as the options that will act as a third premise, and resolve the paradox. The option you choose should address both facts without denying either fact, and justify why the contradiction is happening. If you read the argument along with the correct premise, the argument will make complete sense.

Look at the dialogue between two people in the image. What could be a resolution here?

The following illustration depicts your job for the Resolve the Paradox question type.

> In 1999, America Mart, which previously sold merchandise only through retail outlets, began selling on the intern̶̶̶̶̶̶̶̶̶̶le keeping its retail stores open. Although total sales increased in 1999̶̶̶̶̶̶̶̶̶s than the profits in 1998.
>
> Which of the following, if tru̶̶̶̶̶̶̶̶̶̶̶̶to explaining why America Mart's profits were more in 1998 th̶̶̶̶̶̶̶
>
> A. There was a ̶̶̶̶̶̶̶̶̶̶̶̶̶̶̶̶̶̶̶̶̶̶̶̶hat consumers had to pay on all re̶̶̶̶̶̶
> B. A greater nu̶̶̶̶̶̶̶̶̶̶̶̶̶̶̶̶̶̶̶̶̶ere made available to previous cus̶̶̶̶̶̶̶̶̶̶̶̶̶̶̶̶̶̶̶̶̶ped at America Mart before.
> C. In 1999, Am̶̶̶̶̶̶̶̶̶̶̶̶̶̶̶̶̶̶̶̶̶ased by a smaller amount than ̶̶̶̶̶̶̶̶̶̶̶̶̶̶̶̶̶̶̶̶̶et site.
> D. Customers who had never purchased products from America Mart purchased, on average, fewer products in 1999 than previous customers did.
> E. The increase in costs due to setting up the web site in 1999 was greater than the increase in revenue from sales in 1999.

Only one option will resolve the paradox.

Question Stem

Most discrepancy question stems will include some form of the words "explain" or "resolve", and the vast majority will also contain the words "if true." This means that you have to attempt the question keeping in mind that the information given in the options is unquestionable and is to be taken as fact.

A typical 'resolve the paradox' question stem looks like the following:

- Which of the following, if true, most helps to resolve the paradox described above?

- Which of the following, if true, most helps to explain the discrepancy described in the argument?

- Which of the following, if true, best reconciles the apparent discrepancy described above?

- Which of the following hypotheses best justifies the contradiction occurring above?

11.2 The Process Of Solving Resolve The Paradox Questions

The 4-step approach is the same as in chapter 2.

The 4-step approach

(1) Recognize the question type

(2) Understand the argument construction

(3) Predict the qualifier

(4) Eliminate incorrect options

The first 2 steps are the same for resolve the paradox questions. Let us jump directly to the predict the qualifier step.

Predicting the qualifier

We are already familiar with this step. Let us see how to predict a "resolution" in an argument.

> In 1999, America Mart, which previously sold merchandise only through retail outlets, began selling on the internet while keeping its retail stores open. Although total sales increased in 1999, profits were less than the profits in 1998.
>
> Which of the following, if true, contributes most to explaining why America Mart's profits were more in 1998 than in 1999?

Understand the argument: The argument is easy to understand. It says that in the year 1999, America Mart (AM), began selling merchandise over the internet while keeping its retail stores open. Despite total sales having increased in the year 1999, profits were less than the profits in the year 1998.

The paradox: Sales in 1999 were higher than sales in 1998. Common knowledge plays a role here. It is implied that, when sales increase, profits increase proportionately. However, the argument states that profits decreased.

To resolve the paradox, we must predict possible factor(s) that reduced profits despite good sales. This phenomenon is not new in the modern world. Possible reasons could be that AM sold merchandise at relatively low sale prices to promote the website, or that startup costs to establish the internet portal were substantially high, thus affecting profits.

Predictive Resolution 1: AM sold merchandise at a significantly low sales price.

Predictive Resolution 2: Profit accrued from increased sales could not offset the investment made to establish the internet portal.

Let us see the 5 options to this question.

Critical Reasoning Guide – Resolve the Paradox

(A) There was a two percent increase in sales tax in 1999 that consumers had to pay on all retail purchases.

(B) A greater number of promotions for their internet sites was made available to previous customers than to people who had never shopped at America Mart before.

(C) In 1999, America Mart's wholesale purchase costs increased by a smaller amount than did the selling price of goods on their internet site.

(D) Customers who had never purchased products from America Mart before purchased, on average, fewer products in 1999 than previous customers did.

(E) The increase in costs due to setting up the website in 1999 was greater than the increase in revenue from sales in 1999.

Let us understand each option.

(A) Increased tax was absorbed by the customers, and not by AM, implying no extra cost for AM per product. From AM's perspective, the revenue per product did not decrease. This option does not help explain the paradox.

(B) This is not relevant. Who purchased more of the promotions is not relevant as long as the increased sales happened. Also, a greater number of promotions on the internet site is not sufficient enough to conclude that AM spent huge sums on the promotions, causing lower profits.

(C) This option is an opposite answer. All it means is that in 1999, input costs increased by a smaller amount, but the selling price of the goods on their internet site increased by a relatively larger amount. This further strengthens that profits in 1999 should be more than those in 1998. It increases the discrepancy rather than resolves it.

(D) This option is also an opposite answer. This option implies that in 1999, first-time customers of AM purchased fewer products than did regular customers. This fact is irrelevant as the sales to first-time customers is still additional revenue. This further strengthens that profits in 1999 should have been more than those in 1998. It increases the discrepancy rather than resolves it.

(E) This is the correct answer. It is aligned with predictive resolution 2. The increase in costs could not be offset by the increase in revenue, leading to relatively lower profits in the year 1999. It explains the paradox.

Example Questions

11.3 Examples

Example 1

In the decade beginning in 2000, nine percent of the refrigerators built by WhirlBlue required major compressor and condenser coil repairs. However, the corresponding figure for the refrigerators that WhirlBlue built in the 1990s was only four percent.

Which of the following, if true, most helps to explain the discrepancy?

- **(A)** Government regulation of white goods usually requires all refrigerators, whether old or new, to be inspected for carbon monoxide emission levels prior to sales.

- **(B)** Owners of new refrigerators service their refrigerators more regularly than do the owners of old refrigerators.

- **(C)** The older a refrigerator is, the more likely it is to be discarded for scrap rather than repaired when major compressor and condenser coil work is needed to keep the refrigerator in operation.

- **(D)** The refrigerators that WhirlBlue built in the from the year 2000 onward incorporated simplified compressor and condenser coil designs that made the compressor and condenser coils less complicated than those of earlier models.

- **(E)** Many of the repairs that were performed on the refrigerators that WhirlBlue built in the 1990s could have been avoided if periodic routine maintenance had been performed.

Argument Construction

Major compressor and condenser coil repairs were performed on 9 % of the refrigerators built by WhirlBlue from the year 2000 onward. However, the corresponding figure for the refrigerators that WhirlBlue built in the 90s was only 4 %.

Predictive Resolution

The paradox: Usually it is logical to infer that if any electronic products, such as refrigerators, are in use for a relatively long duration of time, those products will require more repairs and service than those in use for shorter durations of time. The facts presented in the argument, however, contradict the typical situation.

When comparing two things, groups, individuals, or, in this case, products, a reliable issue to check is whether the two things being compared are similar and comparable.

What if the refrigerators produced in the 90s were superior in both technology and manufacturing techniques compared to those produced in the year 2000 onward. It would then be logical that the ones produced later would require more repairs and services than the earlier ones. This resolves the paradox.

Predictive Resolution: The refrigerators produced in the 90s were superior in quality compared to the ones produced in the year 2000 onward.

Answer choice explanation

(A) The stated regulation is applicable to both old and new refrigerators. This information does not help to resolve the discrepancy.

(B) This option is an opposite answer. If owners of new refrigerators service their refrigerators more often than do the owners of old refrigerators, it is likely that new refrigerators would perform better. Instead of resolving the discrepancy, the information further worsens the discrepancy.

(C) This is the **correct** answer. The gap of 5 percentage points (9%-4%) could be because many old refrigerators were discarded for scrap rather than repaired when major compressor and condenser coil work was needed to keep them in operation. Although this option is not aligned with our predictive resolution, it rightly differentiates the comparable products in their characteristics, implying that had the figures of discarded refrigerators been taken into account, the percentage figures from the 1990s and 2000s would be comparable. It helps to explain the discrepancy by providing a reason there seem to be more newer refrigerators needing repairs.

(D) This option is an opposite answer. If the refrigerators built in the 2000s had incorporated simplified compressor and condenser coil designs, it would be likely that new refrigerators would have performed better. Instead of resolving the discrepancy, this information further worsens the discrepancy.

(E) This option is an opposite answer. If many of the repairs on the refrigerators built in the 1990s could have been avoided with periodic routine maintenance, the 4% figure would have been even lower, making the argument unexplainable.

The correct answer is option C.

Example 2

Automobile manufacturers defend their substitution of steel frames in cars with cheaper plastic components by claiming that consumer demand for light cars with crumple zones, rather than corporate profit motives, led to the substitution. However, carbon-reinforced tubing (CRT), which is lighter than steel but stronger, was not employed.

Which of the following, if true, best explains the exclusion of carbon-reinforced tubing while maintaining the manufacturers' claim?

(A) Most consumers prefer steel to plastic components because of their durability.

(B) Prototypes of vehicles with CRT have not been shown at major auto shows.

(C) The manufacturing process for plastic and CRT frame components is quite different from that of traditional steel frames.

(D) Automobile manufacturers have not yet resolved certain quality control problems in the production of CRT in high volumes.

(E) CRT is more expensive than steel.

Argument Construction

Automobile manufacturers have substituted steel frames in cars with cheaper plastic components. They claim that because of consumers' desire for light cars with crumple zones, they chose plastic, and that it was not because of profit motives. However, carbon reinforced tubing (CRT), which is lighter than steel but stronger, was not used instead of plastic.

This question is different from the typical resolve the paradox question. We have to resolve the discrepancy, but we cannot attack the manufacturer's claim, as the question asks us to preserve it.

Predictive Resolution

The paradox: The paradox is that, despite CRT being lighter yet stronger than steel, it was not used instead of plastic to substitute for steel frames in cars. The manufacturers claim that consumers want lighter cars.

There are two underlying assumptions here—one, CRT *is stronger than plastic*. In both aspects – weight and strength – CRT scores well enough, yet it was not used instead of plastic, which is not as strong as CRT. The manufacturers chose to use plastic, and in defending their position, they said that profits did **not** drive the decision.

So, in resolving the paradox, we have to defend the manufacturers for not using CRT without using higher costs or profits as the reason.

Our main task is to provide a non-financial reason for not using CRT. One such reason could be that the manufacturers do not have a dependable supplier of CRT; the paradox will be resolved if we can find some production level problems with CRT.

Predictive Resolution: The manufacturers do not have a dependable supplier of CRT.

Answer choice explanation

(A) This option is **irrelevant.** The argument is about the selection of CRT over plastic; but this option talks about steel.

(B) This option is tempting, but **inconclusive.** Lack of representation of prototype vehicles with CRT at major auto shows does not imply that CRT is not ready for being used in cars. Participation in major auto shows is not a necessary quality certification. It does not explain why CRT isn't being used.

(C) This option is **inconclusive.** We cannot infer anything from this. A different manufacturing process to manufacture CRT does not necessarily mean that it is difficult. Different and difficult are not the same thing. This does not provide an adequate reason for not using CRT instead of plastic.

(D) This option is the **correct** answer. It says carbon tubing has quality control problems making it less safe, or less reliable, than plastic. This resolves the discrepancy because it justifies why the manufacturers did not use CRT instead of plastic.

(E) This option is also correct, but we cannot go against the instruction given in the question stem, which explicitly asks us to preserve the manufacturers' claim that *plastic is not used because of profit motives,* implying that CRT is not employed because of reasons other than profitability.

The correct answer is option D.

Example 3

Teachers' unions are demanding a higher salary for their members. Their principal complaint is that despite the years of study, dedication, and training necessary to obtain their qualifications, teachers earn far less than a mechanic in real terms. These complaints have been rejected by the State Budgetary Commission, which has produced figures compiled by an independent team of auditors proving that mechanics earn far less than teachers.

Which of the following does **NOT** at least partially explain the apparent paradox expressed in the passage above?

(A) The two months' paid leave teachers enjoy annually is offset by the unpaid hours worked in lesson preparation.

(B) Mechanics have the possibility to take advantage of workplace facilities to carry out repairs on their own cars and bikes.

(C) Many teachers also earn money through private tutoring.

(D) Some rich customers gift their old cars to their mechanics.

(E) Pension payments awarded to teachers upon retirement are higher than the pensions awarded to mechanics.

Argument Construction

We have to select an option that does NOT help in any way to resolve the paradox. Four options will at least partially explain the apparent paradox.

The teachers' union's complaint is that despite their years of study, dedication and training, teachers earn far less than a mechanic in real terms. But these complaints have been rejected by the State Budgetary Commission (SBC), which has produced counter facts proving that mechanics earn far less than teachers.

Predictive Resolution

The paradox: The paradox expressed in the passage is that the union claims that teachers earn far less than a mechanic, however, the SBC says exactly the opposite.

While one group claims that another group enjoys more benefits that what their group does, another organization conclusively claims that it is other way round.

A possible resolution in these types of situations is that one group either does not count the benefits it receives or counts non-existent benefits for the other group.

Predictive Resolution: A group either does not count the benefits it receives or counts non-existent benefits for the other group.

Answer choice explanation

(A) This option means that the pay teachers get for summer holiday is, in fact, a justified remuneration to them for their lesson preparation time outside of class hours. So such paid leave is not an undue advantage to the teachers. This option does not resolve the paradox. This option seems to be the **correct** answer.

(B) This option offers a partial resolution. This option provides one reason teachers may be justified in saying that their income is less than that of mechanics in real terms. Mechanics can boost their income by getting free repairs done on their own cars and bikes. One group gets an uncounted benefit, but the other does not.

(C) This option, too, offers a partial resolution. This option provides one reason the SBC may be justified in saying that mechanics' income is less than that of teachers in real terms. If many teachers can earn money through private tutoring, then one group gets some uncounted benefit, but the other does not.

(D) This option, too, offers a partial resolution. This option provides one reason teachers may be justified in saying that their income is less than that of mechanics in real terms. Getting old cars free is a benefit to some mechanics, implying one group gets an uncounted benefit, but the other does not.

(E) This option, too, offers a partial resolution. This option provides one reason the SBC may be justified in saying that mechanics' income is less than that of teachers in real terms. Post-retirement benefits weigh more for teachers than mechanics, implying one group gets an uncounted benefit, but the other does not.

The correct answer is option A.

Example 4

There is statistical evidence that the number of AIDS patients in the US has increased by approximately 8% over the last five years. Surprisingly, those involved in AIDS treatment in San Francisco have reported a sharp decline in the number of patients visiting free clinics over the last five years.

Which of the following, if true, could by itself best explain the difference expressed in the above passage?

- (A) The statistics refer to the US as a whole.
- (B) Many people from cities like San Francisco, Boston, and Philadelphia are not more likely to go to private clinics than free clinics.
- (C) Many people from San Francisco only go to private clinics.
- (D) Globally, there has been an 18% rise in the number of AIDS patients.
- (E) AIDS awareness among US cities is vastly different.

Argument Construction

The number of AIDS patients in the US has increased by 8% over the last five years. However, San Francisco reported a sharp decline in the number of AIDS patients visiting free clinics over the same period. Note that the figures don't include the number of people visiting private clinics.

Predictive Resolution

The paradox: The paradox is that if the number of AIDS sufferers in the US has increased by 8% over the last five years, why is a similar figure not reflected in San Francisco, a popular U.S. city? On the contrary, that city reported a sharp decline in the number of AIDS patients visiting free clinics over the same 5-year period.

The argument has sufficient scope to be resolved with various possibilities. One possibility is that SF is not representative of the US, and differs vastly in the aspect of health care. Another possibility is that while the 8% figure represents the whole country, the average does not mean that the figures for every region must be around 8%. Every region has different demographic, geographic, cultural, and health characteristics that may drastically vary from each other.

Predictive Resolution 1: SF differs widely from the US in aspects that relate to AIDS.

The second premise states that *SF has reported a sharp decline in the number of patients visiting free clinics.* However, no data has been given about the number of patients visiting private clinics.

If the figures for private clinics for the same 5-year period showed a drastic increase in the number of patients visiting them, the discrepancy would be resolved.

Predictive Resolution 2: The figures for private clinics showed a drastic increase in the number of AIDS patients visiting them.

Answer choice explanation

(A) We already know that in the US, the number of AIDS patients increased by 8%. This statement is just a rephrased version. It does not resolve the contradiction.

(B) This option is the opposite of what we need. Considering SF only, the option statement means that almost an equal number of patients visits free and private clinics. This further strengthens that the number of AIDS patients in SF declined, and does not help to explain the paradox.

(C) Although this option is not truly aligned with our predictive resolution 2, it is in line with it. We are trying to answer the question of why although the number of AIDs sufferers nationally has increased, the number of AIDs sufferers showing up at free clinics in San Francisco has declined. This option is a proper justification, as it helps to explain the discrepancy by telling us that though the number of patients visiting free clinics declined, many patients choose private clinics instead.

(D) This option is out of scope. The statistics of the passage relate only to the US.

(E) This option is tempting, but inconclusive. In the real world, we may be swayed by this information, and infer that the difference in the figures between the US and SF has something to do with awareness; but in the GMAT, we can only infer what must be true. We cannot conclude anything on the basis of the variation of awareness. Moreover, the scope of the argument is limited to AIDS patients, and not AIDS awareness, and there's no necessary link between patient visits and awareness.

The correct answer is option C.

Practice Questions

11.4 Practice Questions

11.4.1 Questions

Question 1

Recently many people in a certain county have stopped buying new apartments, primarily because high taxes have been introduced by the county tax office, and because the rate of unemployment in the county is high. However, the average price of a new apartment has almost doubled in the county.

Which of the following, if true, best explains the increase in the average price of a new apartment?

- (A) The price of used apartments has climbed steadily over the past five years.
- (B) There will be a tax reduction later in the year which is expected to aid moderate and low income families.
- (C) The market for new apartments has been unaffected by current economic conditions.
- (D) Economic conditions are expected to get significantly worse before the end of the year.
- (E) In anticipation of low demand for new apartments, there has been a large decrease in construction.

Question 2

The results of an endurance test (comprising three tests) of micro-automobiles showed that models from Japan, France, and Italy were on average 18% more efficient fuel burners than models from the US and England, and possessed 14.5% better braking as well. It was also found that models from the US and Germany were 12% less efficient in the tests relating to engine wear and tear. The final results of the test series announced last week showed the US models to be the clear winners.

Which of the following could best possibly explain why the US models are the clear winners?

- (A) The climatic conditions under which the tests were held favored the Japanese models.
- (B) The judges of the test were drawn from representatives of all the participating automobile producers.
- (C) Only four US models were allowed to participate in the tests.
- (D) All the participating US models were standard and unmodified vehicles.
- (E) The test series was composed of 12 different tests carried out on each vehicle after the completion of 5000 miles.

Question 3

Having urged the government to sign the United Nations Human Rights Charter, the intellectuals of a Balkan country now have a government-sponsored petition appealing against a UN decision that imposes sanctions on their country for human rights violations. Although morally and ethically opposed to the use of torture and imprisonment without trial, those intellectuals nevertheless feel obliged to support authorities in their crackdown on insurgents and they are fully aware that such violations are taking place.

Which of the following, if true, would best explain the apparent paradox expressed in the passage above?

(A) The country is on the verge of being overrun by insurgents.

(B) The intellectuals are related to the insurgents.

(C) The intellectuals support the stand of the insurgents.

(D) The intellectuals are not being pressured by the authorities.

(E) The human rights abuses referred to are of an extreme nature.

11.4.2 Answer-Key

(1) E   (2) E   (3) A

Solutions

11.4.3 Solutions

Question 1

Argument construction

Recently many people in a certain county have stopped buying new apartments. This has happened because of two reasons: one, high taxes levied on buying apartments; and two, the high rate of unemployment in the county. Surprisingly, the average price of a new apartment has almost doubled in this county.

Predictive Resolution

The paradox: The paradox is that despite many people not purchasing apartments (low demand), the average price of new apartments has almost doubled.

There is a paradox because prices reflect the relationship between supply and demand. Low demand should mean low prices and vice versa. Higher unemployment and taxes may decrease demand. A decrease in demand should have decreased the price, but on the contrary, the prices have increased.

Predictive Resolution: We need a factor that explains why prices have gone up despite low demand. Any option that explains what made the prices go up is the right answer.

Answer choice explanation

(A) This option is **irrelevant** since it talks about used apartments. The argument is only concerned with new apartments.

(B) This option is **irrelevant.** It talks about a future scenario which does not impact the paradox right now. It does not justify why prices have gone up despite low demand. At best, this should form the basis for steady prices, but certainly not increased prices.

(C) The information that the market for new apartments has been unaffected by current economic conditions does not answer why new apartment prices doubled. It does not resolve the discrepancy.

(D) This option is an opposite answer. The inference of the information that economic conditions are expected to get significantly worse before the end of the year will make people very cautious while making investments. It may be another reason people stopped buying new apartments, but this option does not resolve the discrepancy.

(E) This option is the **correct** answer. In anticipation of low demand for new apartments, there has been a large decrease in construction. It means that low demand has caused significantly lower supply. Consequently, the lower supply means that apartments on the market are priced high because the supply has gone lower than the low demand. It is possible that because of a large decrease in construction, buyers, however few, have to compete for fewer apartments, leading to the doubling of prices.

The correct answer is option E.

Question 2

Argument construction

The argument is fully loaded with data. After reading the question stem, we know that the question is the "Resolve the Paradox" type. We have to resolve the discrepancy of why the US models are the clear winners. This suggests that the argument provides data that does not seemingly favor the victory of US models. So, let's focus on the US data only.

The endurance test:

Test 1 (Efficiency of fuel burners) - Top place - Models from Japan, France, and Italy - 18% more efficient fuel burners than US models; US models were not the winners.

Test 2 (Efficiency of braking) - Top place - Models from Japan, France, and Italy - 14.5% better braking than US models; US models were not the winners.

Test 3 (Engine wear and tear) - Top place - Do not know - but US models were not the winners. Despite losing 3 tests, the final results of the test series announced last week showed that the US models are the clear winners.

Predictive Resolution

The paradox: The paradox is that despite not being the winners in any of the three mentioned endurance tests, the US models are declared the winners.

This question demands attention while reading the argument. The argument talks about data from the endurance test, but the conclusion is derived for the test series. This implies that there must be more tests other than the endurance tests in the test series, and in a majority of them, the US won. Such a situation would resolve the discrepancy.

Predictive Resolution: US models topped the results in most of the other tests in the test series.

Answer choice explanation

(A) This option is **irrelevant.** It focuses on Japan; we are concerned with the US. A condition favoring Japan further worsens the discrepancy.

(B) This option does nothing in terms of resolving the discrepancy. If the judges of the test were drawn from representatives of all the participating automobile producers, there is more justification to believe that the testing is fair and impartial.

(C) Like option A, this option, too, does nothing in terms of resolving the discrepancy. Even if only four US models were allowed to participate in the tests, the discrepancy stands as to why the 4 US models win, despite losing the three endurance tests.

Critical Reasoning Guide – Resolve the Paradox

(D) Like option A and B, this option too does nothing in terms of resolving the discrepancy. Even if the participating models from other countries were not standard and modified vehicles, the puzzle is unresolved why the US models won despite losing the endurance tests.

(E) This option is the **correct** answer. It explains how the US models won by stating that there were 9 other categories tested, in which the US models must have won. It is aligned with our predictive resolution. So, despite losing in 3 endurance categories, the US models, by winning in most of the other ones, won the series.

The correct answer is option E.

Question 3

Argument construction

The argument is written from the position of intellectuals of a Balkan country. Previously they had insisted the Balkan government sign the United Nations Human Rights Charter (UNHRC), pledging that the government would not carry out a crackdown on insurgents, implying no human rights violations. But now they, along with the government, have appealed against the UNHRC, which impose sanctions for not carrying out a crackdown on insurgents. Although the intellectuals realize that, from a moral and ethical perspective, the use of torture and imprisonment without trial is wrong, they nevertheless feel obliged to support the government's crackdown on insurgents.

Predictive Resolution

The paradox: Previously, the intellectuals were against human rights violations, but they apparently seem to have changed their position now to support the government in carrying out activities against the insurgents, activities that imply human rights violations. The paradox is that intellectuals are supporting human rights violations even though they were initially strictly opposed to them.

The argument deals with moving from one position to another seemingly contradictory position over a period of time. One reason could be that circumstances now are vastly different.

Predictive Resolution Circumstances prevalent now in the Balkans have made the intellectuals change their stance regarding human rights violations.

Answer choice explanation

(A) This option is the **correct** answer. It is aligned with our predictive resolution. While the intellectuals may be strictly against human rights violations, they may have an even-stricter position about insurgency and subverting the government. The intellectuals may have found the insurgents harming the country to such an extent that they may see certain violations as a necessary evil required to get rid of the insurgents. So, earlier, when the situation was not as grave as it is now, they supported UNHRC. In dire situations, principles are sometimes sacrificed.

(B) This option explains why the intellectuals are on the side of the insurgents, but does not explain why the intellectuals are allowing the government to carry out human rights violations against them.

(C) Like option B, this option, too, explains why the intellectuals are on the side of the insurgents, but does not resolve the paradox.

(D) This option is an opposite answer. *The intellectuals are not being pressured by the authorities* implies that the intellectuals have changed their stance on their own and were not influenced by the government. This worsens rather than resolve the discrepancy.

(E) This option does not resolve the paradox why they are allowing human rights violations against the insurgents.

The correct answer is option A.

11.5 References for Official Guide Questions

The Official Guide for GMAT Review, 13th Edition: Question # 3, 6, 9, 13, 17, 22, 24, 44, 49, 57, 61, 86, 92, 94, 99;
Diagnostic test question # 19, and 33

The Official Guide for GMAT Verbal Review, 2nd Edition: Question # 8, 59, 60, 61, 72, and 73

Chapter 12

Inference Argument

12.1 The Inference Argument Question type

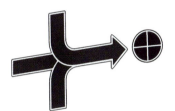
Like 'resolve the paradox' or 'explain the discrepancy' arguments, inference arguments consist only of premises, mostly factual statements, and sometimes claims. Since the arguments contain only premises, the conclusion is missing from the arguments. Inference questions also belong to the evidence-based family.

Inference questions are not as frequent as assumption, strengthen or weaken questions; however, you will see at least a couple of these questions on your GMAT.

Inference questions ask you to select an option that must be true as per the information in the argument. Mostly, the correct option may be inferred using only some of the information in the argument; however, you are free to use all of it.

Look at the dialogue between two people in the image. What could be inferred here?

The following illustration depicts your job for the inference question type.

> Southern Haul Cargo (SHC) Railway owns the entire railroad tracks in the city of Woe-be-gone, Idaho. Because of Woe-b[...]nning to make a metropolitan rail & subw[...]uncil has claimed, however, that if SHC railw[...] an unfair advantage over the city's existing bu[...] could be subsidized by the profits of their mono[...]
>
> Based on the information [...]red?
>
> (A) SHC's subway transport system w[...]'s bus transport.
> (B) If SHC railway were allowed to pr[...]ld not want to do so.
> (C) SHC Railway makes sufficient p[...]
> (D) SHC railway is forbidden to offer bu[...]
> (E) It expected that SHC railway will have a lon[...] monopoly on commuter traffic.

Only one option can be inferred, and must be true.

Question Stem

Most inference question stems will include some form of the words "conclude", "support", or "infer".

A typical 'inference' question stem looks like the following:

- Which of the following can be logically concluded based on the information in the argument?

- The information above most strongly supports which of the following conclusions?

- Which of the following can be properly inferred based on the information in the argument?

- The information above best supports which of the following claims?

- Which of the following must be true based on the information in the argument?

12.2 The Difference Between Strengthen And Inference Question Types

Like strengthen questions, inference question stems, too, may contain the phrase "most strongly support", so it is important to make sure that you do not get confused between the two question types. The following table highlights the differences between the two.

	Inference question type	Strengthen question type
Who supports whom?	The argument supports the correct option.	The correct option supports the argument.
Presence of conclusion	There is no conclusion in the argument.	The conclusion is always present in the argument.
Role of assumption	Since there is no conclusion in the argument, there is no role of assumption.	Since the conclusion is present in the argument, the assumption has a role.
Truthfulness of options	Only the correct option is true. Incorrect options are either not necessarily true or could be false.	All the options are true and unquestionable.
Question stem	The argument above most strongly supports which of the following?	Which of the following most strongly supports the argument above?

Handwritten notes:

Inference → Argument supports options

Strengthen → Options support argument.

12.3 The Process Of Solving Inference Questions

The 4-step approach is the same as in chapter 2.

The 4-step approach

(1) Recognize the question type

(2) Understand the argument construction

(3) Predict the qualifier

(4) Eliminate incorrect options

The first 2 steps are same for inference questions. Let us jump directly to the "predict the qualifier" step.

Predicting the qualifier

We are already familiar with this step. Inference questions test how you treat what is within scope and what "must be true", and not what "could be true". Your inclination to reasonably assume or infer something is cleverly tested by the test maker with a trap of classic wordplay; the key is to think skeptically.

The test maker will tempt you into inferring something beyond the scope of the argument; the incorrect inference will seem true when you supplement the argument with real-world information. However, you must not bring outside information into the argument.

Let us examine the following argument.

Moderate consumption of carbonated soft drinks may keep your sugar level in check. Excess sugar is one of the primary reasons for obesity.

Let us see one of the seemingly correct options.

Option: Excess consumption of colas causes obesity-related diseases. —out of scope.

If we supplement the argument with real-world information, then the option seems correct. However, we must not do so. You can make a "must be true" inference–*Excess consumption of colas may cause obesity.* The above option is wrong because we cannot assume that the excess consumption of colas will surely cause obesity-related diseases. Diseases are out of scope. Also, the second premise states that excess sugar is one of the primary reasons for obesity, but that does not mean that the excess consumption of colas raises sugar level high and causes obesity-related diseases.

Another common trap is a "cause and effect" mix-up. If the argument says that X causes Y, we cannot necessarily conclude that Y causes X, too; however, the test maker will sell just such a tempting option in a way that seems correct.

Critical Reasoning Guide – Inference

Let us see following example.

If Barcelona's star player Messi scores a hat-trick, Barcelona will win the match.

It is simple cause and effect example where the cause, X, is 'Messi scoring a hat-trick', and the effect, Y, is 'Barcelona winning the match'.

Correct inference: If, in a match, Messi scored three or more goals, we can infer that Barcelona must have won the match.

Incorrect inference: If Barcelona won the match, we cannot necessarily infer that Messi must have scored three or more goals. There is a possibility that Barcelona could have won because of superlative performances by other players'.

So, $X \Rightarrow Y \neq Y \Rightarrow X$

Taking the inference to the extreme is another common trap in the answer options.

Let us look at the following example.

Lack of practice affects your marks significantly.

Correct inference: Scoring below the expected level could be due to insufficient practice.

Incorrect inference: One may fail in the exam because of falling short with practice.

↳ just says "affects marks"... could be A→B. etc. not imply FAIL.

The argument does not necessarily mean that due to lack of practice, the marks will be affected to such an extent that one might fail. In the real world, it is reasonable to infer this, but in a GMAT argument, you must avoid inferring something to the extreme until there is a reason to do so.

Let us see how to predict an inference from a GMAT-like argument.

> Major corporations have condemned the doubling of the annual license fee demanded by Microsoft for the use of specialized software as surrender to the organized piracy that continues in a number of S.E. Asian countries. Microsoft has conceded that piracy continues to eat into profits, but claims that the price hike is due to increased research and development costs.

Understand the argument:

The argument is easy to understand. It says that Microsoft has doubled the annual license fee for the specialized software used by major corporations. The major corporations oppose this move. Their viewpoint is that Microsoft is soft on the organized piracy taking place in a number of S.E. Asian countries, resulting in lowered profits and raised costs. Microsoft does acknowledge that the piracy eats into profits; however, it claims that the price hike is required because of the need for more funds for increased research and development.

While understanding the argument and predicting the inferences, you must pay attention to key words in the argument. These key words will dictate the scope of the argument. For example, the argument is limited to "specialized software" only; any inference regarding non-specialized, generic, and popular software like Windows is out of scope. Similarly, it's only major corporations that have condemned the move. If an option talks about ethically upright corporations, then it falls in the category of "could be true" and not "must be true". Another extreme case could be to include all Asian countries. Remember that the scope is limited to South East Asian countries.

Let us predict a few inferences.

Predictive Inference 1: Both Microsoft and the major corporations acknowledge that the piracy of specialized software cannot be fully checked.

Predictive Inference 2: Major corporations strongly feel that the mechanism for controlling software piracy by Microsoft is ineffective.

Predictive Inference 3: Major corporations purchase specialized software through legitimate sources.

The inference immediately above is a "must be true" inference, as major corporations will oppose the move from Microsoft only if they are affected by the price to be paid to the legitimate software seller.

Let us see some of the options for this argument.

(A) The previous license cost was dictated by major companies // There is no evidence in the argument to infer that the previous license cost was dictated by major companies. On the contrary, this may fall into the category of "could be false", as despite condemnation by major corporations, Microsoft doubled the license fee.

(B) Microsoft is lenient towards the piracy of their software // This option is incorrect because the argument states that major corporations feel that Microsoft is lenient towards the piracy of their software, but we cannot infer that Microsoft is necessarily lenient towards it. Such an inference would imply that feelings always reflect reality.

(C) Acquisition of software by major companies is through legitimate channels // This is the correct "must be true" inference. It is aligned with predictive inference 3.

(D) Research and development costs incurred by Microsoft have increased beyond anticipated levels // This is a case of extreme inference. This could be true, but is not a case of "must be true". Justifying the price hike due to the R & D outlay does not necessarily mean that the R & D cost has increased beyond anticipated levels.

(E) Major corporations fear the competition posed by those organizing the software piracy // This option is an example of clever wordplay. It looks promising, but is not correct. While the corporations may fear the competition from those using the pirated software, clearly those organizing the piracy are not their direct competitors. In any case, we cannot say that this is absolutely true. It may or may not be true.

Example Questions

Critical Reasoning Guide - Inference

12.4 Examples

Example 1

According to a recent report on higher education in the United States, the 15 universities with the highest annual tuition fees also gave out the largest financial aid awards to incoming students with outstanding achievements. Because of a belief in equal opportunity, these universities are able to redistribute resources from those who can afford to give to those students who deserve aid by virtue of merit.

Which of the following can be correctly inferred from the statement above?

(A) Following a belief in equal opportunity is a good way to mask charging higher tuition fees.

(B) It is possible for a university that believes in equal opportunity to put different financial demands on different students.

(C) A university that offers large financial aid awards must do so because it believes in equal opportunity.

(D) Universities that have high tuition fees tend to give out little financial aid.

(E) Universities that have large endowments tend to give out lots of financial aid.

Argument Construction

The 15 U.S. universities who charge the highest annual tuition in the country also gave out the largest amount of financial aid to those incoming students who demonstrated outstanding achievements. These universities believe in equal opportunity, and are able to charge more fees for those who can afford to pay, and charge less for those who cannot afford it.

Predict An Inference

The language used in the argument is extreme. The aforementioned 15 universities charge the highest fees, and give out the largest amount of aid. Since the aid is based on the virtue of merit and achievement, the total cost for students varies. If some paid the full 100%, some others may have paid 80%, 60 %, or 40%.

Predictive Inference 1: The annual tuition fee for students in these universities varies.

We have established that the universities charge the full fee for some, and lower fees for others, but still they must be able to collect an ample sum to run the classes.

Predictive Inference 2: Despite charging less for some incoming students, these universities can accrue sufficient funds to run their courses.

Answer choice explanation

(A) We cannot infer that following a belief in equal opportunity is being carried out to disguise charging higher tuition fees. This option is too judgmental and does not go along with the tone of the argument.

(B) Yes, it is possible for a university that believes in equal opportunity to put different financial demands (different fee structures) on different students based on their merit and needs. This is the **correct** answer. It is aligned with predictive inference 1.

(C) It may seem like a rephrased statement from the argument, but it is not. The argument states that a university that offers large financial aid awards would do so because it believes in equal opportunity. However, the language in the option statement uses the verb "must do", implying compulsion. We cannot infer this necessarily.

(D) We cannot infer that all the universities that have high tuition fees tend to give out little financial aid. The scope of the argument is limited to the universities that have the highest fees and that believe in equal opportunity.

(E) We cannot infer that all the universities that have large endowments tend to give out lots of financial aid. Like option D, the scope of the argument is limited to the universities that have the highest fees and that believe in equal opportunity.

The correct answer is option B.

Example 2

Badly hit by the recession, an automobile company decided to split its production into two categories – a division to make private vehicles and a division to make commercial vehicles. It proved to be a wise decision. Over the following four years, the private division, primarily due to increased sales of luxury limousines to the United Nations, accounted for approximately 40% of dollar sales and 20% of overall profit. The commercial division was responsible for the remaining balance.

Which of the following can be inferred concerning the performance of the company over the last four years?

(A) Expensive luxury cars were more profitable products than commercial vehicles.

(B) The private division realized lower profits per dollar than the commercial division achieved.

(C) The commercial division had to face stiffer competition than the private division.

(D) The range of luxury limousines accounted for a higher percentage of profits than any products sold by the commercial division.

(E) The company's program failed to improve overall profits.

Critical Reasoning Guide – Inference

Argument Construction

The private division, primarily due to increased sales of luxury limousines, accounted for approximately 40% of dollar sales and 20% of the overall profit of the company. The commercial division was responsible for the rest.

Predict An Inference

According to the passage, the private division accounted for 40% of dollar sales and 20% of overall profit, so the commercial division would have accounted for 60% of dollar sales and 80% of overall profit.

We can deduce that the private division accounted for 20%/40% = 0.50 profit per dollar sales, and the commercial division accounted for 80%/60% = 1.33 profit per dollar sales.

Predictive Inference: Profits per dollar sales for the commercial division is more than double that of the private division.

Answer choice explanation

(A) We cannot infer that the expensive luxury cars were more profitable products than the commercial vehicles. We can only conclude that the commercial division was more profitable than the private division.

(B) This is the **correct** answer. It is aligned with our predictive inference. The private division has realized lower profits per dollar (0.50) than the commercial division (1.33).

(C) We cannot infer that the commercial division had to face stiffer competition than the private division. This is out of the scope of the argument.

(D) We can infer that the luxury limousines accounted for the highest percentage of profits of any products sold by the private division, but we cannot compare the same with any product in the commercial division.

(E) This is a "must be false" option, as the argument states that it (i.e. splitting the program) proved a wise decision.

The correct answer is option B.

Example 3

Lately many people in a certain post-communist country have decided to emigrate for economic reasons. The people who want to leave the county in search of a job or a better life are either those who have no money or those who know multiple foreign languages.

Of the following persons, who is LEAST likely to emigrate?

(A) A person who knows two foreign languages, but doesn't have any money.

(B) A person who knows two foreign languages, but is afraid to travel.

(C) A person who has no money to travel and knows a second language at an elementary level.

(D) A person who knows no foreign language, but has money to travel.

(E) A person who has no money to leave the country, and is dejected with his/her present situation.

Argument Construction

People will leave the county either for a job or a better life; these people either do not have money or know multiple foreign languages.

Predict An Inference

Read the question stem clearly – Of the following people, who is LEAST likely to emigrate? We have to find the person who is NOT eligible to emigrate. What is the qualifying criterion to emigrate? The criterion is either people who do not have money or those who know multiple foreign languages.

Predictive Inference (LEAST likely to leave): A person with sufficient money and no knowledge of any foreign language.

Answer choice explanation

(A) This person is certain to emigrate. He fulfills both the criteria – knowing two foreign languages, and having no money.

(B) This person is likely to emigrate, too. He fulfills one criterion – knowing two foreign languages. Remember that 'afraid to travel' is not a criterion in the argument. It is a real-world knowledge trap laid by the test maker. They want you to assume that a person won't travel when he is afraid of traveling. However, the argument clearly mentions that a likely emigrant is one who knows foreign languages. By that criterion, this person is highly likely to emigrate.

(C) This person is likely to emigrate, too. He fulfills at least one criterion – having no money. No money to travel is a trap for you to bring in real-world wisdom. We must not use our brain on the details of travel without money. It is beyond the scope of the argument. Knowing the second language is inconclusive, because we don't know whether it is a foreign language. However, the answer to this does not impact the decision, as the person fulfills one criterion – having no money. Thus, according to the argument, this person is very likely to emigrate.

(D) This is the **correct** answer. This person is LEAST likely to emigrate. He does not fulfill any criterion. This person does not know any foreign language, and has money, and so has no reason to emigrate

(E) This person is likely to emigrate. He fulfills one criterion – having no money. Like option C, 'no money to leave', and 'dejected with his/her present situation' are traps for you to bring in real-world wisdom. Moreover, 'dejected with his/her present situation' is not a criterion as per the argument. However, the argument clearly mentions that a likely emigrant is one who doesn't have money. By that criterion, this person is highly likely to emigrate.

The correct answer is option D.

Example 4

The cost of electricity is high because there is no effective competition among those who produce this vital source of energy. The utility companies have blamed the price of electricity on the need to invest in new plants to serve the ever-growing market in the region. This offers little consolation to the consumer, who could be compared to a tourist with diarrhea stranded in a strange city where all the public washrooms cost as high as $100 to use.

The analogy above serves to make which of the following points?

(A) The use of public washrooms has become a luxury and should be free of charge.

(B) The cost of electricity is being kept high by the producers to encourage consumers to use less.

(C) Without electricity, society would be unable to sustain its infrastructure and public services.

(D) Essential products like electricity should be supplied free of cost.

(E) Price-fixing can keep charges for an essential product artificially high.

Argument Construction

The cost of electricity is high because there is no competition among its producers. The companies blame the high price on the need to invest in new plants to serve the ever-growing need for electricity. The argument provides an analogy to ridicule the high price by observing that this scenario is similar to a situation in which a tourist with diarrhea is stuck in a strange city where all the public washrooms cost as high as $100 to use.

Predict An Inference

The key to this question is to understand the question stem. The question stem is unlike a typical question stem used for an inference question. You must identify which of the options that can be inferred, based on the analogy used in the argument.

Let us understand what the purpose of analogy is, and what we can infer from it. The tourist with diarrhea stuck in a strange city has no choice but to use the washroom even if he doesn't want to pay an exorbitantly high price for the service. We can infer that this example is given to draw a parallel to the high cost of electricity. We can conclude that the analogy serves to illustrate that, due to the monopoly of utility companies, consumers have no choice but to pay high prices for electricity.

Predictive Inference: Due to the monopoly, consumers have no choice but to pay high prices for essential commodities.

Answer choice explanation

(A) This is a classic real-world trap, but it is an incorrect option. The question stem wants us to infer something from the example about public washrooms, but it is not about the example. The argument is not about why the service of a washroom should be free; instead it is about the high price of electricity.

(B) We cannot infer that the cost of electricity is being kept high by the producers to encourage consumers to use less. The motive behind the producers' actions is not discussed.

(C) This is again a classic real-world trap, but it is an incorrect option. It is true that without electricity, society would be unable to sustain its infrastructure and public services, but this aspect is not mentioned in the argument. So, this option is out of scope.

(D) This option is tricky and tempting, but too extreme to be the right answer. From the analogy, we cannot infer that the argument is about offering the services of essential products free; rather it is concerned about unjustifiably high prices.

(E) This is the **correct** answer. For both essential products – electricity and washroom facilities, price fixation can be unjustifiably, or artificially, high.

The correct answer is option E.

Practice Questions

12.5 Practice Questions

12.5.1 Questions

Question 1

A private bus company wanted to increase profits. For 20 years it worked to make its buses more economical and faster by reducing the number of bus stops. Although the company was in some measure successful, the economy grew worse, and the industry almost went bankrupt. Assumptions and realities were vastly different. The real problem came not from passengers who wanted faster transport, but from the number of passengers who stopped using the bus service because of the limited number of bus stops.

Which of the actions below would most likely lead to a solution to the problem faced by the bus company as it is analyzed above?

(A) Providing buses with engines that run on a cheaper type of fuel than that traditionally used

(B) Providing double-decker buses that will stop at more bus stops

(C) Providing buses that have more seating room than any other existing buses

(D) Implementing a system to ensure that buses are loaded to capacity

(E) Implementing a market plan that focuses on routes that are known to be less used by other bus companies

Question 2

Southern Haul Cargo (SHC) Railway owns all the railroad tracks in the city of Woe-be-gone, Idaho. Because of Woe-be-gone's sudden population explosion, SHC is planning to make a metropolitan rail & subway system using its pre-existing tracks. The city council has claimed, however, that if SHC Railway were to offer subway transport, it would have an unfair advantage over the city's existing bus routes because SHC's subway transport system could be subsidized by the profits from their monopoly on cargo transport.

Based on the information given above, which of the following can be inferred?

(A) SHC's subway transport system would be as efficient as the city's bus transport.

(B) If SHC Railway were allowed to provide bus transport, it would not want to do so.

(C) SHC Railway makes sufficient profit in the cargo transport business.

(D) SHC Railway is forbidden to offer bus transport.

(E) It is expected that SHC Railway will have a long-term monopoly on commuter traffic.

Question 3

An electric piano designed to have perfect frequency for each note would sound different from the best Baldwin or Steinbach grand piano currently available.

To professional pianists, a piano that sounds different from the best grand pianos sounds less like a piano and, therefore, worse than the best-sounding existing pianos.

Professional pianists are the only acceptable judges of the quality of pianos.

Which of the following would best be supported by these statements?

- **(A)** Only amateur pianists should be asked to judge the sound of electric pianos.
- **(B)** Professional pianists assist in designing electric pianos.
- **(C)** The best sounding grand pianos have been around for more than 100 years.
- **(D)** It is currently impossible to create an electric piano that accepted judges will evaluate as being an improvement on existing grand pianos.
- **(E)** It is possible to create an electric piano that sounds better to everyone except a professional pianist.

Question 4

The level of financial aid given by rich nations to poorer nations in order to raise the poorer nations' industrial capacity is directly influenced by the extent to which the donors fear competition and the threat of diminished exports. The amount of aid recommended by Congress is invariably reduced and redistributed by presidential decree according to the findings of a select committee judging aid packages purely from an American business perspective. As a consequence, many poorer nations have to find areas of industrial activities that pose no threat to the industrial global order.

If the above statements are true, which one of the following must also be true?

- **(A)** The most needy countries are those with the smallest industrial output.
- **(B)** The amount of aid received by poorer nations for industrial projects is in proportion to the extent to which they develop new industrial bases that pose no threat to rich nations.
- **(C)** Poorer nations depend on foreign aid to advance their industrial economies.
- **(D)** The wealth of richer nations has expanded thanks to a policy of withholding foreign aid.
- **(E)** The amount of foreign aid given to poorer nations by richer industrialized nations has been reduced to safeguard existing export markets.

12.5.2 Answer-Key

(1) B | (2) C | (3) D | (4) B

Solutions

12.5.3 Solutions

Question 1

Argument construction

The argument is simple to understand. A private bus company wanted to increase profits. Over the years, it worked to make its buses more economical and faster by reducing the number of bus stops. The real problem came from passengers who stopped using their bus service because they wanted a greater number of bus stops.

Predict A Solution

The question stem of this one may stump you. Which category does this question belong to? The question stem asks for the solution. The solution will come from the information given in the argument. This is what we do in an inference question.

What is the problem with the bus company's logic? They kept cutting out bus stops to decrease transit time until they had virtually no customer base left. The only way to have a bus route that makes money is to have it pick up plenty of people from different stops to make a profit. If you have too few stops, how do you correct this? By adding more stops.

Predictive Solution: Make the buses stop at an optimum number of places.

Answer choice explanation

(A) Providing buses with engines that run on a cheaper type of fuel than that traditionally used will certainly reduce operational costs, but they would still lack the customer base. The solution should address customers' convenience regarding catching buses. This option does not address that.

(B) This is the **correct** answer. By providing double-decker buses, the company can cut costs, and making the buses stop at more bus stops will ensure that the increased capacity of the buses is available to more customers who will use the buses because of more bus stops.

(C) Providing buses that have more seating room than any other existing buses will certainly increase revenue, but they would still lack the customer base. The solution should address customers' convenience regarding getting on buses. This option does not address that.

(D) Like option C, this option, too, does not address the core issue of customers' convenience regarding bus stops.

(E) On the same lines as options C and D, this option, too, does not address the real problem.

The correct answer is option B.

Question 2

Argument construction

Southern Haul Cargo (SHC) Railway owns all the railroad tracks in the city. SHC is planning to make a Metropolitan rail & subway system using its pre-existing tracks. The city council is skeptical about this plan; it fears that if SHC Railway were to offer subway transport, it would affect the city's existing bus routes and transport because SHC has the capacity to reduce commuting costs substantially. The council claims that SHC would subsidize a subway transport system with the profits they accrued through the cargo transport business over the years.

Predict An Inference

Since SHC Railway owns all the railroad tracks in the city, we can infer that no other company offers subway transport services, and so city council claims that bus routes would be affected by SHC. We can infer that only SHC can offer subway services because the city council seems concerned about SHC's impact on bus routes if SHC provides a subway system.

Predictive Inference 1: No other railway company offers metropolitan rail & subway transport services in the city.

Predictive Inference 2: The network of SHC's railroad tracks is widespread enough to affect many major bus routes.

Answer choice explanation

(A) The argument did not talk about the efficiency of any transport system. We cannot infer that SHC's subway transport system would be as efficient as the city's bus transport. We don't even know that the bus transport is efficient to begin with.

(B) From the information in the argument, we cannot infer that SHC Railway would not provide bus transport if it were allowed to do so. SHC's position on providing bus transport is not given in the argument.

(C) This is the **correct** answer. SHC's expansion plan and the council's claim that SHC may subsidize its proposed subway service imply that SHC Railway has been making sufficient profit in the cargo transport business.

(D) No legal aspect is discussed in the argument. We cannot infer that SHC Railway is forbidden from offering bus transport.

(E) This option is based on future projections that haven't been made in the argument.

The correct answer is option C.

Question 3

Argument construction

An electric piano has been designed to have perfect frequency for each note, and sounds different from (but not necessarily better than) the best Baldwin or Steinbach grand piano currently available. Professional pianists, who are the only acceptable judges of the quality of pianos, find that when the sound of the electric piano (or any piano) is different from the best grand pianos, the sound is worse than that from best-sounding existing pianos. Their measure of a good-sounding piano is based on the best grand pianos, and any piano that does not sound like the best grand pianos cannot be deemed acceptable by those pianists.

Predict An Inference

It is currently impossible to create an electric piano that the acceptable judges will evaluate as being an improvement on existing grand pianos. The argument clearly states that professionals consider a piano that sounds different from the best grand pianos worse than the best-sounding existing pianos. So, it is not possible for an electric piano to sound better than a grand piano because an electric piano is currently made such that it will sound different from a grand piano. Nothing is said about technical improvements etc. to prove this false. Also, the argument does not state that the electric piano is *better* than a grand piano, just that it is different.

Predictive Inference: It is impossible for an electric piano to sound better than a grand piano.

Answer choice explanation

(A) This option directly opposes the premise stating that it is not amateur pianists, but professional pianists, who are the only acceptable judges of the quality of pianos.

(B) There is nothing mentioned about professional pianists designing these pianos; the argument only talks about judging the quality of pianos. Thus, this option cannot be inferred.

(C) Nothing in the argument tells us anything about the age of these pianos. This is out of the scope of the argument.

(D) This is the **correct** answer. It is aligned with our predictive inference that it is impossible to create an electric piano that sounds better than a grand piano.

(E) We are not told about how people other than professional pianists might perceive perfect frequencies. Note that we cannot necessarily infer that the electric piano, just because it has perfect frequency, will sound **better** than the grand piano. The argument mentions only that the electric piano will necessarily sound different from the grand piano. Hence, we cannot infer that people prefer perfect frequencies and will like the electric piano.

The correct answer is option D.

Question 4

Argument construction

How much financial aid should be given by rich nations to poorer nations to raise their industrial capacity depends on the extent to which the rich nations fear competition from would-be competent poorer nations and the consequent threat of reduced exports. The amount of aid recommended by the U.S. is invariably reduced and redistributed by a select committee judging aid packages purely from an American business perspective. As a consequence, many poorer nations have to find areas of industrial activity that pose no threat to the industrial activities of rich nations if they want to receive donations from those rich nations.

Predict An Inference

The passage states that the proportion of U.S. aid relates to the extent that the industries being aided compete with U.S. industries. The more the poorer nations compete, the less the aid given by the U.S. is.

Predictive Inference: The amount of financial aid to poorer nations will be proportionately less if the industrial activities of the receiving nations affect America's business interests. Otherwise, the aid will be optimum.

Answer choice explanation

(A) We cannot conclude that the neediest countries are those with the smallest industrial output. The argument does not imply this. A nation can be rich even if industrial output isn't high, but the economy is based on agriculture or the export of abundant natural resources.

(B) This is the **correct** answer. It is almost a restatement of the provided facts. It is aligned with our predictive inference.

(C) We cannot conclude that poorer nations depend on rich nations for developing their industrial economy as a whole. The argument implies that poorer nations get reduced financial aid to develop their industrial base if it is in areas other than ones the U.S. deals in.

(D) We cannot conclude that the wealth of richer nations has expanded because of a policy of withholding foreign aid. The argument does not imply this. This is too judgmental.

(E) The argument does not say that aid is reduced as a rule. The aid is reduced and redistributed by judging aid packages purely from an American business perspective. We can infer that if American business is unaffected because of the aid, the aid will not be reduced.

The correct answer is option B.

12.6 References for Official Guide Questions

The Official Guide for GMAT Review, 13th Edition: Question # 26, 38, 54, 55, 60, 66, 91, 103, 104, 105;
Diagnostic test question # 24, and 31

The Official Guide for GMAT Verbal Review, 2nd Edition: Question # 12, 14, 19, 43, 53, 57, 64, and 75

Chapter 13

Complete the Argument

13.1 The Complete the Argument Question type

Recently the importance of "Complete the Argument " (CA) questions has been increasing. CA questions cannot be categorized into any one family of questions. These question types are not followed by any question stem after the argument. The argument ends with a blank space that you complete with one of the options.

The "fill-in-the-blank" statement could be a conclusion, a premise either strengthening or weakening the argument, or even an inference or a reconciling statement. Mostly, however, most CA arguments are similar to assumption or strengthen questions. Most CA questions will ask us to select an option that makes a claim or conclusion true, or more likely to be true. The correct option may even be a restatement of the argument.

Look at the dialogue between the two people in the image. What can complete the argument?

The following illustration depicts your job for 'complete the argument' questions.

Which of the following best completes the argument below?

In an internet ~~~~~~~~~~~~~~~~~~~~~~~~~~~~~~~~ to cheating on their wive~~~~~~~~~~~~~~~~~~~~~~~~~~~~~~~~nate the proportion of~~~~~~~~~~~~~~~~~~~~~~~~~~~~~~~~ because_____

Only one option can correctly complete the argument.

A. some ch~~~~~~~~~~~~~~~~~~~~~~~~~~~~~~~~rvey to be faithful

B. some generally faithful ~~~~~~~~~rvey might have claimed on the survey to be chea~~~

C. some people who clai~~~~~~~~~ve cheated at least once may be very cheat

D. some people who claimed on the survey to have cheated may have been answering faithfully)

E. some people who are not married males have probably cheated at least once

Question Stem

CA question do not contain any question stem, hence it becomes important to understand what the question intends to ask. The key is to read the preceding word before the blank space, which may start with "therefore", "since", "because", or other words or phrases. Read the following table and you will understand this type of question.

Preceding word	Option statement	Question type
since, because, as, etc.......	premise / FACT	assumption/ strengthen/ weaken/ or resolve
therefore, thus, hence, as a result, etc.........	conclusion	inference
The argument is flawed because........	abstract statement describing the flaw, or true statement describing the weakness	find the flaw or weaken
The above situation is similar to........	parallel analogy	parallel argument or mimic the argument

Critical Reasoning Guide – Complete the Argument

13.2 The Process Of Solving Complete The Argument Questions

The 4-step approach is the same as in chapter 2.

The 4-step approach

(1) Recognize the question type

(2) Understand the argument construction

(3) Predict the qualifier

(4) Eliminate incorrect options

The first 2 steps are the same for CA questions. Let us jump directly to the "predict the qualifier" step.

Predicting the qualifier

Since CA questions can be of any type of CR question, we must first see which category the question belongs to, and, accordingly, we must apply the approach we have learned for each of those question types. Say the question type is 'strengthen the argument', then we must predict a strengthener best supporting the conclusion. Similarly, if it belongs to the 'weaken the argument' type, we must predict a weakener shattering the conclusion; likewise for inference or other question types.

Let us take a look at an example to better understand the approach.

> Which of the following best completes the argument?
>
> Since an experienced, top-rated race car driver is now constantly losing races he had always won before he acquired a certain race car, he plans to junk the race car he is currently using and replace it with a better model. The new improved race car model is more likely to improve the race car driver's performance than any other factor will because..........................

Reading the word that precedes the blank space, we understand that the question asks for a premise, but we are still not sure whether it asks for an assumption, strengthener, or weakener.

Understand the argument:

An experienced, top-rated race car driver is constantly losing races he had always won. He blames the loss on the model of car he is using. He intends to raise his performance by replacing the car with a new improved race car model.

Conclusion: The new improved race car model is more likely to improve the race car driver's performance than any other factor will.

The word "because" following the conclusion indicates that we must plug in a strengthener to support the claim that the new improved race car model is more likely to boost the race car driver's performance than any other factor will. So, this is a "strengthen the argument" question.

Let us predict a couple of strengtheners.

Predictive strengthener 1: Over the years, top racers have observed that the quality of the car constitutes 80% of the factors in winning races.

Predictive strengthener 2: Some advanced systems used in the new model keep it in control even at very high speeds.

Let us see some of the options to this argument.

(A) the driver may have new personal problems that have nothing to do with his car's performance. *weakener*

This cannot be the answer as the option lays the onus of losing the race on the driver rather than the car. The importance of the car is diluted, and the argument is weakened rather than strengthened.

(B) racers tend to judge the quality of the car more than the quality of the driver.

This is the **correct** answer. It is aligned with our predictive qualifier. This is a strengthener. It emphasizes the importance of the quality of the car in winning races and strengthens the argument.

(C) decisions to switch race cars should be based on that particular model's success rate. *irrelevant*

This option focuses on the selection of a particular model of car for racing, whereas the argument is concerned about whether the quality of the car itself is the most important factor in races.

(D) the driver may not necessarily have been able to overcome other obstacles during recent races. *weakener*

Like option A, this cannot be the answer as the option lays the onus of losing the race on the driver rather than the car. Again, the importance of the car is diluted, and the argument is weakened rather than strengthened.

(E) improved race cars are very expensive and difficult for many teams to afford. *irrelevant*

This option focuses on the price aspect of the car for racing, whereas the argument is concerned about whether the quality of the car itself is the most important factor in races.

Example Questions

13.3 Examples

Example 1

Many airlines have been pushing the federal government for assurances of greater security in case of terrorist attacks on board flights. One of these airlines expects the improved security to help increase revenue by $20 million a year, mostly from people who ....

Which of the following most logically completes the argument above?

- **(A)** are afraid of traveling by plane because of terrorist attacks.
- **(B)** travel by luxury trains.
- **(C)** spend more money on traveling.
- **(D)** travel by plane because such travel is a status symbol.
- **(E)** travel by plane when they are pressed for time.

Argument Construction

Airlines have been pushing the government for greater security in being prepared for terrorist attacks on board flights. One of these airlines expects improved security to increase revenue by $20 million a year. The increased revenue will mostly come from the class of people who ....

Predict An Inference

With an understanding of the argument, we can infer that this is a question on inference. If it is true that improved security will increase revenue by $20 million a year, what type of people will bring in the increased revenue?

Certainly, people who were scared of insufficient security on board flights will now feel confident and start taking flights more often.

Predictive Inference: ...those who were scared of insufficient onboard flight security.

Answer choice explanation

This is an easy question. As discussed, the answer is A. It is aligned with our predictive inference.

The correct answer is option A.

Example 2

Which of the following best completes the argument below?

Critical Reasoning Guide – Complete the Argument

The main disadvantage of the new promotion scheme is that it places more emphasis on seniority than on capability. While not wishing to degrade the work record of certain executives who have faithfully served the company for a good many years, ...

- **(A)** other more qualified personnel have been promoted before them.
- **(B)** they clearly should be in positions of more responsibility.
- **(C)** perhaps it's time to let them go.
- **(D)** one has to ask oneself whether they deserve automatic promotion.
- **(E)** they might well consider such an appointment as a demotion.

Argument Construction

The author criticizes the new promotion scheme. He reasons that it places more emphasis on the seniority of the employees in the workplace than on their capability. **Although** he acknowledges the work record of certain senior employees, ...

Predict An Inference

With an understanding of the argument, we can infer that while the author is against the new promotion scheme for basing its decisions on seniority rather than on merit, he does not refute the contribution of ALL the senior employees, and even acknowledges the contribution of some of them.

Understand the tone and the intent of the author. The word "while" shows that he does not shrug off the value of some senior employees, but that he also wants capability to be a factor in the promotion process. He therefore implies that not all senior employees deserve promotion just because they are senior. The correct option would be the one that goes against senior employees, or one that emphasizes capability as a basis for promotion.

Predictive Inference 1: Capability should also have its say while considering promotion.

Predictive Inference 2: Many competent employees of junior rank work alongside senior staff that is not as competent.

Answer choice explanation

- **(A)** "Other more qualified personnel have been promoted before them" is a factual statement. It does not support capability over seniority. The correct option must be author's opinion. This is incorrect.
- **(B)** "They clearly should be in positions of more responsibility" is obviously in favor of senior staff. We want something against them. This is incorrect.

(C) "Perhaps it's time to let them go" is certainly against senior employees, but is an extreme statement. The author does not refute the contribution of ALL the senior employees; he even acknowledges the contribution of some of them. This is incorrect.

(D) This is the **correct** answer. "One has to ask oneself whether they deserve automatic promotion" is against senior staff, and is the justified inferable opinion of the author.

(E) "They might well consider such an appointment as a demotion" is out of scope. The author cannot conclude the argument with senior employees considering such promotions as demotions. There's no indication for such a deduction.

The correct answer is option D.

Example 3

Which of the following best completes the argument below?

The price of computers is dictated more by the price of computer chips than by any other computer component. Due to this fact, the fortunes of computer chip manufacturers have risen dramatically as computers have now become an indispensable element of modem life. When the prices of computer chips rise in any given year over the prices of the previous year, the prices of computers rise accordingly. This has the effect of the sales of new computers falling when purchase costs increase. In 1999, sales of home computers went up by 29%, therefore, it can be concluded that ....

(A) the cost of computer chips in 1998 was at least as high as it was in 1999.

(B) the cost of chips rose by at least 29% in 1999.

(C) the prices of all models of computers in 1998 were 29% lower than prices in 1999.

(D) sales by computer chip manufacturers rose by 29% in 1999.

(E) total sales by computer manufacturers rose by 29% in 1999.

Argument Construction

The crux of the argument is that whenever the price of computer chips rises in any given year, the price of computers also then rises accordingly. This in turn causes sales of new computers to go down. In 1999, sales of home computers went up by 29%, therefore, it can be concluded that ....

Predict A Conclusion

As stated, the crux of the argument is that whenever the price of computer chips rises, the price of computers rises accordingly. We need to draw a conclusion from the argument.

The meaning of *the price of computers rises accordingly* is that if the chip price drops, then the computer price must go down. The data given for 1999 states that sales of home computers went up by 29%, therefore, it can be concluded that the price of home computers must not be higher in 1999 than it was in 1998. This further concludes that the price of chips must not be higher in 1999 than it was in 1998.

Predictive conclusion: the price of chips must not be higher in 1999 than it was in 1998.

Answer choice explanation

(A) The meaning of this option statement is that the cost of computer chips in 1998 was almost equal to what it was in 1999. So, if sales of home computers went up by 29%, the price of home computers and chips could not have risen. So, option A is the only valid conclusion.

(B) This is an opposite answer. It is inconsistent with the fact that *when the prices of computer chips rise in any given year over the price of the previous year, the prices of computers rise accordingly.*

(C) We cannot conclude this. The data given in the argument is regarding home computers only, and not for all computer models.

(D) Like option C, we cannot conclude that sales by all computer chip manufacturers rose by 29% in 1999, as the data given in the argument is regarding home computers only.

(E) Similarly, like option C and D, we cannot conclude that sales by all computer manufacturers rose by 29% in 1999, as the data given in the argument is regarding home computers only.

The correct answer is option A.

Example 4

Which of the following best completes the argument below?

Chrysler has been undergoing some dramatic changes. Gone is the image of a company focused solely on the U.S. Now both the products and the work force have begun to reflect the global nature of the company. The new works team is composed of engineers from all over the world. All of the mechanical engineers are the product of an in-house training program, although, as yet, none of the engineers specializing in hydraulics has won the prestigious Order of Merit bestowed by the Mechanical Engineers Union. So far, only engineers winning the Order of Merit have gone on to become department heads. Therefore ....

(A) all of the department heads have received the Order of Merit.

(B) all of the winners of the Order of Merit have received in-house training.

(C) none of the department heads who have specialized in hydraulics are the product of an in-house training program.

(D) none of the department heads are from the U.S.

(E) none of the non-U.S. mechanical engineers who are products of in-house training have the Order of Merit.

Argument Construction

The argument is long in size, but easy to understand. The crux of the argument is that the new works team at Chrysler is composed of engineers from all over the world. All of the mechanical engineers are the product of an in-house training program, but no engineer specializing in hydraulics has won the Order of Merit award. Till now, only engineers winning the award have become department heads (HoDs). Therefore ....

Predict An Inference

We can further simply the facts for better understanding.

- All the mechanical engineers received a training program.
- No engineer specializing in hydraulics (a branch of mechanical engineering) has won the award.
- Only award-winning engineers became department heads (HoDs).

Let us see what we can conclude from this information. Since only engineers who have won the award have become HoDs, and none from hydraulics have won it so far, we can infer that the HoD for the hydraulics department would be not an in-house-trained mechanical engineer specializing in hydraulics.

Predictive inference: The HoD for the hydraulics department is not an in-house-trained mechanical engineer specializing in hydraulics.

Answer choice explanation

- **(A)** This option can be eliminated, as the argument merely states that of the engineers promoted to department head, all had won the Order of Merit, but maybe non-engineers were made department heads. The HoD for the hydraulics department may be a non-award-winning/non-engineer person, or an outside recruit who has not been promoted internally.

- **(B)** This option can be discarded as the argument only states that all the mechanical engineers are the product of in-house training schemes.

- **(C)** This is the **correct** answer. It is just a restatement of the facts provided by the argument. It is aligned with our predictive inference.

- **(D)** This can easily be eliminated as the argument does not differentiate between the U.S. and non-U.S. works teams.

- **(E)** For the same reason as option D, option E is incorrect.

The correct answer is option C.

Practice

Questions

13.4 Practice Questions

13.4.1 Questions

Question 1

Which of the following best completes the argument below?

In an internet survey of married males, 23.78 % admitted to cheating on their wives at least once. However, the survey may have underestimated the proportion of married males who are cheats because............................

(A) some cheats taking the survey might have claimed to be faithful.

(B) some generally faithful people taking the survey might have claimed to be cheats.

(C) some people who claimed to have cheated at least once may have cheated much more often.

(D) some people who claimed to have cheated on the survey may have been answering faithfully.

(E) some people who are not married males have probably cheated at least once.

Question 2

Which of the following best completes the argument below?

The prospects for the future of the seal are far from rosy. Poaching and the abuse of quotas have become endemic throughout the sealing regions of Canada and Russia. Seal-hide dealers, motivated by the high profits to be made selling hides to the fashion industry, are ignoring the distinctive markings on the skins which show that hides come from illegally culled animals. An internationally-supported initiative to police the trade was launched last year............................

(A) and has been very successful.

(B) but has proved highly effective.

(C) which goes some way to explain the current situation.

(D) although much has been achieved.

(E) but has had little practical effect.

Question 3

Which of the following best completes the argument below?

Each time X grocery store raises the price of goods by 10 percent, sales drop by 20 percent. However, when the price of apples increased, the quantity of apples sold was the same as before the price increase. This is because ....

(A) whenever there is an increase in price, the amount of a certain product sold must drop.

(B) shop assistants should take care to try to interest clients in other fruits besides apples.

(C) the drop in sales is consistent with quarterly trends forecast by the grocery store.

(D) apples are, on average, more expensive than other fruit in the grocery store.

(E) the sale of apples is dependent not only on the price, but on other factors as well.

Question 4

Which of the following best completes the argument below?

Recent research by the tropical disease division of the Army Medical Corps suggests that the malaria parasite's incubation period is accepted to be a maximum of 90 days.

Surprisingly, studies of more than 80 male and female service personnel who were infected have revealed that, although the 90-day limit remains generally true, 18 of the patients had succumbed to the parasite more than 90 days after returning to the U.S. from a zone containing malaria-bearing mosquitoes. The longest was a pilot who had developed malaria 133 days after returning to the U.S. from a spell of duty in Africa. This exception is understandable because ....

(A) insecticide-resistant mosquito swarms have become a common phenomenon in the U.S.

(B) pilots have frequently complained of mosquitoes getting trapped aboard planes.

(C) the malaria parasite's incubation period is accepted to be a maximum 90 days barring an exception to a maximum of 1% of cases.

(D) the incubation period of the malaria parasite varies according to the species of mosquito as host.

(E) anti-malaria immunization has become less effective over the last 20 years.

13.4.2 Answer-Key

(1) A | (2) E | (3) E | (4) B

Solutions

13.4.3 Solutions

Question 1

Argument construction

The argument is simple to understand. In an internet survey of married males, 23.78% admitted to cheating on their wives at least once. However, the author is skeptical about the survey results. He is of the opinion that the figure may be higher because................................

Conclusion: The survey may underestimate the proportion of married males who are cheats.

Predict A Strengthener

The conclusion states that the figure 23.78% may be even higher. We must think how survey respondents can make this figure skewed. It is possible that some cheats incorrectly claimed on the survey that they are faithful. Such a situation would show how the survey can underestimate the number of cheats.

Predictive strengthener: Some cheats claimed on the survey that they are faithful.

Answer choice explanation

(A) This is the **correct** answer. It is aligned with our predictive strengthener.

(B) If some generally faithful people taking the survey claimed to be cheats, the survey would overestimate, rather than underestimate, the proportion of married males who are cheats.

(C) This option is irrelevant. It talks about the degree of cheating.

(D) This information serves neither to underestimate nor overestimate the proportion of married males who are cheats.

(E) Cheating by non-married males is outside the scope of the argument.

The correct answer is option A.

Question 2

Argument construction

The author laments the prospects of the existence of seals, and the likelihood of their survival. Poaching and the abuse of quotas are to blame. Seal-hide dealers sell hides to the fashion industry, and ignore the distinctive markings on the skins of seals which show that the seals come to them illegally. An internationally-supported initiative to regulate the trade was launched last year................................

Conclusion: The prospects for the future of the seal are far from rosy.

Predict A Strengthener

The clue is the negative idea suggested in the first sentence – the conclusion: the prospects of seal livelihood are in danger. The author lists the threats to the seal and concludes with one inadequate positive step. It can be inferred that the concluding statement would be in a negative tone supporting the conclusion that seals are in danger despite measures taken to ensure the survival of their species. Hence this is a strengthen question.

Predictive strengthener: however, little could be reaped from it.

Answer choice explanation

Options A, B, and D are positive in meaning, while option C is neutral. The only option that is aligned with our predictive strengthener is option E.

The correct answer is option E.

Question 3

Argument construction

The argument is simple to understand. Each time the grocery store raises the price of goods by 10 percent, sales drop by 20 percent. However, the price of apples and their subsequent sale did not follow this rule. This is because ....

Predict A Resolution

This question can be treated as the "resolve the paradox" type.

The paradox: Despite an increase in the price of apples, the quantity of apples sold did not decrease.

Predictive resolution: The price of apples was lower than normal; the increase in price did not make any difference to customers.

Answer choice explanation

- **(A)** This option is merely a mandate which states the rule. It does not help to explain the paradox.

- **(B)** This option is irrelevant. Whether shop assistants should take care to try to interest clients in other fruit besides apples does not relate to the paradox.

- **(C)** Consistency in a drop in sales with a quarterly trend that was forecast does not explain the paradox.

- **(D)** Comparing the price of apples with other fruit does not help to resolve the paradox.

- **(E)** This is the **correct** answer. If the sale of apples is dependent not only on price but also on other factors, the increase in price will not significantly impact the quantity sold.

The correct answer is option E.

Question 4

Argument construction

Recent research suggests that the malaria parasite's incubation period is 90 days at most. Some surprising studies of infected service personnel showed that 18 of them who were victims of the parasite became so more than 90 days after returning to the U.S. from malaria zones, and for one person it took 133 days for their malady to surface. This exception is understandable because ....

Predict A Resolution

This is a question on "resolve the paradox".

The paradox: The malaria parasite's incubation period is a maximum of 90 days, but 18 out of 80 patients were found to be infected with malaria well after the 90-day period.

We have to resolve the discrepancy while maintaining that the malaria parasite's incubation period is a maximum of 90 days, but 18 out of 80 patients got malaria more than 90 days after returning to the U.S. from a zone containing malaria-bearing mosquitoes.

It is possible that malaria-bearing mosquitoes bit those 18 patients after they returned to the U.S.

Predictive resolution 1: Malaria-bearing mosquitoes bit those 18 patients after they returned to the US.

It is possible that the top medical research body refutes the findings presented by the tropical disease division of the Army Medical Corps by suggesting that the malaria parasite's incubation period may go well over 90 days.

Predictive resolution 2: The top medical research body suggests that the malaria parasite's incubation period may go well over 90 days.

Answer choice explanation

(A) This option states that swarms of mosquitoes will take over the U.S., but the puzzle is over the incubation period of the parasite, not the mosquito. Also, this option discusses malaria infections occurring in the U.S., but the argument talks about 18 infected patients returning to U.S. (thus getting infected outside the U.S.).

(B) This is the **correct** answer. The mosquitoes getting trapped aboard planes may have made their abode in the workplace of the patients in the U.S. and bit them there.

(C) 1% of 80 patients is approximately 1 patient. So, as per this option, there can be an exception of 1 patient, but the data suggests that there are as many as 18 infected patients. This information does not resolve the discrepancy.

(D) This option can be eliminated because the argument states that the maximum incubation period is 90 days, so any variations according to species must be below this limit.

(E) The argument is concerned about the incubation period of the parasite, not about the effectiveness of anti-malaria immunization.

The correct answer is option B.

13.5 References for Official Guide Questions

The Official Guide for GMAT Review, 13th Edition: Question # 12, 33, 39, 59, 65, 69, 74, 81

The Official Guide for GMAT Verbal Review, 2nd Edition: Question # 10, and 38

Chapter 14

Summary

14.1 Approaches for different question types in a nutshell

Question family	Question type	Area of focus	Option	Approach
Assumption-based	Find the Assumption	Conclusion	Premise	Identify the **unstated assumption derived from the argument filling the logical gap in the argument** and making the conclusion believable.
	Strengthen the argument	Conclusion	Premise	Make the conclusion more believable with the help of **additional information.**
	Weaken the argument	Conclusion	Premise	Identify the logical gap in the conclusion, and make the conclusion less believable with the help of additional information.
	Evaluate the argument	Conclusion	Premise in question form	Raise a question, which when answered "yes" and "no" will **strengthen and weaken** the argument.
	Find the Flaw	Conclusion/ Assumption	Premises in generic and abstract form	Identify the logical gap in the conclusion, and **attack the assumption** made to reach the conclusion. Paraphrase the flaw in generic and abstract form.

Structure-based	Boldface/ Role Play	Structure of the argument; role of each statement	Describing the role reach each boldface portion plays.	Understand the structure of the argument, and the role of each statement. Paraphrase the **predictive role play** answer, and look for the correct option.
	Method of Reasoning (MoR)	Author's reasoning and logic	Describing author's reasoning	Ignore the subject matter; **focus on the reasoning**; paraphrase the description and look for the correct option.
	Parallel Reasoning/Mimic the argument	Structure of the argument, and reasoning	Similar argument with premise(s) and conclusion	**Understand the structure and reasoning of the argument.** Ignore the subject matter. Understand each option one-by-one and select the one that is similar to the question argument.
Evidence-based	Resolve the paradox/ Explain the discrepancy	Contradiction of two premises (facts)	Premise	Select the premise that resolves the contradiction in the argument. The correct option will make the two contradictory premises sensible not paradoxical.
	Inference	Premises (Mostly facts/claims)	Conclusion	Select the option that **"must be true"** based on the information given in the argument. Beware of "could be true" and true based on "real world information".

Critical Reasoning Guide – Summary

| No family | Complete the Argument | This is a question type which is not independent. The area of focus depends on the category of question. | Conclusion or premises | The approach depends on the category of question. |

14.2 References for Official Guide Questions

Find the Assumption

The Official Guide for GMAT Review, 13th Edition: Question # 21, 41, 46, 48, 75, 77, 83, 93, 96, 106, 109, 113; Diagnostic test question # 28

The Official Guide for GMAT Verbal Review, 2nd Edition: Question # 7, 34, 44, 52, 56, 63, 67, 76

Strengthen the Argument

The Official Guide for GMAT Review, 13th Edition: Question # 1, 5, 11, 14, 16, 19, 23, 29, 30, 31, 35, 40, 45, 50, 52, 56, 64, 67, 95, 101, 102, 108, 111, 118, 120, 121; Diagnostic test question # 25, 27, and 32

The Official Guide for GMAT Verbal Review, 2nd Edition: Question # 1, 2, 6, 9, 13, 17, 21, 23, 25, 29, 30, 32, 33, 35, 37, 45, 51, 55, 58, 62, 65, 68, 69, 77, 78, 82

Weaken the Argument

The Official Guide for GMAT Review, 13th Edition: Question # 2, 4, 20, 25, 32, 37, 43, 51, 58, 62, 71, 73, 79, 80, 82, 87, 88, 90, 97, 107, 112, 115, 117, 119, 122; Diagnostic test question # 18, 20, 23, 26, 30, and 34

The Official Guide for GMAT Verbal Review, 2nd Edition: Question # 4, 5, 11, 15, 16, 18, 20, 22, 24, 26, 27, 31, 36, 39, 41, 46, 47, 49, 50, 71, 80, 81, 83

Evaluate the Argument

The Official Guide for GMAT Review, 13th Edition: Question # 7, 10, 15, 27, 36, 42, 47, 53, 68, 70, 72, 110, 114, 124; Diagnostic test question # 21, 22, and 29

The Official Guide for GMAT Verbal Review, 2nd Edition: Question # 3, 28, 40, 42, 54, 66, and 70

Find the Flaw

The Official Guide for GMAT Review, 13th Edition: Question # 2, 8, and 100

Method of Reasoning

The Official Guide for GMAT Review, 13th Edition: Question # 34, 84, 85, 123

The Official Guide for GMAT Verbal Review, 2nd Edition: Question # 79

Bold Face/Role Play

The Official Guide for GMAT Review, 13th Edition: Question # 18, 28, 63, 76, 78, 89, 98, and 116

The Official Guide for GMAT Verbal Review, 2nd Edition: Question # 48, and 74

Resolve the Paradox

The Official Guide for GMAT Review, 13th Edition: Question # 3, 6, 9, 13, 17, 22, 24, 44, 49, 57, 61, 86, 92, 94, 99; Diagnostic test question # 19, and 33

The Official Guide for GMAT Verbal Review, 2nd Edition: Question # 8, 59, 60, 61, 72, and 73

Inference

The Official Guide for GMAT Review, 13th Edition: Question # 26, 38, 54, 55, 60, 66, 91, 103, 104, 105; Diagnostic test question # 24, and 31

The Official Guide for GMAT Verbal Review, 2nd Edition: Question # 12, 14, 19, 43, 53, 57, 64, and 75

Complete the Argument

The Official Guide for GMAT Review, 13th Edition: Question # 12, 33, 39, 59, 65, 69, 74, 81

The Official Guide for GMAT Verbal Review, 2nd Edition: Question # 10, and 38

Chapter 15

Practice Questions

1. Doctors face an ethical dilemma with glaucoma patients over the choice between prescribing a legal drug with harmful side effects or recommending the illegal drug cannabis, which works better despite the hallucinations it causes. The American Medical Association (AMA) has posted an official warning to medical practitioners that advising patients to use an illicit drug is forbidden under federal law, and punishment can include prison sentences. While no doctor has been arrested yet, it is inevitable that doctors cannot avoid arrest for long.

   Which of the following, if true, would undermine the conclusion derived in the argument?

   (A) A glaucoma patient suffers no side effects from using cannabis.

   (B) For doctors, ethics weigh below the American Medical Association's (AMA) mandates.

   (C) Lawyers, with professional discretion, can withhold information if the information is damaging to clients.

   (D) Many patients have been arrested for following the advice of doctors.

   (E) Some drugs now commonly used, such as Novocain, were once illegal to use.

2. This question is based on the argument of the question given above.

   Which of the following is imperative to determine the validity of the conclusion derived in the argument?

   (A) Whether the law allows for any extenuating circumstances in which the law isn't necessarily enforced

   (B) Whether any other illegal drug is being used by doctors in treating fatal diseases

   (C) Whether glaucoma patients themselves have any issues with using cannabis

   (D) Whether adequate research about any other legal drug without harmful side effects to treat glaucoma has been made

   (E) Whether patients will get arrested, too, for using cannabis on the advice of their doctors

3. A wave of redundancies has led state governments to appeal to the federal government for emergency funding to alleviate unemployment. Following publication of a report on the viability of garage enterprises, a consortium of banks and investment houses has proposed the establishment of an investment fund to provide capital for such enterprises. This has elicited a chorus of criticism from various quarters, who have pointed out that federal light industry programs aimed at assisting skilled but redundant workers by stimulating the growth of garage enterprises frequently end up harming other U.S. social groups unconnected to the enterprises.

   Which of the following, if true, provides the most doubt for the critics' claim above?

   (A) Garage enterprises in the state now produce almost 12% of the vehicle components previously imported from Southeast Asia.

   (B) The funding of the light industry program depends on the reallocation of resources earmarked for the refurbishment of run-down areas.

(C) Light industry programs have previously produced employment opportunities that last no longer than a decade at most.

(D) The viability report was commissioned and published by the Union for Light Industry Workers.

(E) Much of the proposed Investment derives from government and treasury investment houses.

4. This question is based on the argument of the question given above.

   Which of the following, if logical, provides the most support for the claim made by the critics above?

   (A) Light industry programs have recently invested heavily in R&D of the automation of car-servicing.

   (B) Garage enterprises, while being viable, are not as profitable as eating establishments.

   (C) Existing garages and mechanic shops are currently run and managed by immigrants because of a shortage of trained mechanics in the U.S.

   (D) The viability report was commissioned and published by the Union for Light Industry Workers.

   (E) Many environmental pressure groups are against setting up garage enterprises.

5. Seeking to improve his business, a restaurant owner places a number of extra tables and seats on an outside terrace during summer. This has an immediate impact and raises the clientele by 22%, although a good many of the customers simply stop by for a drink or a dessert. Over the course of the year, surprisingly, the restaurant owner discovers that his sofas and lounge chairs, the most comfortable seating in his café, are fetching much less profit than his tall stools and standing tables. This can be explained by the fact that..........................

   Which of the following, if true, most logically concludes the argument given above?

   (A) his most profitable table is the smallest and most dimly lit sofa, almost hidden behind some plants.

   (B) most of his patrons are office workers from the nearby business district meeting with clients for lunch.

   (C) his bakery products are fetching him higher profits than anything else on the menu.

   (D) students find the cafe very relaxing to sit in to study and work on projects for long hours.

   (E) the more cozy and comfortable the seating, the more likely it is that a person will linger.

6. The economic downturn has run its course and all the indications of a recovery appear to be present, although some analysts remain skeptical. The paper's recently published predictions for employment trends between 2000 and 2010 clearly suggest that the greatest increase in the number of people employed will be in the low-paying catering sector. However, surprisingly, the low-paying catering sector will not increase its percentage share of overall employment, but the catering sector involving high-paying catering positions will do so, proving skeptical analysts wrong.

If the predictions listed above are accurate, which of the following best reconciles the surprising situation described above?

   (A) The overall number of people employed in the catering sector will decrease.

   (B) There will be more high-paid catering workers than low-paid catering workers.

   (C) The number of people employed in others sectors, excluding low paid workers, will increase.

   (D) The number of low-paid catering workers will approximately equal those in other higher-paid sectors.

   (E) The overall number of people employed in the catering sector will increase.

7. This question is a modified version of the argument from the previous question.

The economic downturn has run its course and all the indications of a recovery appear to be present, although some analysts remain skeptical. The paper's recently published predictions for employment trends between 2000 and 2010 clearly suggest that **the greatest increase in the number of people employed will be in the low-paying catering sector**. However, surprisingly, **the low-paying catering sector will not increase its percentage share of overall employment**, but the catering sector involving high-paying catering positions will do so, proving skeptical analysts wrong.

In the argument given, the two portions in boldface play which of the following roles?

   (A) The first is a premise that has been used against the author; the second supports the main conclusion.

   (B) The first is a statement accepted by the author; the second is a consequence of the critics' claims.

   (C) The first is a consideration that the author offers in support of his conclusion; the second is a fact that the author believes does not contradict his conclusion.

   (D) The first is evidence used by the critics in making their argument; the second is evidence offered by the author to explain his position.

   (E) The first is evidence that undermines the author's position; the second is a statement that follows from that position.

Critical Reasoning GuideTraining Set – Critical Reasoning   303

8. The Dalyan sea turtles in Turkey, a huge tourist attraction, will soon become extinct. Tourist developments including neon-lit hotels and discos obscure the moonlight, disorienting the female turtles as they seek out beaches to lay their eggs. The turtles assume that hotel pools are the sea and end up laying their eggs in flower beds. Once the eggs hatch, the hatchlings are unable to find their way to the sea and die. The stringent building regulations protecting the turtles are flouted openly by the corporate sector while the number of turtles dwindles.

    Which of the following can be inferred from the above passage?

    (A) The dwindling number of turtles does not affect the number of tourists visiting Turkey.
    (B) Turkish building regulations are no longer enforced as stringently as they were before.
    (C) If the turtle hatchlings are in the sea, they will not die.
    (D) Female Dalyan sea turtles are guided only by moonlight when laying their eggs.
    (E) The corporate development sector is known to ignore building restrictions norms.

9. A month after the completion of national elections, a Gallop Poll measured the popularity of politicians and **placed the prime minister of the country 25 points below the leader of a small party. The same poll placed the leader of the opposition 10 points above the PM.** Subsequently, a telephone poll carried out by a leading newspaper confirmed the findings of the poll, but suggested that the figures were only an accurate reflection of voters' opinions within a ten percentage range. Clearly, however, **the electorates are more swayed by the policies of a party than its leader.**

    In the argument given, the two portions in boldface play which of the following roles?

    (A) The first is a claim that the argument disputes; the second is a conclusion that has been based on that claim.
    (B) The first is a claim that has been used to support a conclusion that the argument accepts; the second is that conclusion.
    (C) The first is evidence that has been used to support a conclusion for which the argument provides further evidence; the second is the main conclusion of the argument.
    (D) The first is support for a claim whose implications suggest a particular inference; the second is a claim presented in order to argue against deriving such an inference from that finding.
    (E) The first is a finding whose accuracy is evaluated in the argument; the second is evidence presented to establish that the finding is accurate.

10. This question is based on the argument in the question above.

    Which of the following, if true, would most seriously undermine the conclusion given in the argument?

(A) In most countries, the elected leaders are never as popular as the opposition leaders.

(B) The Gallop Poll formulates its ratings from a representative sample of voters and not all the voters.

(C) In the same poll, the president was the most popular politician chosen by voters.

(D) The opposition has been acquiring fame by taking up the most controversial issues in the country.

(E) Voters vote according to the track record of a politician, and not by the policies of the party at any given time.

11. People think of cars as an investment, whereas in reality they are depreciating assets. Even if one religiously follows the maintenance schedule set out in the car manual, within just three years discernible changes inevitably accrue, even with the most responsible driver. Such a car appears as good as new to the owners, who think the car's value would only have depreciated marginally. However, any dealer will tell the owners that they will be lucky to get even 50% of the purchase price, regardless of whether it's a domestic or a foreign car.

    Which of the following, if true, calls the claim above into question?

    (A) A bigger market than new cars is that of second-hand cars.

    (B) Not all people who buy cars wish to sell them off within three years of purchase because they give them to their relatives.

    (C) Many car parts, especially those of foreign cars not easily available, are sold at disproportionately high prices.

    (D) Car dealers are notoriously well known for disproportionately inflating the price of cars they sell, and disproportionately diminishing the price of cars they buy.

    (E) Every year, most car companies come out with at least 4 new models of cars, other than variants of existing cars.

12. This question is based on the argument from the above question.

    Which of the following, if true, supports the above claim the most?

    (A) The moment the car is driven out of the dealer showroom, its value depreciates thirty percent, and, for every subsequent year onwards, double-digit depreciation is inevitable.

    (B) Many people purchase cars to use casually, only to pass them off to their kids or someone close to them at a later date.

    (C) For those people who purchase a car the first time round, the car has more sentimental value attached than material value.

    (D) Some drivers make a habit of reckless driving and intermittent servicing as far as their cars are concerned.

    (E) In most cases, car rental companies are always willing to buy used cars of foreign models from the market.

13. In a speech, Senator Wiley criticized frequent flyer programs, now operated by virtually all major U.S. airlines, as nothing less than a bribe to acquire the accounts of major corporations who are willing to pay over the top in order to give untaxed rewards to their employees. Thus, the price of tickets for the general public is kept artificially high. Walter Healey, the Vice President of America Airlines, responded by saying the frequent flyer program was enjoyed by millions of Americans who were able to acquire program points from supermarket purchases and credit card transactions.

    Which of the following, if true, best weakens Healey's response to Wiley's criticisms?

    (A) Only some supermarket chains and credit card companies offer frequent flyer points to customers.

    (B) More people acquire frequent flyer points through airline ticket sales than through supermarket purchases.

    (C) Many airline companies offer bonus points with special meal perks for long haul flights.

    (D) More than two-thirds of airline tickets sold in the U.S. are bought by companies for their representatives.

    (E) Ticket prices are regularly reviewed by a committee of government and airline representatives.

14. This question is based on the argument in the above question.

    Which of the following, if true, would it be important to determine the correctness of Healey's response to Wiley's criticisms?

    (A) Whether the best supermarket chains and credit card companies offer frequent flyer points to customers

    (B) Whether most Americans acquire frequent flyer points through their supermarket purchases or through their airline tickets?

    (C) Whether most fliers are flying international or within US territories

    (D) Whether the general public feels the tickets are overpriced and difficult to bear

    (E) Whether the corporations pay taxes on the frequent flyer points they acquire for their employees

15. The designers of a revolutionary automobile engine for race cars have claimed that it can achieve a 25% reduction in fuel consumption compared to similarly-sized engines in current use. Developed using technology borrowed from NASA, the weight of the engine is 50% less than that of other engines of similar capacity. However, critics have pointed out that the fuel consumption reduction is dependent on the use of such a lightweight chassis as to be not only impractical but also downright dangerous. The critics are understandably upset about this finding because.....................

    Which of the following, if true, most logically concludes the argument given above?

(A) lightweight car parts cannot sustain wind pressure at high speeds and cave in or crumble.

(B) fuel consumption is not the slightest concern for race car drivers, who need to attain high speeds very quickly on the track.

(C) the engine was designed for different purposes, and not originally meant for cars.

(D) NASA has made faulty technology before that has resulted in astronauts' deaths.

(E) other engines can be altered to be lighter in weight without reducing fuel consumption.

16. Utility companies have to pay a changeable levy governed by the amount of fuel sold, the price of fuel, and the degree of state-supported investment. Increases in the first two variables or a decrease in the third generates higher levies. To ensure fairness, regular assessments of all three variables are required. In reality, the levies are determined according to computer-simulated scenarios extrapolated from assessments. Rather than just figures, the simulations are expressed as deviations from a 'norm', a mean based on the average level of the least volatile variable, which is the market price of fuel.

The method of calculation described above to calculate the levy is most flawed because it fails to consider that

(A) simulations need not be adequate representatives of the actual scenario.

(B) market price is not a good indicator to determine the price of any item being sold.

(C) the less deviation in a governing factor, the less changeable any calculation based on it.

(D) changeable levies allow for less control over the consumption and sale of resources.

(E) levies based on three factors make simulations difficult to generate.

17. After a visit to the municipal swimming pool, almost the entire schoolbody of Washington Junior High School contracted a mysterious skin ailment. The ailment took the form of a severe rash, which the school doctor diagnosed as an allergy caused by a chemical irritant present in the pool's water, and accordingly prescribed a course of treatment. Although the municipal authorities initially questioned the doctor's findings, because within two days of beginning the prescribed course of treatment most of the children were cured, they hurriedly accepted responsibility, thus opening themselves to the possibility of law suits.

Which of the following is it necessary to determine to judge the decision of the municipal authorities to accept culpability?

(A) Whether all children who visited the pool contracted the rash on that day, and to the same degree of intensity

(B) Whether the water supplied to the pool by the municipal corporation is potable

(C) Whether all children responded equally to the treatment prescribed by the doctor

(D) Whether the prescribed treatment works in cases of other non-chemically-induced ailments

(E) Whether the rashes took more than four days to clear up completely

18. This question is based on the argument in the above question.

Which of the following, if true, would show support for the author's judgment that the decision of the municipal authorities to accept culpability was hasty?

(A) Some types of berries can cause a severe reaction to chlorine if they are consumed right before coming into contact with chlorine.

(B) Laws mandate that any government body must award damages to any citizen if found guilty of misconduct or carelessness.

(C) Not all children suffered from the same degree of intense rashes that some children did.

(D) The science of detecting allergens has improved much in recent times, enough to be accepted as valid proof in a court of law.

(E) School doctors are usually known to make hasty diagnoses when faced with lots of patients.

19. In cases of cardiac arrest, prompt action is vital to increase the chances of a full recovery in victims. However, particularly in sparsely populated rural areas, consistently prompt response is impossible to achieve mainly because of the travel distances involved. For this reason, emergency operators have been issued a diagnostic question list to go through with those reporting cases of cardiac arrest in order to ascertain the severity of the attack prior to the dispatch of mobile treatment teams. It is clear that patients will suffer with this extra procedure, and that very few will benefit from it.

Given that the above statements are true, which of the following also has to be true?

(A) Cardiac arrest, if not treated properly, will lead to fatality.

(B) Some patients in rural areas do not get timely care for cardiac arrests.

(C) Medical facilities in sparsely populated rural areas are inadequate.

(D) Cardiac arrests get quick responses in densely populated urban areas.

(E) Many patients of cardiac arrest are denied chances of a full recovery.

20. This question is based on the argument in the above question.

In making the conclusion above, the author has necessarily assumed which of the following?

(A) The distance, without using the extra procedure, would not have affected the promptness of response, and the chances of full recovery.

(B) Those who report such emergency cases of cardiac arrest are ill-equipped to handle a diagnostic questioning procedure at that time.

(C) There are other ways of ensuring chances of full recovery other than a speedy response in the case of cardiac arrests.

(D) Ascertaining the severity of the attack is not possible through a list of diagnostic questions asked over a telephone.

(E) No patient suffering from cardiac arrest in rural areas can benefit from this extra step of diagnostic procedure.

21. With the invention of digital TV, many TV channels face the dilemma of whether to switch to digital. Although the advantages of digital TV are many, there are also pitfalls. To raise the funds to switch to digital, BBC decreased subscriptions to analogue channels and fired program makers, leading to a drop in quality. This alienated the public to such an extent that there's been a dramatic shortfall in the expected number of subscribers to the new BBC digital channels and a financial disaster looms, from which recovery seems unlikely. And so, many channels have resisted switching.

    If the above statements are true, which of the following must also be true, especially from the TV channels' perspective?

    (A) Digital TV is unlikely to spread to the masses.
    (B) BBC represents most of the TV channels adequately.
    (C) BBC's program quality would have gradually improved again.
    (D) The public is not concerned about the reputation of the TV channel.
    (E) There are as many disadvantages as advantages in switching to digital.

22. This question is based on the argument in the question above.

    The author assumes which of the following in the argument?

    (A) It is possible for most channels to switch to digital TV and maintain their public base.
    (B) The other channels, like BBC, will fail in successfully switching to digital.
    (C) A channel cannot switch successfully if the existing quality of programs isn't maintained.
    (D) BBC can regain its public base and popularity again.
    (E) Digital TV is not a beneficial proposition for most TV channels.

23. The annual fiscal report from the Washington State Highways Commission revealed that the Highway Maintenance Department (HMD), at the end of 1997, had a large surplus in its highway materials fund, yet exactly a year later, the same fund had a deficit of almost $500,000. This discrepancy was investigated by a team of accountants commissioned by the state government, but their report after an exhaustive examination of HMD finances made it clear that from the beginning of 1997 to the end of 1998, not only had expenses remained generally unchanged, but also in some months there had been significant

declines.

Which of the following, if true, will justify the apparent discrepancy mentioned in the argument?

(A) The Highway Maintenance Department received more funding in 1997 than it received in 1998.

(B) The expenses incurred by the HMD in the period 1997 to 1998 were less than had been anticipated.

(C) In some months, the HMD incurred unusually large expenses in conducting repairs due to wear and tear from weather.

(D) The auditors commissioned by the state government used statistical methods such as standard deviation and arithmetic mean in compiling their report.

(E) The HMD failed to utilize its resources to the maximum and fell short of expectations.

24. The annual fiscal report from the Washington State Highways Commission revealed that **the Highway Maintenance Department (HMD) at the end of 1997 had a large surplus in its highway materials fund, yet exactly a year later the same fund had a deficit of almost $500,000.** This discrepancy was investigated by a team of accountants commissioned by the state government, but their report after an exhaustive examination of HMD finances made it clear that from the beginning of 1997 to the end of 1998, **not only had expenses remained generally unchanged, but also in some months there had been significant declines.**

In the argument given, the two portions in boldface play which of the following roles?

(A) The first is a general fact accepted by the author as true; the second is a consequence that naturally follows from the truth of that fact.

(B) The first is evidence that supports one of two contradictory points of view; the second supports the point of view that first opposes.

(C) The first is support for a contradictory point of view; the second is the support for an opposite point of view.

(D) The first is the basis of a perplexing situation given in the argument; the second is a finding that intensifies that situation.

(E) The first concedes a consideration that weighs against the viewpoint of the author; the second is that viewpoint.

25. The Federal Inland Revenue Department has launched a new initiative to improve its image because it believes that the general public erroneously believes that the system by which taxes are calculated is inequitable. The department just needs some correctly placed publicity. Public relation experts contend that the mistrust for the Revenue Department is so indelibly entrenched in the consciousness of the general public that even the slickest PR campaign would be doomed to failure.

Which of the following, if true, supports the department's belief?

(A) Tax collectors have always been disliked everywhere in first world regions.

(B) Megalithic corporations and rich individuals get special consultations allowing them to minimize their taxes.

(C) Some allegations have been made about corruption in customs officials and inspectors.

(D) Most government departments are generally mistrusted because of lack of transparency.

(E) Most people object to the taxes that are created and find them unfair in general.

26. This question is based on the argument in the question above.

    Which of the following, if true, would cast the most serious doubt on the prediction of the PR experts' contention?

    (A) Most government departments generally are mistrusted because of lack of transparency.

    (B) Opinion for the government's policies was at an all-time low during the Vietnam War, but campaigns eventually changed people's opinions.

    (C) PR campaigns are not always successful in changing the general opinion about strongly felt issues.

    (D) The Revenue Department was not always mistrusted, but has been since the 1920s.

    (E) Some PR experts feel that the general distrust of the public towards the government can be overcome.

27. In a landmark decision, an Arkansas judge recently threw out a $10M claim for flood damage by Little Rock Municipal Council against Sun Insurance. The judge said that, as science and technology had progressed to the point where natural disasters could almost be predicted, it was the responsibility of municipal councils to seek expert scientific advice on possible dangers, and take precautions accordingly. Seismic researchers have mapped out the precise regions of the globe that, within the next two years, will probably suffer seismic activity of sufficient strength to cause structural damage, loss of life, and hospitalized casualties.

    If the above statements are taken into consideration, which of the following must be true for a three-year-long community center project being undertaken by the municipal council in one of the earthquake-prone zones?

    (A) The construction site of the community center will suffer major seismic activity in the next two years.

    (B) The project will be scrapped altogether because of the danger of major seismic activity in the next year.

    (C) The community center project will not receive any insurance against major seismic activity.

(D) The community center project can get insurance payments for seismic activity damage only if precautions for earthquakes are in place.

(E) It is uncertain which insurance company will step forward in the event of major seismic activity.

28. This question is a modified version of the argument in the previous question.

   In a landmark decision, **an Arkansas judge recently threw out a $10M claim for flood damage by Little Rock Municipal Council against Sun Insurance** saying that, as science and technology had progressed to the point where natural disasters could almost be predicted, it was the responsibility of municipal councils to seek expert scientific advice on possible dangers and take precautions accordingly. Seismic researchers have mapped out the precise regions of the globe that, within the next two years, will probably suffer seismic activity of sufficient strength to cause structural damage, loss of life, and hospitalized casualties.

   Which of the following best explains the role played by the portion in boldface in the above argument?

   (A) It states the position that the argument, on the whole, opposes.
   (B) It provides evidence against the position that the argument, on the whole, supports.
   (C) It lends support for the claim that the argument agrees with in the main conclusion.
   (D) It affirms the position that the argument, overall, does not nullify.
   (E) It presents a position that is thoroughly negated by the argument in its conclusion.

29. Imran: BCCI, a top cricketing body in India, is contemplating increasing the penalty for its contracted players who are caught betting. The punishment will still not be harsh, though, so betting cannot be curbed. Subsequently though, BCCI will increase its revenue.

   Alex: You are right. The betting will not be curbed. The players, on the other hand, will likely bet instead through their agents, who are not under the contract of BCCI.

   Alex responds to Imran's argument by doing which of the following?

   (A) Indicating that a measure taken is not potent enough to have the effects Imran predicts it should have
   (B) Calling Imran's prediction into question by indicating an alternative possible effect of a certain measure taken
   (C) Alluding that Imran's conclusion would have been better supported had Imran cited an example for what he predicts will happen
   (D) Questioning Imran's conclusion by predicting that a possible consequence could in fact bring about the possible effect multifold
   (E) Showing that the cause that Imran claims will produce a certain effect is not the only cause that could produce that effect

30. Some people think that it is fine to do things that are ethical, but not legal. The act of slaughtering a cow, though legal, is unethical.

In which one of the following does the reasoning most closely parallel that employed in the passage?

- **(A)** Some people think that it is fine to jump a traffic signal, but not to drive a car without having a license. Bigger crime must be avoided, though it may seemingly look petty.
- **(B)** Some parents think that it is fine for their children to do a little copying on an exam rather than failing. Success with help is a bigger stigma than failure.
- **(C)** Some executives think that it is better to work for a company that pays less, but offers opportunities to learn new things. A telemarketing job, though monotonous, is high-paying.
- **(D)** Some mothers think that it is fine to overfeed their kids, but not to underfeed them. Though a cup of milk more looks like overfeeding, it is better than underfeeding.
- **(E)** Some athletes do not run as fast as they can in practice matches. It is fine to promote aspiring talents in practice matches rather than in tournament matches.

31. The decrease in the number of accidents can be attributed to the adoption of the road design suggested by NHAI, since control of fast-moving vehicles improved only when that design was implemented.

The reasoning in the above argument most closely parallels that in which one of the following?

- **(A)** At most, it can be inferred that Morton Confectionaries' stock devaluation is not due to inefficient control over the market; however, it cannot be attributed to ineffective operation.
- **(B)** Ever since the data bandwidth of most tele-service companies in the country increased, 3G data plans have shown exponential growth in sales. The high revenue registered by these companies can be attributed to the high sale of 3G data plans.
- **(C)** Since the currency devaluated due to a widening of the current account deficit and not due to low forex reserves, the appreciating dollar can be attributed to the after-effect of narrowing the current account deficit.
- **(D)** Since the improvement in inter-departmental ties began to occur after the CEO's new restructuring plan was put in place, the plan can be credited with the improvement in these ties.
- **(E)** Since the post-mortem concluded that death was caused by a blockage in the carotid artery, the possibility of the rupture of a brain tumor was ruled out.

32. If you run daily for an hour, your heart rate will improve. If your heart rate improves, you are healthy. So, if you run daily for an hour, you are healthy.

Which one of the following most closely parallels the reasoning in the argument above?

(A) If you practice math daily for an hour, your logic will improve. If your logic improves, you can solve many reasoning-based questions. So, if you practice math daily for an hour, you can solve Integrated Reasoning questions.

(B) If you don't drink sufficient water, you will feel dehydrated. If you drink sufficient water, your skin will look plump. So, if you don't drink sufficient water, your skin will not look plump.

(C) If the currency is devalued, the import bill increases. If the import bill increases, inflation increases. So, if the currency is appreciated, inflation decreases.

(D) If you work for less than five hours a day, you feel discontented and lethargic. If you feel discontented and lethargic, you lose interest in life. So, if you work for less than five hours a day, you lose interest in life.

(E) If females cook food, you like the taste. If you are a foodie by nature, you must be expert in cooking. So, if you are a foodie by nature, you are a female.

33. No scholar can lack logic, but students are not scholars. Therefore, the argument that students lack logic is not justified.

The flawed reasoning in the argument above is most closely paralleled in which one of the following?

(A) Many animals are sluggish, but fish are not animals. Therefore, it is right to conclude that small fish are sluggish.

(B) Every corporation must pay taxes, however NGOs are not corporations. So, it is not rational to tax NGOs.

(C) No company can skip filing an income tax return, therefore the argument that Dexter and Sons Inc., which operates in tax-free zone, must file an income tax return is justified.

(D) When a pond is full of water, fish feed on ants, however when the pond is empty ants feed on fish. Therefore, it is wrong to say that small animals cannot conquer large animals.

(E) The justification that 'capital punishment should be abolished because God creates man, so only God can set a man free' is flawed because if the same man can kill another man, God would not have created a killer.

34. A premium black tea brand advertises its tea as healthy tea since its brand contains ginger, basil leaves, and ginseng. It is ironic that the company overlooks the fact that it contains caffeine, too. If you mix caffeine with a glass of milk, milk will not be healthy anymore.

Which one of the following most accurately describes the method of reasoning used in the argument?

- (A) Citing a claim to prove a point
- (B) Citing an example to establish a theory
- (C) Citing a claim to disapprove a theory
- (D) Leveraging on the veracity of a cited fact to challenge a claim
- (E) Leveraging on an arguable claim to challenge a claim

35. The IT company Dexter Solutions is one of the most successful consulting companies around. It primarily deals in cloud computing. Dexter Solutions wins over most business deals in cloud computing services. Alex is an IT consultant whose primary specialization is in IT infrastructure services, so Alex surely cannot be an associate at Dexter Solutions.

    The reasoning in the argument is flawed because the argument

    - (A) assumes that a person is not part of a group on the basis that the person does not have an attribute that the group possesses
    - (B) misses an explanation of why a group is not interested in the services the person specializes in
    - (C) misses the likelihood that a person can work as an IT consultant without being an associate at an IT company.
    - (D) misses the likelihood that a person may also have a secondary interest which is the same as the primary interest of the group.
    - (E) overlooks the possibility that a group may also be equally successful in other services too

36. A recent study on brand preference showed that brand M ice cream is considered the best of all brands among all age groups. It beats the next two preferred brands – brand Q and brand D – by a wide margin. Yet sales figures revealed that brand Q and brand D each sold many more cartons of ice cream than brand M.

    Which of the following would most help to resolve the apparent paradox described in the passage?

    - (A) Brand D sold more cartons than brand Q and brand M combined.
    - (B) The price of brand Q ice cream is less than that of brand D.
    - (C) The study was conducted only in select clusters where the distribution network of brand M is strong, not nationwide.
    - (D) The price of brand M ice cream is not significantly higher than that of brand D and brand Q.
    - (E) A few food stores refuse to stock brand M ice cream because the distributers demand that brand M be stocked exclusively.

37. A regular fare-dodger travels daily to a station for which the ticket costs $5 and does not buy a ticket. Upon getting caught without a ticket and fined $50, his friends asked him whether he would buy a ticket from then on. He answered, "No. I know that the chance of getting caught without a ticket is 1 in 10, so it is immaterial whether I buy a ticket."

    The man's reasoning is flawed because he is ………………

    (A) assuming the chances of getting caught without a ticket could be even less than what they are currently.
    (B) assuming the price of the ticket for the station could increase significantly.
    (C) assuming that he would be caught and fined at regular intervals and not more.
    (D) ignoring the possibility that he could even save some money if he buys a ticket for every trip.
    (E) ignoring the scenario of when the price of a ticket may increase significantly and the amount of the fine may decrease significantly.

38. Suzy: Numerology is a myth. It is a fad based on an illusion that destinies can be altered.

    How can the behavior patterns of a person change with the interplay of letters in the spelling of a name?

    Brian: By adding a couple of letters to the spelling, one feels that one's problems are then taken care of, and, due to this confidence, the person takes the world in stride and attains success.

    On which of the following points would Brian disagree with Suzy?
    (A) Numerology is a myth.
    (B) Behavior patterns of a person cannot change .
    (C) Letters of a spelling are not linked with destiny.
    (D) Self-confidence influences one's conduct.
    (E) Destinies cannot be altered.

39. Normally the per carton price of Alphonso mangoes ranges from $80 to $100; however, due to untimely rain playing havoc with mango farms in the western part of the country, which supplies over 80 percent of Alphonso mangoes, it was feared that the average price may shoot up to $120 per carton. Surprisingly, it has remained in the range of $90 to $100.

    Which of the following information, if true, would best explain the fact above?
    (A) There was no untimely rain in other parts of the country that grow Alphonso mangoes.
    (B) The normal number of Alphonso mangoes from other parts of the country was not reduced significantly.

- (C) "Langda", another popular mango that is relatively cheaper and tastes similar to Alphonso mangoes, had record-breaking production in the northern part of the country.
- (D) Per capita consumption of Alphonso mangoes in the northern part of the country reduced drastically.
- (E) Three leading beverage companies in the country invested heavily in fruit beverages other than mango-based ones.

40. Many of the articles written by editors lie far below the scope outlined. Such articles do not qualify to be published in the newspaper.

    Which one of the following can be properly inferred from the statements above?

    - (A) Some of the articles written by editors lie above the scope outlined.
    - (B) All the articles that do not qualify to be published in the newspaper lie far below the scope outlined.
    - (C) The newspaper publishes articles that lie above the scope outlined.
    - (D) If an article is not published in the newspaper, but lies within the scope outlined, it is not written by an editor.
    - (E) At least one such article does not qualify to be published in the newspaper.

41. A successful media tycoon always seeks to build up his portfolio of media outlets but has acquired a reputation for his aggressive pursuit of failing newspapers. When the tycoon embarked on a campaign to gain control of a fading but respected political magazine in a country where he already owns a satellite TV station and several national dailies, media observers accused him of trying to control public opinion, and filed a petition in court for the sale to be stopped. The lawyers of the tycoon rebut this accusation, pointing out that the tycoon has promised that he will not influence the editorial policies of the target magazine, and have requested that the acquisition be allowed by the court.

    Which of the following, if true, would most weaken the media tycoon's case?

    - (A) He has a reputation for making failing companies profitable.
    - (B) He has a reputation for firing the senior journalists of the failing newspapers he acquires.
    - (C) Generally newspaper proprietors refrain from meddling in editorial matters.
    - (D) To save costs, content from the news collection bank serving his other media outlets will be used.
    - (E) Laws governing the acquisition of newspapers are badly enforced.

42. This question is based on the argument in the question above.

    Which of the following, if true, would most strengthen the media tycoon's case?

    (A) The national dailies owned by him are not as influential as his satellite TV channel.
    (B) The senior journalists of the target magazine are very competent.
    (C) Under the acquisition contract, the existing board members will have powers equal to new board members.
    (D) The editorial board of a political magazine he owns in a neighboring country to the one he is targeting is respected and seen as impartial.
    (E) Laws governing the acquisition of newspapers are badly enforced.

43. The decline in the value of the Euro is proving to be a mixed blessing. The German economy in particular is booming with sales in everything from heavy industry to hotels and service providers. France is experiencing a similar phenomenon with a special emphasis on defense products. However, the European Central Bank (ECB) has issued its starkest warning yet that if the value of the euro doesn't increase by at least 3% over the next six months, intervention will become vital.

    Which of the following, if true, would most strengthen the conclusion?

    (A) The decline in the euro's value has led to an 8% increase in exports from the European Economic Community (EEC) as a whole.
    (B) The EEC has become a net importer of a wide range of staple products.
    (C) Certain EEC manufacturers have experienced higher exports than would normally be associated with the current value of the euro.
    (D) Many businesses are taking advantage of low interest rates and borrowing.
    (E) Some economists have predicted that the current boom will turn into a sharp recession once the euro's value rises.

44. This question is based on the argument in the question above.

    Which of the following can be properly inferred from the argument above?

    (A) All European countries other than Germany and France import more than export.
    (B) If the value of the euro does not increase by at least 3% within six months, the ECB will pare down imports to a sustainable level.
    (C) A significant number of European countries are suffering due to the decline in the value of the euro.
    (D) Imports by Germany and France are less than that of all other European countries.
    (E) Exports by Germany and France are more than that of all other European countries.

45. This latest move to shift fiscal obligation away from the federal government to local communities is being promoted as a step forward on the road to democracy. Its proponents claim that by making communities responsible for funding everything from health, welfare, education, emergency services, and housing, not only will services improve, but it would also foster a greater sense of community. Although they accept that such a move would mean densely populated areas, which have a greater tax base, would be better off, rural communities could be given top-up subsidies from federal sources.

    Which of the following, if true, would weaken the argument that rural communities could be given top-up subsidies from federal sources?

    (A) Rural services require less funding than metropolitan services.

    (B) Many services are currently provided on a statewide basis.

    (C) The federal government has traditionally funded specialized higher educational facilities.

    (D) Most rural communities are engaged in the agriculture business; the agriculture trade is not tax-free in the country.

    (E) Many private health and education facilities are currently privately run and financed.

46. This question is based on the argument in the question above.

    Which of the following can be properly inferred from the argument?

    (A) The expenses of rural communities are less than those for metropolitan communities.

    (B) Rural communities cannot generate sufficient funds on their own that are needed to meet their expenses.

    (C) Rural communities are sparsely populated areas.

    (D) Employment opportunities in metropolitan communities are more than those in rural communities.

    (E) The lesser the capability of a rural community to generate funds, the more top-up subsidies from federal sources that will be provided.

47. At its first press conference, the People's Information Party (PIP) spokeswoman promised that PIP's cross-party appeal would change the whole political horizon. Its central policy of mandatory fiscal transparency will undoubtedly be popular with the electorate as, according to a recent Morri Poll, 82% of those polled placed the abuse of expense accounts as the major complaint they have against politicians from mainstream parties. Aware of the Morri Poll results, most politicians from all parties have accepted the fact that such a step must ultimately be taken to retain the credibility of the government. However, the PIP's mandatory fiscal transparency proposal was rejected without even a reading during yesterday's session of Parliament.

Which of the following would best explain the apparent paradox expressed in the above passage?

- (A) A majority of those polled had no fixed political affiliation.
- (B) The governing party plans to introduce its own fiscal transparency bill.
- (C) PIP membership is growing faster than any party's membership in the region's history.
- (D) The attendance figure at Parliament on the day of the PIP proposal was unusually high.
- (E) A large number of politicians in Parliament abuse their expense accounts to increase their incomes.

48. This question is based on the argument in the question above.

    Which of the following can be properly inferred from the argument?

    - (A) If polls were conducted today, PIP would secure a majority of votes.
    - (B) According to voters, widespread corruption is a major issue in the country.
    - (C) Passing a financial transparency bill is the only way to retain the credibility of the government.
    - (D) At least 18% of voters are staunch supporters of the ruling party.
    - (E) A significant number of politicians in Parliament abuse their expense accounts to increase their incomes.

49. A study done by a psychologist shows that spending too much time in front of a computer causes insomnia. Two groups of adults took part in this study. During the study, the first group spent three hours or less per day working on a computer; the second group spent six hours or more working on a computer. A greater proportion of the second group had trouble falling asleep during the period of the study than members from the first group.

    Which of the following, if true, most challenges the psychologist's conclusion?

    - (A) Some adults who spent more than six hours per day working on a computer had fewer problems falling asleep than others in the same group.
    - (B) Some adults who spent three hours per day working on a computer did not have problems falling asleep.
    - (C) Some adults voluntarily stopped spending too much time in front of a computer after the study.
    - (D) Some adults spent time working on the computer without any breaks, while others took frequent breaks.
    - (E) Many of the adults in the second group had problems falling asleep before the study began.

50. This question is based on the argument in the question above.

   Which of the following, if true, most strengthens the psychologist's conclusion?

   (A) Sleepiness is often caused by the constant occupation of the mind with one activity.
   (B) Even frequent breaks of less than 2 minutes are not enough to get rid of sleepiness.
   (C) Some adults continuously sit in front of a computer for more than three hours daily.
   (D) The experiment was repeated with the first group being asked to sit in front of a computer for more than six hours daily and showed that a greater proportion of members felt sleepy.
   (E) Most of the members of the first group used desktop computers while those of the second group used laptops.

51. Because of the soaring number of fatalities incurred in accidents on major interstate highways, the Interstate Highways Commission has put forward a proposal to be considered by the state government that only vehicles less than ten years old be allowed to use major interstate highways. Under the terms of the proposal, older vehicles would be confined to using minor interstate highways. Despite vocal opposition, particularly from classic car clubs, the Commission has stated that such a reform would dramatically reduce the number of highway fatalities.

   Which of the following, if true, would undermine the conclusion derived in the argument?

   (A) The Interstate Highway Commission cannot pass laws without government approval.
   (B) Vehicles older than ten years are less reliable than newer vehicles.
   (C) Major interstate highways are overused.
   (D) Major interstate highways are favored by high performance older vehicles.
   (E) The proportion of vehicles ~~less~~ more than ten years old is significantly less.

52. **Icarus Airline Manufacturing Corporation has continuously made greater profits by supplying airlines with quality airplanes** which are equipped with increased seating capacity. In an effort to continue this financial trend, the company is set to launch a double-decker jumbo jet.

   Which of the following describes the role played by the boldface portion?

   (A) It is a general belief that the argument seeks to establish.
   (B) It is fact based on which the next strategy is laid out.
   (C) It is a conclusion that the argument seeks to establish.
   (D) It is an intermediate conclusion that is consistent with the main conclusion.
   (E) It is the main conclusion that is consistent with the intermediate conclusion.

53. The government of Akhlazia should stop permitting mafia-run opium companies to subtract shipping expenses from their revenues in calculating the amount of kickbacks that go to the central government. These opium companies must pay higher kickbacks. However, as a consequence, they would have to raise the price of opium, and this price would then discourage buyers on the world market from purchasing Akhlazian opium.

Which of the following, if true, would undermine the apprehension that Akhlazian opium companies would have to raise their price?

(A) The shipping charges are now significantly less than what they used to be.

(B) Opium companies would need government approval before they could change the price of opium.

(C) The closest competitor to the Akhlazian opium companies does not charge as much as they do.

(D) The money the government would earn as a result of increased kickbacks would be used to educate the public about the dangers of drug addiction.

(E) A research paper presented at the World Pharmaceutical Council speaks highly of the therapeutic use of opium.

54. Among those automobile mechanics who own their own garages and have completed a qualifying course at Main Street Technical School, 35 percent earn above $80,000 a year. Among those who have their own garages but did not complete the qualifying course at Main Street Technical School, only 10 percent earn above $80,000 a year. These figures indicate the importance of technical education in getting a higher salary.

While drawing the conclusion about the importance of technical qualification in getting a higher salary, the argument above fails to consider which of the following?

(A) Whether the cost of the course is affordable to the members of the other group

(B) Whether the average salary of the other group is significantly less than that of the first group

(C) Whether the value of the course undertaken by the members of the first group is significant

(D) Whether the members of the other group are more competent than those in the first group

(E) Whether the minimum salary earned by a member of each of the groups is comparable

55. Now that the babies of the post-war baby boom have reached retirement age, there is a burgeoning population of elderly people. Yet **despite a chronic lack of workers throughout the U.S., employers are still reluctant to take on elderly workers**. Age Concern, an elder citizens' rights protection organization, campaigns for greater employment of those past the age of retirement. **The elder citizens' rights protection organization cites numerous examples of successful companies that have an active**

policy of employing elder citizens, and, therefore, claims that employing older people is good for business.

Which of the following best describes the roles played by the two boldfaced portions in the argument?

- (A) The first is a fact that defies the second; the second is the conclusion.
- (B) The first is a fact consistent with the conclusion; the second is a claim that goes against the conclusion.
- (C) The first is a consideration that defies the second; the second is a consideration that forms the basis for the conclusion.
- (D) The first is the conclusion that defies the second; the second is a fact.
- (E) The first is an objection that the argument rejects; the second presents a conclusion that could be drawn if that objection were allowed to stand.

56. Finance Minister: Last year was disastrous for our manufacturing sector, which has traditionally made up about 75 percent of our national budget. It is therefore encouraging that there is evidence that the IT sector is growing stronger. Taxes from the IT sector accounted for 15 percent of our national budget, up from 8 percent last year.

On the basis of the statements above, which of the following best reveals the flaw in the above conclusion?

- (A) It fails to consider whether investment in the IT sector is growing equally.
- (B) It fails to consider the views of other ministries such as the commerce ministry.
- (C) It fails to consider that the ignorance of the manufacturing sector, a traditional sector, can boomerang on the economy in the long run.
- (D) It fails to consider that the taxes from other sectors are comparable with that from the IT sector.
- (E) It fails to consider that the current national budget could be significantly lower than last year.

57. After losing the 5-set final of the Open Tennis Tournament, the runner up, James Maddy, blamed the partisanship of the spectators for his loss. Against the advice of his trainer, he appealed to the Tennis Association for the result to be annulled and the final to be restaged. As evidence to support his case, Maddy explained he had already won the first two sets, 6-1 and 6-2, when the audience began to loudly support his opponent, Alex Hogan. Maddy claimed that the deafening noise had hampered his concentration, causing him to lose the match.

Which of the following, if true, would NOT provide justification for Maddy's case?

- (A) It was considered that Maddy had more stamina than Hogan did.
- (B) Pre-match betting in favor of Maddy was as high as 7:3.
- (C) Hogan hydrated himself more often than Maddy did during the third set.

(D) Maddy complained to his physiotherapist of hamstring pain during the interval between the second and the third sets.

(E) Both Maddy and Hogan raised the issue of loud noise to the referee during the third set.

58. The incessant monsoon rains are adding to the misery of urban dwellers. As the water level of Yamuna River constantly rises, panic in low-lying areas is growing. More water was released from Hathnikund barrage on Monday, and it will reach the Yamuna by Tuesday evening. The district administration is contemplating evacuation of over 50,000 people from low-lying areas.

Which of the following must be justified before making a decision to evacuate over 50,000 people from low-lying areas?

(A) Has Yamuna River surpassed the highest water level mark it has ever crossed in the last decade?

(B) Has the state where Hathnikund barrage is located also carried out evacuation procedures?

(C) Have boats, divers, and the Disaster Management Force been deployed to take care of any eventuality?

(D) Will Yamuna River cross the danger level mark if incessant rains and more water released from Hathnikund barrage reach Yamuna on Tuesday?

(E) Has the city government planned to set up a sufficient number of relief camps to tackle the threat and the aftermath of a flood?

59. Medicare has announced the introduction of a computer system to streamline the registration of new applicants throughout the U.S. The system will eliminate the possibility of fraudulent claims by cross-checking the names of applicants against past work records and birth certificates. Government officials claim that, once it is up and running, the new system will be able to save more than $500M every year currently paid for assorted medication that is then sold to individuals ineligible to receive Medicare assistance.

Which of the following, if true, most weakens the claim of the government officials?

(A) The provider of the computer system has an impeccable reputation of trustworthiness.

(B) The experts anticipate that the annual maintenance of the computer system would be as high as 20% of the cost of the system.

(C) The computerized registration system will not stop all fraudulent claims.

(D) Many doctors have expressed concern that Medicare staff cannot be fully trained in the handling of the new system.

(E) Critics claim that the new system will prevent some impoverished patients from receiving vital medication.

60. **Acme University receives 2,000 applications a year from high school students who wish to attend college.** The university's admission committee would like to ensure constant standards of quality in the incoming class each year. The admissions committee has decided, **therefore, to accept only the best 200 students for admission each year, selected on the basis of the quality of their personal statements.**

Which of the following best describes the roles played by the two boldfaced portions in the argument?

(A) The first is a fact that forms the basis for the conclusion; the second is the conclusion.

(B) The first is a fact that the argument discusses; the second is a claim that goes against the conclusion.

(C) The first is a fact that forms the basis for the second; the second is the conclusion.

(D) The first is the general consideration presented in the argument; the second is the strategy to help reach the desirable outcome presented in the argument's conclusion.

(E) The first is a challenge that forms the basis for the second; the second is the strategy to help reach the conclusion.

61. Recently, there was a huge flood in Hunan, China, during the rice-growing season. This will lead to the doubling of the price of rice this season, and ultimately to the cost of making rice cakes more expensive. Unfortunately, rice cake consumers in Hunan will now have to pay more for rice cakes.

Which of the following best describes the flaw in the reasoning?

(A) Treating the outcome of an event as also dependent on other events.

(B) Treating many causes as capable of affecting one event.

(C) Treating a cause as capable of affecting many events.

(D) Treating the outcome of an event as solely dependent on another event.

(E) Treating the law of supply and demand as inapplicable.

62. **Enshrined in the U.S. Constitution, a clause protecting the right of the citizen to bear arms** remains the most potent argument used by the gun lobby in their resistance to those wishing to ban possession of handguns. Their opponents cite the most recent UN statistics that prove conclusively that **globally there exists a clear correlation between the number of violent gunfire incidents and the laxity of gun control legislation.**

Which of the following best describes the roles played by the two boldfaced portions in the argument?

(A) The first is a finding whose implications are at issue in the argument; the second is a claim presented in order to argue for the deriving implications from that finding.

- (B) The first is a general consideration that supports the main conclusion; the second is a claim that goes against the conclusion.
- (C) The first is the evidence that strengthens a position; the second is the evidence that strengthens counter-position.
- (D) The first is the consideration that opposes the conclusion; the second is the conclusion.
- (E) The first is the consideration that forms the basis for the conclusion; the second is the conclusion.

63. Although Milton International School provided competent teachers and a revamped curriculum, social science and geography scores for grade 10 students failed to reach the expected level. Therefore, parents suggested to the principal that social science and geography be taught in the native language instead of in English.

    The parents' proposal presupposes which of the following?
    - (A) Unlike subjects such as math and science, social science and geography can be better comprehended by teachers in native language.
    - (B) Math and science can be better explained by teachers and comprehended by students in the English language than in the native language.
    - (C) The average scores for grade 10 students in subjects other than social science and geography must be significantly above the expected level of parents.
    - (D) There are at least a sizable number of English-medium schools in town where a few subjects are taught in the native language.
    - (E) Comprehension of the coursework of subjects such as social science and geography would be significantly higher if these were taught in the students' native language.

64. Which of the following best completes the argument?

    Statistics demonstrate that children who are beaten usually grow up believing that it is appropriate to beat their children as well. This cycle is just one instance of violence perpetuating violence. A certain religious sect claims, however, that beating children is a form of discipline, not violence, and that this discipline is necessary to develop certain good habits in children because..

    - (A) young children often, for no apparent reason, burst into fits of tears or laughter, thereby showing mixed emotions at times.
    - (B) if beaten adequately, they become tough enough to withstand the vicissitudes of the world.
    - (C) at an early age, children are capable of differentiating right from wrong and understanding why things should or should not be done.
    - (D) at an early age, children who are more intelligent are beaten for different reasons than less intelligent children are.
    - (E) child-beating is an acceptable social practice.

65. This year the UK's tax hike on tobacco and alcohol places Britain at the head of what many experts call a worrying global trend. The government has defended the rise, which now makes the UK proportionally the world's leading collector of excise tax, as being the only effective deterrent against tobacco and alcohol abuse. However, critics claim that such policies are a sham and are intrinsically flawed, as the vast sums gathered annually finance so many governmental activities and expenses that if tobacco and alcohol consumers were really deterred, the government would collapse.

Which of the following can properly be inferred based on the information given above?

- **(A)** The high taxes fund medical and other services in the country.
- **(B)** Britain charges the highest amount of tax on tobacco and alcohol throughout the world.
- **(C)** Extreme tobacco and alcohol use is common in many countries.
- **(D)** Incremental tax rises compensate for the gradual decrease in tobacco and alcohol use and the derived revenue.
- **(E)** Government considers that a qualitative measure to control tobacco and alcohol abuse is not as effective as a quantitative measure such as high taxation.

66. Country Y has appealed to the United Nations that sanctions against it have severely curtailed vital exports and should be lifted. The sanctions were originally put in place to punish Country Y for repeated use of torture in military prisons and the failure of the ruling military junta to hand power over to democratically-elected civilian leaders. As a basis for the appeal, Country Y has officially announced its intention to return to civilian rule, **blaming any continuing instances of torture upon rogue officers.**

Which of the following best describes the roles played by the two boldfaced portions in the argument?

- **(A)** The first is a claim which the argument contests; the second is a claim that goes against the conclusion.
- **(B)** The first is a claim which the argument discusses; the second is a claim that Country Y believes does not go against the conclusion.
- **(C)** The first is a claim that contains the conclusion; the second is a prediction consistent with that claim.
- **(D)** The first is a claim that contests the conclusion; the second is a prediction that goes against that claim.
- **(E)** The first contains the continuance of the implications if a certain policy is not annulled; the second is the fact whose implications form the main point of discussion.

67. To claim that computer-industry revenues are declining is overstated. It is a fact that the computer manufacturers' share of industry revenues declined from 75 percent three years ago to 60 percent today, but, for the same period, companies selling computer parts had their share increase from 15 percent to 25 percent, and service companies such as dealers, resellers, and repairers had their share increase from 10 percent to 15 percent.

Which of the following can properly be inferred based on the information given above?

(A) The amount of revenue declined for computer manufacturers equals the amount of revenue increased for computer-part sellers and service companies.

(B) The revenue for at least one of the three companies – computer manufacturers, computer-part sellers, and service companies – increased.

(C) The computer manufacturers' share of industry revenues has been declining for three years.

(D) The collective share of computer-part sellers and service companies in the industry has increased.

(E) The revenue four years ago was more than what it was three years ago.

68. The wholesale price of mustard has increased substantially in the last six months, whereas that of groundnut has decreased. Thus, although the retail price of mustard oil at grocery shops has not yet increased, it will predictably increase.

The prediction about the retail price of mustard oil at grocery shops is based on which of the following presuppositions?

(A) The retail price of groundnut oil at grocery shops increased marginally.

(B) The wholesale price of mustard oil is usually more than that of groundnut oil.

(C) Though the cost of the processing of groundnut oil has decreased in the last year, that of mustard oil has not.

(D) The cost of harvesting mustard has increased in the last two quarters.

(E) The proportion of the consumption of mustard oil with respect to groundnut oil has doubled over the last six months.

69. **When students do not find their projects challenging, they become disinterested and so accomplish less than their abilities would have otherwise allowed.** On the other hand, **when students find their projects too challenging, they give up and so again accomplish less than what they are capable of accomplishing.** It is, therefore, clear that no student's full potential will ever be realized.

Which of the following best describes the roles played by the two boldfaced portions in the argument?

(A) The first is a general consideration that goes against the conclusion; the second is a general consideration that goes with the conclusion.

(B) The first is a general consideration that goes with the conclusion; the second is a general consideration that goes against the conclusion.

(C) Both portions are being argued against in the conclusion.

(D) Both portions are mutually contradicting claims.

(E) Both portions form the basis for the conclusion.

70. The demand for large, family-sized vehicles will slump dramatically over the next ten years; major automobile companies are cutting orders for steel plating usually placed five years in advance of delivery to obtain maximum price reduction.

    Which of the following can properly be inferred based on the information given above?

    (A) Different kinds of steel plating are used for vehicles other than large and family-sized.

    (B) The major automobile companies manufacture a significantly large number of large and family-sized vehicles.

    (C) The price of steel plating ordered now will usually be more than that ordered five years in advance.

    (D) The demand for small-sized vehicles will not slump dramatically over the next ten years.

    (E) The proportion of the cost of steel plating is the highest among other components in a large and family-sized vehicle.

71. Investing in the fishing boat business could be very profitable at this time, despite seeming like a bad idea. A survey done by Hook, Line & Sinker magazine shows that 75 percent of the magazine's readers want to buy a new fishing boat during the summer. However, fishing boat manufacturers can only produce enough boats to satisfy 30 percent of total potential buyers.

    Which of the following, if true, would help explain the seemingly incompatible evidence cited above?

    (A) The fishing boat industry is a highly labor-intensive business.

    (B) Fishing boats are not evenly distributed across the country.

    (C) The number of fishermen who buy fishing boats has been growing each year for the past six years.

    (D) The number of readers of Hook, Line & Sinker magazine is far less than that of other consumers who want to buy a fishing boat.

    (E) The magazine's readers are keener to invest in fishing boats than any other customer.

72. Although we manufacture one hundred types of mobile phones, we currently limit our stock to only the ten best-selling models. However, in a bid to increase our profits, our plan is to increase the number of mobile phones we sell by expanding our stock to include the twelve most popular types.

    Which of the following, if true, points out a major weakness in the plan above?

    (A) The capabilities of the four most popular mobile phones are approximately equivalent, with no model having consistent superiority in all respects.

(B) The nine most popular types of mobile phones account for almost all mobile phones sold.

(C) As users of mobile phones have become more sophisticated, they are more willing to buy less well-known models.

(D) Less popular types of mobile phones often provide less profit to the retailer because prices must be discounted to attract customers.

(E) The leading type of mobile phone has been losing market position to less popular types that offer similar capabilities for less money.

73. In a certain socialist country, party members earn twice as much as non-party members do, but party members happen to work in businesses that generally have higher wages. Non-party members who also work in these particular businesses earn about as much as party members. Therefore, higher incomes do not necessarily result from a connection to the party.

    Which of the following, if true, most seriously weakens the argument above?

    (A) Besides wage increases, party members also receive other benefits.

    (B) Some of the most highly-paid business people in that country are capitalist executives in special economic zones, and are not party members.

    (C) Wages in many industries vary from one part of the country to another, whether or not workers are in the party.

    (D) Non-party members in a given industry often receive higher wages as a result of the lobbying done by party members, which in turn increases the wage for the entire industry.

    (E) Becoming a member of the party within a given industry or business often encourages others to follow suit.

74. The Hale Burton Oil Pipeline Construction Corporation has had a bad quarter. Rather than lay off workers to cut costs, it will simply defer salaries for 30 days and hold the money in a mutual fund to earn interest to cover expenses. By doing this, the company and its employees will avoid the negative consequences often associated with earnings shortfalls.

    Which of the following, if true, is the best criticism of the corporation's plan?

    (A) Employees will not be able to control which mutual funds their salaries will be diverted into.

    (B) The corporation cannot save money by cutting staff because it is already understaffed.

    (C) Some employees will have to borrow money until the 30 days are up and they will consequently have 30 days of interest on these loans.

    (D) Some employees will not be affected by the rollover because they have savings.

    (E) The corporation's budget was cut by 15 percent last year.

75. Countries that legalized drug X 20 years ago, because a significant percentage of the population had been using X on a daily basis without any apparent harm to the community at large, reset the benchmark for what is appropriate and proper behavior among their citizens. Since X's legalization, there has been an increase in manic depression, suicide, and certain kinds of cancer. In order for Andovia, a country that has not yet legalized X, to avoid the development of such undesirable tendencies and prevent the social problems that stem from broad usage of drug X, it should close its borders and not issue visas to any tourists from countries where drug X is legal.

    Which of the following, if true, may most seriously jeopardize the plan above?
    - **(A)** Drug X emits only a faint smell that makes it very difficult for trained canines to identify it at border control points.
    - **(B)** The detrimental side effects of drug X only become visible after several years of usage.
    - **(C)** Andovia is surrounded on three sides by water, but has an excellent naval border police force.
    - **(D)** Drug X resembles several other designer drugs currently on the market.
    - **(E)** Drug X is very easy to extract chemically from certain consumer products and is taken in droplet-sized doses that can easily be camouflaged as items such as hairspray or nail polish remover.

76. The Flerenchian government decided to limit the import of chocolate from the four countries that export the greatest amount of chocolate to Flerenchia. An analyst hired by the government maintains that in the near future this will cause a large increase in domestic sales of chocolate produced in Flerenchia.

    Which of the following, if true, would most likely render this prediction inaccurate?
    - **(A)** A new tax bill that would discourage foreign investment in the chocolate industry is being debated by the Flerenchian government.
    - **(B)** Flerenchian companies' orders for milk chocolate, which accounts for 60 percent of sales by chocolate companies, rose faster than for other types of chocolate during the past year.
    - **(C)** Worldwide orders for chocolate made in Flerenchia dropped by more than 15 percent during the past year.
    - **(D)** Substantial inventories of foreign-made chocolate were stockpiled in Flerenchia during the past year.
    - **(E)** Companies in the chocolate industries of many countries showed a significantly increased demand for chocolate during the past year.

77. This question is based on the argument above.

    Which of the following should be thought over before taking such a move to limit the import of chocolate?

(A) Whether Flerenchian companies are capable of producing sufficient chocolate to feed the domestic need

(B) Whether the Flerenchian government can impose quantitative tariffs on exported chocolate from the four countries

(C) Whether the exporting countries can build plants in Flerenchian and produce locally

(D) Whether imposing trade restrictions on the four countries would earn similar sanctions upon Flerenchia

(E) Whether natives will offset the deprivation of foreign-made chocolate with Flerenchian-made chocolate.

78. When a major fire occurs in the city of Springfield, the number of media reports about fires increases fear-factor responses that often last many months after the original incident. These media sources also include discussions about fire safety. Emergency response officials in Springfield claim that the fear frenzy whipped up by the media is responsible for the increased number of reports that appear in the city's media outlets, rather than an increase in the number of actual fires causing the reports.

Which of the following, if true, would seriously weaken the claim of the emergency response officials?

(A) The publicity surrounding fires is largely limited to the city in which the incident happened.

(B) Fires tend to occur more often during certain summer months when it is dry and hot.

(C) News organizations do not have any guidelines to help them decide how severe or close a fire must be for it to receive coverage.

(D) Fires receive coverage only when news sources find it advantageous to do so.

(E) Studies by the government show that the number of fires in Springfield is almost the same every month.

79. Save-a-Tot Corporation is a manufacturer of safety seats for bicycles and automobiles. Children often die unnecessarily in collisions because they were not properly fastened into seats that conform to their fragile bodies. Save-a-Tot has recently designed a new type of safety seat that is able to conform more closely than ever to curves in the spines and necks of small children. This new design also cushions the head in a better way. Save-a-Tot claims that the usage of these safety seats will decrease child mortality rates in serious collisions by up to 60 percent.

Which of the following, if true, represents the strongest challenge to Save-a-Tot's claim?

(A) The child safety seats that Save-a-Tot has designed are made of a lighter plastic compound that turns brittle during a collision.

(B) The government demands that Save-a-Tot produce these child safety seats to very strict specifications.

(C) By providing Save-a-Tot seats free with new cars, automobile sales will increase.

(D) The proposed child safety seats will add too much weight to bicycles.

(E) As production costs increase, Save-a-Tot will have to raise the price of its safety seats.

80. Environmental activists: The appearance of three-eyed fish in the river is the result of radioactive material produced at your plant.

    Nuclear Power Plant Management: Our study indicates that the number of three-eyed fish is abnormally high throughout the entire valley because water sources in the area are polluted.

    Which of the following, if true, most weakens the management's claim?

    (A) The study does not differentiate between different types of pollution.
    (B) Communities in the valley have not changed their fishing locations.
    (C) Toxic chemicals discharged at the plant find their way into local water sources.
    (D) The plant both uses and produces nuclear waste that has been shown to cause mutations.
    (E) There had been incidents of three-eyed fish reported on several occasions before the nuclear power plant was built.

81. Many high schools send students to special courses to prepare them for language exams. Some language teachers criticize these courses and point out that the high schools that do not send their students to special courses have reported a higher average score than those that do since 1995. The language teachers say that the courses are a waste of time and money.

    Which of the following, if true, would most effectively support the argument?

    (A) Those schools that send students to the courses have better knowledge of the exams since they are the only schools that participated in the exams prior to 1995.
    (B) Schools that have sent students to the courses since 1995 have not experienced a score drop in their scores compared with prior to 1995.
    (C) The cost of these courses run by outside teachers has risen dramatically since 1995.
    (D) The poor design of courses to prepare students for the language exams is not the only reason for their ineffectiveness.
    (E) Since 1995, the number of students who have passed the language exams has risen by 20 percent.

82. Six months after the city of Nodlin began a traffic safety experiment to decrease red-light runners at its main intersection by installing cameras to catch would-be violators, the program was discontinued. The city claims that the program led to an increase in the number of red-light runners.

    Which of the following, if true, would most effectively help explain why the traffic safety experiment reported an increase in red-light runners rather than a decrease?

    (A) The intersection chosen for the system had a higher frequency of traffic violations than other intersections in the city.

    (B) The rate of increase in traffic violations was higher in the intersection with the system than at other intersections.

    (C) The number of all traffic violations at the main intersection reported increased as a result of the ability of the system to catch traffic violators who might otherwise have gone unnoticed.

    (D) The six-month period during which the system was in place was representative of regular traffic violation statistics.

    (E) Such systems installed on highways have also been helpful in catching motorists who drive too fast.

83. Some experts in the Sepharian Federation believe that an embargo by Kalistan of a certain petroleum derivative, if implemented, would drive up the price of that derivative in Sepharia by a factor of 20. They also point out that few other countries have that particular derivative, and that, with an embargo, Sepharia might have to depend on yet unproven synthetic fuel technologies to acquire a reasonable substitute for the derivative.

    Which of the following, if true, most seriously supports the analysis above?

    (A) Kalistan's economy relies on earnings derived from the export of the petroleum derivative to other countries.

    (B) There are economic steps that Sepharia could take to negotiate with Kalistan, and perhaps avoid the embargo.

    (C) Petroleum experts believe the derivative might possibly exist in yet unexplored regions of Sepharia.

    (D) Only a small portion of Sepharia's import expenditure is devoted to acquiring the derivative.

    (E) In the case of an embargo, Sepharia could buy the same amount of the derivative indirectly on the world market at less than one-fourth an increase in price.

84. This question is based on the argument given above.

    Which of the following can be properly concluded from the passage above?

    (A) Kalistan is the most dependable supplier of the aforementioned petroleum derivative from the Sepharian Federation's perspective.

(B) Among all the countries in the region, the aforementioned petroleum derivative from Kalistan is the only petroleum derivative that is processed with scientifically proven technologies.

(C) The price of a reasonable substitute for the aforementioned petroleum derivative from other countries would be more than the regular price of that derivative from Kalistan.

(D) The price of a reasonable substitute for the aforementioned petroleum derivative from other countries must be less than 20 times the regular price for it from Kalistan.

(E) The Sepharian Federation and Kalistan do not enjoy a cordial relationship currently.

85. Though technological innovations are necessary to make things affordable at less time and cost, they also make workers feel secondary. Furthermore, due to this, workers do not feel gratified because they do not face challenges in their work, and feel dissatisfied since they realize that their skills are not key to the production. Therefore, we can conclude that technological developments ──────.

Which one of the following most logically completes the argument?

(A) are solely responsible for the efficiency in production.

(B) drive up the remuneration of white-collar workers compared to blue-collar ones.

(C) at work are more whole-heartedly welcomed by managers than workers.

(D) are responsible for making workers' key expertise less critical in their work.

(E) are responsible for laying off many workers.

86. Introverts frequently engage themselves wholly in online activities so that they can feel a sense of belonging, even if it is with machines. During the process, they more easily foster relationships with cyber-friends. However, when they get disillusioned with the virtual world, they go back into their shells. Therefore, committing oneself solely to an imaginary world is not a fruitful approach in an attempt to be social.

Which one of the following assumptions does the argument depend on?

(A) Other approaches in an attempt to be social are not as effective as engaging in online activities.

(B) Once introverts come out of their shells, they become social.

(C) One needs enduring friends to be social.

(D) Online activities impair interpersonal skills.

(E) By making cyber-friends, introverts feign being extroverts.

87. Mahatma Gandhi viewed hardships as opportunities. Throughout his life, he did not compromise on principals, so anyone who does not compromise on principals leads a life of contentment.

The conclusion of the argument follows logically if which one of the following is assumed?

(A) Anyone who sees hardships as resolve leads a life of contentment.
(B) Anyone who leads a life of contentment sees hardships as resolve.
(C) Anyone who does not lead a life of contentment compromises on principals.
(D) Anyone who does not view hardships as resolve compromises on contentment.
(E) Anyone who compromises on principals does not see hardships as resolve.

88. Jack: The reason for the debacle of the ruling party in the recent election can be explained by acknowledging the fact that only the winning opposition projected its leader as the Prime Ministerial nominee leading to connect the people of the country well.

Mary: In my opinion, it was the charisma of the opposition party leader that charmed everyone and led to his party winning by a landslide.

Mary's response to Jack proceeds by

(A) denying the truth of one of the stated premises of Jack's argument.
(B) demonstrating that Jack's conclusion is not consistent with the premises he uses to support it.
(C) implying she agreed with Jack's argument and building the rational for his argument.
(D) calling into question an assumption on which Jack's conclusion depends.
(E) drawing a conclusion which is in contrast with that of Jack's.

89. Chanakya-Today, a lesser known agency among many polling agencies, was the closest in predicting how many total constituency seats the winning opposition would take in the national election. Though its exit poll forecast of 340 came true with a deviation of just plus 5, I disagree with the deviation figure. Out of a total of 28 states in the country, each state's prediction deviated from between minus 7 to plus 10; if we calculate the total absolute deviation, we reach a figure of 42. On this parameter, the less talked about NDTV survey did a better job.

Which of the following is the most necessary assumption to conclude that the NDTV survey did a better job?

(A) The NDTV survey's exit poll forecast had a deviation of more than plus 5 or minus 5.
(B) The total deviation of constituency seats predicted by Times Now, another respected agency, must be more than that of Chanakya-Today and NDTV.

- **(C)** The absolute deviation of seats (considering 28 states) predicted by Chanakya-Today must be less than that by NDTV.
- **(D)** The NDTV survey is the most accurate in predicting constituency seats in each state in the country.
- **(E)** Chanakya-Today's and NDTV's predictions are the two most accurate for total constituency seats.

90. Equipping our classrooms with large-sized, Techo-make digital white boards satisfies our 'value for money' criterion. So, the school must plan to buy new digital white boards since the school should always make a decision that satisfies this criterion.

    The conclusion drawn above follows logically if which one of the following is assumed?

    - **(A)** The school should buy large-sized, Techo-make digital white boards.
    - **(B)** Cost-effective digital white boards are an indispensable part of the classrooms of the school.
    - **(C)** Investing in new large-sized, Techo-make digital white boards makes a better 'value for money' choice than many of the other options open to the school.
    - **(D)** New, large-sized, Techo-make digital white boards are affordable in price.
    - **(E)** The school needs new large-sized, Techo-make digital white boards.

91. The manifesto of the 'All People' party states that the core committee must select some women with lower caste backgrounds, but no women from poor economic classes have yet registered in the party. It therefore follows that the party is not currently complying with its manifesto.

    The conclusion of the argument follows logically if which one of the following is assumed?

    - **(A)** The party presently has no women belonging to poor economic classes.
    - **(B)** The party should register women with lower caste backgrounds.
    - **(C)** The only women with lower caste backgrounds are women belonging to poor economic classes.
    - **(D)** The party's manifesto cannot be altered to exclude the mandatory clause of including women with lower caste backgrounds.
    - **(E)** All women from poor economic classes have lower caste backgrounds.

92. Standard bottle sizes of shampoo are 100 ml, 250 ml, 500ml, and 1000 ml. Compared to the per milliliter price of shampoo in the 100 ml bottle, the price of the 250 ml bottle decreases by 20%, that of the 500 ml bottle decreases by 30%, and that of the 1000 ml one decreases by 40%. Thus, it follows that buying a larger bottle makes better sense.

    Which of the following must be considered before choosing a bottle size EXCEPT?

(A) Is there any time limitation regarding the quality of the shampoo?

(B) Is the per ml. price of shampoo going to come down significantly in the near future?

(C) Is the brand of shampoo being considered one you know for a fact you like?

(D) Is the brand of shampoo being considered the product of a reputable company?

(E) Do any non-standard sized bottles offer greater cost reduction?

93. Which of the following logically completes the argument?

    Analyst: Your company cheats artifact collectors by selling some artifacts as 'antique'; however, those items are relatively common, and accessible on the market at significantly lower prices.

    Company executive: That is incorrect because ....

    (A) Our company is one of the largest artifact dealers in the world.

    (B) Our company authenticates the artifacts we sell through a government-recognized firm.

    (C) Our company operates a licensed artifact dealership.

    (D) Our company buys antique-tagged artifacts from the National Archeological Department.

    (E) The National Archeological Department is the only authorization agency that can tag artifacts as 'antique'.

94. Moterra Motor Company claims that despite coming into the market after 2005, as many as 42% of the most fuel-efficient motorbikes on the market are their flagship model, the 125 cc bike, a figure almost double that of the leading player in the market.

    Which of the following, if true, most strongly supports the company's claim?

    (A) Moterra Motor Company procured advanced engine technology from a leading Japanese motor company.

    (B) 100 cc bikes, which are sold in greater proportion compared to 125 cc, 150 cc, and 200 cc bikes (the only other categories in terms of capacity), are comparatively less fuel-efficient than 125 cc bikes.

    (C) Moterra Motor Company offers three years of free service for bikes compared to other companies that offer only one year.

    (D) The price of a 125 cc bike from Moterra Motor Company is more than one from other companies.

    (E) The highest proportion of all 125 cc bikes on the road is manufactured and sold by Moterra Motor Company, and they are the most fuel-efficient of all bikes of any category.

95. Decrease in purchasing power has not been the primary reason for the current slump in the realty sector in this region. Low interest among potential property buyers is primarily caused by the fact that, in recent years, buyers have not experienced any improvements in infrastructure services in the region, and the amenities promised to them for their apartments have not been provided.

Which of the following, if true, would most support the claims above?

(A) Today more buyers are investing with a higher budget than in the past.

(B) Many buyers would not have bought their apartments under the current economic scenario.

(C) Some buyers have cited a decrease in purchasing power as a reason for the current slump in the reality sector in this region.

(D) Many prospective buyers have cited a decrease in purchasing power as a reason for not buying properties in this region.

(E) Many buyers have cited poor commuting facilities and indoor security as reasons for selling their properties.

96. When the economy is booming, people are more inclined to develop skills rather than earn a college degree, but when the economy slows down, people prefer to earn degrees. It follows that the anticipation of the economy turning to shambles dampens enthusiasm for learning new skills, and sends people to colleges for degrees.

The argument above assumes that ...

(A) people who develop skills earn more than those who earn degrees.

(B) the anticipation of an economic slowdown has amplified over the years.

(C) the likelihood of people preferring to develop new skills depends on the degree to which the economy is thriving.

(D) there are more vocational courses available when the economy is booming.

(E) people's anticipation of the economy slowing down determines how many people are inclined to earn a college degree.

97. Which of the following most logically completes the argument?

In town X, schools that follow the CBSE system of education charge significantly higher fees per student than schools that follow the state recommended system of education. Therefore, it follows that students studying under the CBSE system of education are more knowledgeable than students studying under the state recommended system of education because..........................

(A) The average salary of a teacher in a CBSE school is significantly more than that of a counterpart in a state school.

(B) The efficacy of all the teaching resources in a CBSE school is significantly more than that in a state school.

(C) Expenditure on infrastructure in a CBSE school is significantly more than that in a state school.

(D) CBSE schools are driven with a profit motive, whereas state schools are non-profit organizations.

(E) Teachers of CBSE schools are known to teach students privately, too.

98. The effort to curb betting on teams during the World Cup was not successful. If it had been successful, the decades-old legal business of lotteries would not have flourished during that time.

    The argument in the passage depends on which of the following assumptions?

    (A) Many first-timers preferred betting on teams during the World Cup than taking a chance on traditional lotteries.

    (B) Betting on traditional lotteries acted as a catalyst for people to try their luck betting on teams during the World Cup matches.

    (C) A significant number of bookies who run a traditional lottery business also accepted bets on teams during the World Cup.

    (D) The number of bookies who solely accepted bets on teams during the World Cup grew in lesser proportion than those who run traditional lottery businesses.

    (E) The amount of business done by traditional lottery bookies was more than that done by bookies who bet solely on matches.

99. Schools are given a fixed subsidy per non-paying student to induce them to build their student body so at least 25% of students belong to a lower economic class. Such students are not charged any fee. This practice is unfair to big schools located in urban areas, which are actually subsidizing these students by themselves. Clearly, therefore, small schools in rural areas are, in actuality, earning money from this subsidy outlay.

    Which of the following must be compared before reaching the conclusion?

    (A) the amount of total subsidies received by a rural school and the fee collected by that school from regular students

    (B) the average fee per regular student charged by big schools in urban areas and that by small schools in rural areas

    (C) the average amount of expense per student borne by big schools in urban areas and that by small schools in rural areas

    (D) the amount of subsidy per student received by a rural school and the fee collected by the school per regular student

    (E) the average total number of students in big schools in urban areas and that in a small schools in rural areas

100. A potential buyer: Too many bike-makers today focus too much on style, body, features, digital consoles, and television commercials showing how capable their bikes are of doing stunts, but they ignore the aspects of mileage and power – the foremost reason to own a bike. When I watch a TV commercial of a bike claiming itself to be an uber-cool bike with an ergonomically-designed body, for example, I know that at least one bike is not worth buying.

Which of the following is a presupposition of the potential buyer's argument?

(A) TV commercials unduly exaggerate the capabilities of a bike.

(B) The bike referred to in the TV commercial is unlikely to be a leader among bikes in mileage and power.

(C) The bike referred to in the TV commercial is probably expensive.

(D) A focus on mileage and power and a focus on style are mutually exclusive.

(E) A bike focusing on features other than mileage and power is unlikely to be considered for purchase.

15.1 Practice Questions' Answerkey

Critical Reasoning Guide Training Sets - Answer Keys

(1) B	(30) C	(59) D
(2) A	(31) D	(60) D
(3) A	(32) D	(61) D
(4) C	(33) B	(62) C
(5) E	(34) D	(63) E
(6) E	(35) A	(64) B
(7) C	(36) C	(65) E
(8) D	(37) C	(66) B
(9) D	(38) B	(67) D
(10) E	(39) C	(68) C
(11) D	(40) E	(69) E
(12) A	(41) D	(70) C
(13) D	(42) C	(71) D
(14) B	(43) B	(72) B
(15) A	(44) C	(73) D
(16) C	(45) D	(74) C
(17) D	(46) B	(75) E
(18) A	(47) B	(76) D
(19) B	(48) E	(77) E
(20) A	(49) E	(78) B
(21) B	(50) D	(79) A
(22) C	(51) E	(80) C
(23) A	(52) B	(81) A
(24) D	(53) A	(82) C
(25) E	(54) B	(83) D
(26) B	(55) C	(84) D
(27) D	(56) E	(85) D
(28) D	(57) D	(86) C
(29) B	(58) D	(87) B
		(88) C
		~~(89) C~~ Book Issue
		(90) E

(91) C	(95) E	(99) D
(92) D	(96) C	(100) E
(93) D	(97) B	
(94) E	(98) C	

15.2 Practice Questions' Solution

1. Doctors have two choices in the case of glaucoma patients – to prescribe a legal drug with harmful side effects or recommend cannabis, which though illegal, works better. The AMA can imprison doctors for recommending illegal drugs. The argument concludes that the doctors will get arrested eventually, implying that many doctors do recommend cannabis.

   Conclusion: Doctors cannot avoid arrest for long.

   We have to weaken the argument.

   (A) This is **incorrect** because it does not weaken the conclusion. Just because patients don't get any side effects from using cannabis does not mean the doctors won't get arrested for recommending an illegal drug. Having no side-effects does not make cannabis a legal drug.

   (B) This is the **correct** answer. If doctors respect the mandates of the AMA over their ethics, they are likely to adhere to the AMA warning and comply with its instructions, implying that they will not prescribe an illicit drug. This weakens the conclusion by showing the doctors won't be arrested because they won't get implicated.

   (C) This option is **irrelevant**. What lawyers can do does not have any necessary relation to doctors and their professional rights.

   (D) This is also **irrelevant** to the conclusion that deals with the arrests of doctors.

   (E) Some drugs might have been legal before they were made illegal, but no basis for comparison between those drugs and cannabis has been established (whether those drugs are similar to cannabis), and thus we cannot conclude on the basis of this option whether cannabis will be legalized. Also, "some" is a vague word, because it can mean 1-99%. This option is **incorrect.**

   The correct answer is option B.

2. We have to find information that helps us to evaluate the argument.

   (A) This is the **correct** answer. This information will help us strengthen and weaken the conclusion. If we answer "yes" to this option, that the law allows extenuating circumstances and makes exceptions, then the conclusion will be weakened. If we answer "no" to the option, that the law does not allow it and enforces the law in every case, then the conclusion will be strengthened.

   (B) This option is **irrelevant**. The conclusion is concerned with the doctors recommending cannabis for glaucoma. Even if there are other illegal drugs being used to treat fatal diseases, we cannot assume that every case of glaucoma is necessarily fatal, thus justifying the use of illegal cannabis.

   (C) This option is **incorrect** because this wouldn't impact the conclusion either. The patients may have issues with using cannabis; the doctors will get arrested for recommending illegal drugs, and even if the patients don't have an issue with using cannabis, the doctors will still get arrested for recommending illegal drugs.

   (D) This is **incorrect** because this would not impact the conclusion, which deals with illegal recommendations already being made. The research might help doctors in the future, but won't prevent their prison sentences now.

(E) This is **incorrect** because patients getting arrested will not halt the arrest of doctors for recommending forbidden drugs.

The correct answer is option A.

3. There have been job losses (redundancies) in the state, and this unemployment has driven the state government to ask for the federal government's help by funding some programs to generate employment. Garage enterprises have been found to be a viable option according to a report; after which, banks and funding houses have proposed funding such enterprises to generate employment. However, some criticized the funding program (the federal light industry program) by stating that these programs always harm other social groups in the U.S..

We have to weaken the conclusion and establish that the funding will not harm other social groups.

(A) This is a **weakener**. This is the **correct** answer. It shows that the funding programs will reduce our imports. Garage enterprises are making 12% of parts we used to import. Thus, funding garage imports will not only generate employment in the U.S., but also will not affect other social groups in the U.S.

(B) This is a **strengthener**. This is **incorrect** because it shows that the funding will be generated from another program, which now will end up being canceled. Thus, the people who might have gotten employed in refurbishment work will now remain unemployed. So, the funding will hurt another social group in the U.S.

(C) This option is **irrelevant**. A decade-long employment is neither necessarily good nor bad. Hence, we cannot say that a decade is insufficient or too much.

(D) This is **incorrect** because the union publishing reports won't necessarily hurt other social groups unless we assume that they are doing it with vested interests only.

(E) This option is **irrelevant**. Where the funding is derived from is irrelevant until we know that sourcing in that manner will hurt other social groups.

The correct answer is option A.

4. We have to strengthen the critics' case and prove that the funding will either not generate adequate employment, or it will hurt other social groups.

(A) This option is **inconclusive**. Investing heavily in R&D of the automation of the car-servicing unit of light industry programs does not prove that it will necessarily harm the prospects of other social groups in the U.S. Eating establishments are irrelevant to garage enterprises and funding for garage enterprises. We don't know whether eateries generate as much employment as garage enterprises. This option is **irrelevant**.

(B) This is the **correct** answer. If this is true, the funding will generate employment among immigrants and it won't help U.S. social groups, thus verifying the critics' claims. This proves that the money will be spent on non-US citizens, thus depriving

U.S. citizens of a chance of betterment from the funds generated – and therefore hurting U.S. social groups.

- (C) This is **incorrect** because a union publishing reports won't necessarily hurt other social groups unless we assume that they are doing it with vested interests only.
- (D) This option is **irrelevant** till we know the reason the environmental groups are against garage enterprises. We cannot necessarily assume that they are right and garage enterprises are bad.

The correct answer is option C.

5. The above argument is simple to understand. A restaurant owner puts out more seats and tables on the outside terrace, leading to increased business. However, he surprisingly finds that his most comfortable seats are less profitable than his other seats. The argument ends with saying that this can be explained by the fact that.............................

So, we need to find an option that will explain why his most comfortable seats are not as profitable as the other ones.

This is a 'complete the argument' question; however, we can look at the question as being of the 'resolve the paradox' type to form an approach.

- (A) This is **incorrect** because it is talking about one hidden table and **sofa** being the most profitable. It goes against the facts slightly. The facts state that the sofas, the most comfortable place, are less profitable than his other seats.
- (B) This option is **irrelevant**. It does not explain why the most comfortable seats are less profitable than his other seats.
- (C) This is **incorrect** because the argument does not discuss which products are more profitable. We need to explain why the most comfortable seats are less profitable than his other seats.
- (D) This might be the answer if no other option works because students might linger in the café and not buy as much (due to limited money). However, this is not immediately correct because we have to assume that students linger and that they don't purchase as much as other patrons of the café.
- (E) This is the **correct** answer. This explains why the most comfortable seats are less profitable than his other seats. The seats are so comfortable that a patron lingers longer on these seats than he would on the other seats. So the number of people in a day on sofas is lower than the number on other seats. That's why the most comfortable seats are less profitable than his other seats.

The correct answer is option E.

6. The paradox in the above argument is that though the greatest increase in the number of people employed will be in the low-paying catering sector, the percentage share of the low-paying catering sector will not increase, while the high-paying sector will increase its percentage share.

We have to resolve this paradox. Let's assume that, initially, there were 100 people in the catering sector, of which 80 were low-paid and 20 high-paid. Thus, their respective share in the catering sector is 80% and 20%. The argument says the greatest increase in number is in the low-paying sector. Let's say 100 new people are entering the catering sector, of which 60 join the low-paying one. So, only 40 maximum can join the high-paying sector.

Thus now the number of low-paid and high-paid workers is 140 and 60, respectively. Thus the percent of low-paid and high-paid staff now becomes 70% and 30% respectively. So, the conclusion remains true that the high-paying sector increased its percentage share. The low-paying one did not increase its share (it reduced or remained the same) and the greatest increase in number is still in the low-paying sector.

So, clearly, the paradox is resolved only when the overall number of people in the catering sector increases.

- **(A)** This will worsen the paradox. This option is **incorrect.**
- **(B)** This will also worsen the paradox. This does not resolve the issue. In our analysis, we deduced that for the paradox to be resolved, initially low-paid workers must be higher in number than high-paid workers, and the increase in the workforce of low-paid workers is more than that of high-paid workers. So, the number of workers in the low-paying sector will always be more than the number in the high-paying sector.
- **(C)** This option is **out of scope.** Other sectors are not discussed.
- **(D)** As explained in option B, this will also worsen the paradox.
- **(E)** This is the **correct** answer. It matches our deduction.

The correct answer is option E.

7. **Conclusion:** The economic downturn has run its course; the analysts are wrong in being skeptical.

   Statement 1 (The economic downturn ... remain skeptical): This is the main conclusion of the author – his main point.

   Statement 2 + BF 1 (The paper's recently ... **low-paying catering sector**): The author uses this report as proof that the downturn has run its course.

   Statement 3 + BF 2 (However, ... **low-paying catering** ... but the ... wrong). In this statement the author presents a fact that could be the reason the critics are being skeptical, but he counters it later and proves critics wrong.

   So, BF1 is the author's evidence/fact. BF2 is a fact that the author concedes might be construed wrongly, but something he believes does not weaken his conclusion.

   - **(A)** BF1 is not a fact used against the author. BF2 can be taken as supporting the main conclusion.
   - **(B)** BF1 is accepted and furnished as proof by the author, but BF2 is not a consequence of critics' claims. It's probable proof of critics' claims that the author believes does not weaken his conclusion.

(C) BF1 is consideration/fact offered by the author in support of his position. BF2 is probable proof of critics' claims that the author believes does not weaken his conclusion. This is the **correct** answer.

(D) BF1 is not used by the critics, but by the author. BF2 is not used by the author to explain his position, but rather acknowledged by the author as not weakening his conclusion.

(E) BF1 is not a fact used against the author. BF2 is not a position; it's a fact that the author believes does not weaken his conclusion.

The correct answer is option C.

8. The above argument states that the Dalyan sea turtles will soon be extinct because the bright lights of hotels and discos, which obscure the moonlight, are disorienting female turtles. The turtles' eggs are laid in flower beds, and the hatchlings die because they cannot reach the sea. Stringent building regulations are flouted by developers.

   We have to find a possible inference from the argument.

   (A) This option is **incorrect.** We cannot infer this. The argument says that the turtles are a big attraction, but does not say that the turtles are the **only** attraction.

   (B) This option is **incorrect.** While we can conclude that the regulations are not being enforced stringently now, we cannot say that they were being enforced before. It is possible that the regulations were being flouted from the time development started, now leading to the possible extinction of the turtles.

   (C) This option is **incorrect.** One way for hatchlings to die is by not reaching the sea, but this does not mean that once they reach the sea, the hatchlings won't die.

   (D) This is the **correct** answer. This is directly present in the argument - the lights obscure the moonlight and disorient female turtles, which end up laying eggs in the wrong place. If moonlight weren't their only guide, they still could have laid eggs in the right place.

   (E) This is **irrelevant** because although we can draw the inference that the corporate sector ignored building restriction norms, we cannot infer that the sector is known to ignore such norms.

   The correct answer is option D.

9. In the above argument, a Gallop Poll finds that the PM of the country is less popular than the opposition leader and a leader of a small party. A telephone poll also confirms the above findings with some margin of error. However, the argument concludes that the voters vote according to the policies of the party and not just popularity of the leader.

   We have to find the role of the boldface portions in the argument.

   Statement 1: BF1 (A month after ......above the PM): This statement includes the facts about how the PM is less popular than other politicians.

Statement 2: (Subsequently, a .... percentage range): This is another set of facts that confirm the above facts mentioned in BF1.

Statement 3: BF2 (Clearly, however, the .... than its leader.): This is a claim that the author makes, in which he says that despite the above facts, the PM must have been elected because the voters choose the party and not just the leader.

So, BF2 is the author's claim that is slightly against what the facts implied in the argument.

- **(A)** This is **incorrect** because BF1 is not a claim, but a fact. BF2 is not based on BF1.
- **(B)** This is **incorrect** because BF1 is not a claim, but a fact. BF2 is not supported by BF1.
- **(C)** This is **incorrect.** While BF1 can be used as evidence, it is not evidence for a conclusion by the argument. The argument clearly defies the facts (using the word "however"). BF2 can be the main conclusion of the argument.
- **(D)** This is the **correct** answer. BF1 is support for a claim that suggests a particular inference - the leader of the small party is the most popular, and might win. BF2 is the author's claim -party scores over its leader - to keep us from deriving such an inference from BF1.
- **(E)** This is **incorrect** because while BF1 can be called a finding, BF2 is not evidence; it is a claim.

The correct answer is option D.

10. We have to weaken the conclusion that voters choose the party and not just the leader.

    Conclusion: Voters vote according to the policies of the party and not just the popularity of the leader.

    - **(A)** This is **incorrect** because it strengthens the conclusion that voters choose the party and not just the leader.
    - **(B)** This is **inconclusive.** A representative sample may or may not adequately represent the whole set. Due to lack of concrete data, we cannot conclude anything based on this.
    - **(C)** This option is **inconclusive.** It may be possible that the president belonged to the party voters liked the most, and it was a mere coincidence that he belonged to that party.
    - **(D)** This is **incorrect** because it still does not prove that that voters won't choose the party.
    - **(E)** This is the **correct** answer. It shows that voters choose the politician for his track record, and do not place more importance on the policies of the party.

Critical Reasoning GuideTraining Set Solutions – Critical Reasoning   351

The correct answer is option E.

11. The above argument is easy to understand. People buy cars some and maintain them well. The car seems like new. However, as per the dealers, in just three years, the value depreciates more than 50%, regardless of the make or model of the car.

    The question is to weaken the dealer's claim that car value necessarily goes down by at least 50%.

    (A) This option is **irrelevant**. It does not necessarily say that the bigger market of used cars fetches more than 50% of the original car price.

    (B) This option is **irrelevant**. The argument discusses the value of the car three years after purchase. It does not state whether the owner should sell it, but makes the point that if the owner sold the car, he would get less than 50% of the original car price.

    (C) This is **inconclusive**. First, it is limited in scope to foreign cars only. Secondly, it could be that the many car parts that are sold at disproportionately high prices could be the least expensive parts among all the parts. If true, other relatively expensive parts could be sold at disproportionately low prices, making the valuation of the car less than 50%.

    (D) This is the **correct** answer because the devaluation of cars more than 50% in three years came from the dealer's side, so if their creditworthiness is in doubt, the conclusion is weakened.

    (E) This is **irrelevant**. That most car companies come out with at least 4 new models of cars does not mean that the variants of existing cars would depreciate by more than 50%. Even if it is true, this option would have been a **strengthener**.

The correct answer is option D.

12. The purpose of this question is to strengthen the conclusion that car value goes down by at least 50%.

    (A) This is the **correct** answer. If the value depreciates by 30% on the day the car is bought, and thereafter it depreciates by at least 10% per annum, we can conclude that the car will depreciate by at least 50%. It is a **strengthener.**

    (B) This option is **irrelevant**. The argument discusses the value of the car three years after purchase. It does not discuss the scenario of when an owner passes on the car.

    (C) This option, too, is **irrelevant**. The argument discusses the value of the car three years after purchase. Sentimental value associated with cars is irrelevant to the argument.

    (D) This is inconclusive because reckless driving and intermittent servicing cannot necessarily be taken to mean that those cars would depreciate by 50%.

    (E) This is **incorrect** because even though rental companies may buy foreign models of cars, it does not say that they buy them at more than 50% of the original car price.

The correct answer is option A.

13. In the above argument, the senator says that frequent flyer (FF) programs are comparable to deliberate bribes to major corporate corporations for their accounts. He further criticizes the programs by saying that fares are kept artificially high because companies are willing to pay extra in order to give employees untaxed bonuses. However, a VP of one of the airlines responds by stating that FF programs are not exclusively meant for corporations, but are available to the general public through supermarket and credit card transactions.

    The question asks us to weaken the VP's response and prove the senator correct.

    This question is tricky. We must read the question stem carefully. Unlike a typical weaken question which asks us to weaken the conclusion – that the price of tickets for the general public is NOT kept artificially high – this question asks us to weaken the VP's response and prove the senator correct.

    (A) This is **incorrect** because the number of supermarket chains and credit card companies is not relevant, but their size is important to the issue of FF points and how many average people they serve.

    (B) This is **inconclusive** because the actual number of people belonging to the general public is unknown. It says that more acquire points through one way than another, without revealing any actual statistics.

    (C) This option is **irrelevant**. We need to know how many of the FF programs are for the general public.

    (D) This is the **correct** answer because if two-thirds of the tickets are sold to companies, there is little incentive for the airlines to care whether tickets are over-priced for the general public.

    (E) This option is **irrelevant** with respect to this question. This could have been the correct answer had the question stem asked to weaken the conclusion, because if the ticket prices are regularly reviewed by a government committee, it validates the fact that the price is not kept artificially high.

The correct answer is option D.

14. The question asks us to find information that will help us to evaluate the VP's response to the senator.

    (A) This option is **irrelevant**. Whether the chains are the best does not change whether they provide FF programs to the general public, and in what number.

    (B) This is the **correct** answer. If we find out the answer to this question, the VP's response will be strengthened or weakened. If the answer to this question is 'through supermarket purchases', the VP is right in his claims. If, however, the answer to this question is 'through airline tickets', the VP is wrong in his claims. It would mean that for the general public to benefit from FF programs, they have to purchases costly airline tickets, proving the senator right.

(C) This is **incorrect** because where travelers go is irrelevant to whether the public is being overcharged on airline tickets for corporate benefits.

(D) This may sound correct but it is **incorrect** because what the public feels does not necessarily reflect the actual situation, and does not reflect the facts of the situation.

(E) This is **incorrect** because the argument already states that the companies don't have to pay taxes on the airline benefits they give to their employees.

The correct answer is option B.

15. A new engine designed for race cars will be 25% lower in fuel consumption because the weight is 50% that of similar engines. This technology is borrowed from NASA. Critics say the engine is impractical and dangerous. The argument ends by saying that critics are right in being upset because ....

We need to complete the argument with an option that will explain why the critics are right in saying that the lighter, lower fuel-consuming engine is impractical and dangerous.

(A) This is the **correct** answer. If lightweight parts cannot sustain wind pressure at high speeds, a race car part should not have light parts because race cars will necessarily need safety at high speeds. This option will explain why the critics are right in saying that the lighter, lower fuel-consuming engine is impractical and dangerous.

(B) This is **incorrect** because it does not show anything impractical or dangerous about the new engine at all.

(C) This is also **incorrect** because it, too, does not show anything dangerous. Saying that a thing was meant originally for something else does not mean it cannot be used in the current scenario.

(D) This option is **incorrect**. Just because NASA has made some errors earlier does not mean everything it makes is impractical and dangerous. Also, the engine is not directly made by NASA. It is based on NASA's technology.

(E) This is **incorrect** because it does not show anything impractical or dangerous about the new engine at all.

The correct answer is option A.

16. Companies pay a levy that is determined by 3 factors - amount of fuel sold, price of the fuel, and degree of state investment. The first two are directly proportional to the levy, i.e. if they go up, the levy goes up. The third variable is inversely proportional, i.e. if state investment goes up, the levy goes down and vice versa.

To ensure fairness, levies are determined on the basis of computer simulations based on scenarios, and use deviations in the average price of fuel, rather than actual figures.

The question asks us to find the flaw in the method used in calculating levies. The answer to this lies in the last line of the argument, which states that levies are calculated from simulations which use deviations in one factor – the average price of fuel (the least volatile among all three factors) and are not based on actual figures.

- **(A)** The flaw isn't that simulations cannot be adequate representations, but that the simulations are not based on actual figures, but on mere deviations on only one factor – the average price of fuel (the least volatile of the three factors). Even if you assume that the simulations cited in the argument are not adequate representatives of the actual scenario, this cannot be chosen as the most flawed option compared to option C.
- **(B)** Market price is mentioned as one of the factors used for levies, and thus using market price to calculate levies cannot be a flaw in the method.
- **(C)** This is the **correct** answer. The argument mentions that the levies are changeable. So, they should be calculated based on the three factors. However, they are calculated using only one factor. Also, that factor's actual figures are not used, but deviations are. Because the factor used is the least volatile, the deviation is minimum. Therefore, the levy is not as changeable as it would otherwise be.
- **(D)** Control through changeable levies is not the flaw in using simulations to calculate levies.
- **(E)** Difficulty in generating simulations is not mentioned. Also, since the levy is based on three factors, all three factors should be taken into consideration.

The correct answer is option C.

17. The argument states that after a visit to a municipal school, children contracted a severe skin rash for which chemicals in the pool were deemed responsible. The authorities accepted that a chemical irritant had been present in the pool water and that this had caused most of the children to suffer a skin complaint similar to a known reaction to the irritant. The evidence that convinced them of this was the fact that most of the children were cured after being treated for this condition.

The question is to find information that would help us evaluate the conclusion that the authorities accepted the fact that the chemical irritant was responsible.

- **(A)** This option is **irrelevant**. As long as the children contracted the ailment after using the pool, the severity and intensity of the rash does not impact the conclusion.
- **(B)** This option is **irrelevant**. There is need to supply water that is potable; the quality of water must be as per standards for pools.
- **(C)** This option is **irrelevant**. As long as the children did respond to the treatment, the degree of response to the treatment does not impact the conclusion.

(D) **This is the correct answer.** The argument states that the authorities initially questioned the fact that the pool had contaminants. However, later they conceded because the children responded to treatment for that ailment. However, if the treatment prescribed works well in other non-chemically-induced ailments too, one cannot conclude that the rash was necessarily caused by the contaminant present in the pool. It may be the result of something else that is contagious. This will weaken the decision to accept culpability. However, if the treatment prescribed is used only for treatment of those types of rashes, there's no doubt that the children contracted it from the pool, and hence the decision to accept culpability is strengthened.

(E) This option is **irrelevant.** As long as the children did respond to the treatment, the number of days for treatment does not impact the conclusion.

The correct answer is option D.

18. The question is to strengthen the conclusion that the authorities accepted that the chemical irritant was responsible too quickly. They should not have done so.

(A) This is the **correct** answer. If there's a possibility of something ingested having caused the rash, the chemicals in the pool cannot be solely to blame. This strengthens the conclusion that the authorities should not have accepted culpability so quickly.

(B) This is **inconclusive.** This shows that the authorities would have to pay damages if found guilty. We cannot conclude from that point that the authorities were right in accepting culpability.

(C) This option is **irrelevant.** As long as the children did contract the ailment after using the pool, the severity and intensity of the rash does not impact the conclusion.

(D) This is a **weakener.** This shows that the doctor might be correct and that the authorities would be faulted, and thus they were right in accepting culpability.

(E) This is **incorrect** because this is too general and cannot be used to specifically weaken the given doctor's analysis.

The correct answer is option A.

19. Full recovery after a cardiac arrest is possible if prompt medical attention is given. In sparsely populated rural areas, accomplishing this is difficult because of the great distances involved. To manage this issue, a new procedure has been put into place. Whenever anyone calls to report a patient suffering from cardiac arrest, a list of questions is asked to ascertain the severity of the arrest. This might help in better managing the limited resources available. The argument concludes that the patients will suffer due to this time-consuming process.

The question asks us to draw an inference from the given argument.

(A) This is **out of scope** of the argument. The argument states that full recovery after a cardiac arrest is possible if prompt medical attention is given, but not what happens if attention is not given. Secondly, treating a cardiac arrest **properly** is not discussed in the argument.

(B) This is the **correct** answer. This can be inferred from the last line of the argument, which states that **very few** will benefit from it (the new procedure). The author implies that the extra procedure will lead to some patients not getting prompt attention.

(C) This is **incorrect** because we cannot infer that **medical facilities** in sparsely populated rural areas in general are inadequate. We can only infer about the availability of prompt medical attention for cardiac arrests in such areas.

(D) This is **out of scope** because the argument only talks about rural areas.

(E) This is **out of scope** because we cannot necessarily infer this. Maybe some get prompt attention and some don't, but the chances of a full recovery are not discussed in the argument.

The correct answer is option B.

20. The question asks us to find the assumption in the given argument.

    (A) This is the **correct** answer. The author concludes that the new procedure will result in patients suffering because he assumes that the actual distance itself would not have hurt the chances of full recovery for the patient. He is assuming that the patients would suffer more only because extra time is being wasted on the diagnostic questions, and that, otherwise, full recovery is possible, despite the distance.

    (B) This is **incorrect** because the author does not mention that the patients would suffer because the ones who report cardiac arrest are incompetent.

    (C) This is **incorrect** because if the author assumed that there were other ways to treat cardiac arrest, he would not imply that the extra procedure will cost some patients dearly. This weakens the conclusion.

    (D) This is **incorrect** because the author does not imply at all that the questions will not help to determine the severity. He implies that more time will be wasted by the questions themselves.

    (E) This option is **incorrect**. It is too extreme to be the author's assumption. He says more will suffer and very few will benefit. So, some **will** benefit.

The correct answer is option A.

21. The above argument states that digital TV has created a dilemma. There are advantages, but there are problems too. BBC, when it tried to go digital, decreased subscriptions to its analog channels. It also fired some program makers, impacting quality. This upset the public, leading to a reduced viewer base. BBC is facing financial disaster. Because of this, many other channels have resisted trying to switch to digital.

The question is on drawing an inference. It asks us to draw a conclusion on the basis of the argument – something that should be true from the TV channels' perspective.

(A) This option is **incorrect** because this is too extreme. BBC failed because, in trying to switch to digital TV, it lowered quality. If other channels do not lower quality, digital TV might spread. Hence, we cannot conclude this.

(B) This is the **correct** answer. The argument states that after BBC's fiasco, most channels resisted digital TV. So, in their opinion, they have concluded that whatever BBC faced, they would face, too. Thus, they concluded that BBC adequately represents TV channels in general.

(C) This option is **incorrect** because we cannot necessarily infer this. BBC's quality may or may not improve again.

(D) This is **incorrect** because we cannot necessarily assume that the TV channels feel that BBC's reputation was not considered by the public. Maybe some viewers remained true to BBC because of its reputation.

(E) This is **inconclusive** because there is no reason to believe that the TV channels would like to equate the number of disadvantages with the advantages,

The correct answer is option B.

22. The question asks us to find the author's assumption in the above argument.

(A) This cannot be the author's assumption. He has said that when BBC tried to switch, it ended up losing its viewer base. Hence, the author cannot assume that it is possible to switch without losing this base.

(B) This is close, but not the author's assumption. The author mentions at the end that other channels resisted switching, but whether he agrees with that is unknown to us.

(C) This is the **correct** answer. The author says that BBC's recovery seems unlikely and financial disaster looms, all because BBC lowered quality by firing program makers. Thus, he assumed that BBC could have transitioned better if it had maintained its quality.

(D) This is **incorrect** because the author says that recovery seems unlikely for BBC.

(E) This is **incorrect** because this is too extreme.

The correct answer is option C.

23. The above argument states that HMD in 1997 ended with a surplus, but in 1998 ended with a deficit. This despite the fact that expenses remained unchanged, and, in some cases, declined.

The paradox is that despite declining expenses, somehow the HMD ended up with a deficit, though a year earlier, with slightly higher or similar expenses, it had ended up with a surplus.

The question asks us to resolve the paradox.

(A) This is the **correct** answer. If this is true, this would explain the paradox. Let's assume that the HMD got $2,000,000. At the end of 1997, it had a surplus – say 500,000 after spending 1,500,000. The next year, HMD again spent 1,500,000. However, if it had received funding of only 1,000,000, it would face a deficit of 500,000 that year.

(B) This is **incorrect** because even if expenses were less than expected, the fact remains that they were the same as last year's expenses.

(C) This is **incorrect** because this goes against the premise, which says that expenses remained generally unchanged, and in some months there had been significant **declines** rather than unusual increases.

(D) This is **irrelevant** to the given facts because it changes nothing.

(E) This is **incorrect** because even if resources were not utilized to the maximum, the fact remains that they were the same as ones in the previous year.

The correct answer is option A.

24. The above argument states that HMD in 1997 ended with a surplus, but in 1998 ended with a deficit. This despite the fact that expenses remained unchanged in most months, and declined in others.

The paradox is that despite declining expenses, somehow the HMD ended up with a deficit, though a year earlier, with slightly higher or similar expenses, it had ended up with a surplus.

Statement 1: BF1(The HMD... of almost $500,000): This is data from a report and thus is a fact that is showing a different trend. The trend is that HMD, in 1997, had a surplus, but a year later had a huge deficit.

Statement 2: BF2(Not only...significant declines): This is another statement. This outlines the situation that the differences in account balances were explored by accountants, who found that expenses had remained the same, and perhaps declined a little.

Hence, both BFs are facts that together present a paradoxical situation.

(A) While BF1 might be a fact accepted by the author, BF2 is not a natural consequence of BF1 because BF2 presents a totally confounding situation.

(B) BF1 and BF2 are facts, but they don't support any points of view in the argument. No point of view has been mentioned.

(C) BF1 and BF2 are facts, but they don't support any points of view in the argument. No point of view has been mentioned.

(D) This is the correct answer. BF1 is a fact that presents a paradoxical situation, and BF2 further worsens the confusion/paradox.

(E) While BF1 may be a consideration, it does not weigh against the author, and BF2 is not a viewpoint.

The correct answer is option D.

25. The above argument is simple to understand. The Revenue Department wishes to improve its image. It believes that the public has its image wrong because people think that the tax system is unfair. However, PR experts are of the opinion that improving the image is a losing battle.

    The question asks us to strengthen the department's belief that the public wrongly believes that the tax system is unfair.

    (A) This is **irrelevant** because it does not address the issue that the tax calculation system is unfair. The argument is not concerned about tax collectors.

    (B) This is **irrelevant** because providing consultations to megalithic corporations and rich individuals that in turn help them to minimize their taxes is not a special privilege to them.

    (C) This is **irrelevant** because it does not address the issue that the tax calculation system is unfair. The argument is not concerned about corruption in the department.

    (D) This is a tricky option, but **inconclusive**, because first, we cannot count the Revenue Department in most government departments, and second, an inequitable tax calculation system cannot be treated as having a lack of transparency.

    (E) If this is true, this would **strengthen** the department's belief that the public has the wrong image of the Revenue Department because the public thinks that the tax system is unfair.

The correct answer is option E.

26. The question asks us to weaken the PR experts' opinion that the image of the Revenue Department cannot be changed. So, we need to provide some option that shows that the image can be changed.

    (A) This is **irrelevant** because an inequitable tax calculation system cannot be treated as having a lack of transparency.

    (B) This is the **correct** answer. If this is true, there is one situation where the image of the government was very low but campaigns eventually changed it. So, even now, the Revenue Department's image can be changed.

    (C) This is **incorrect** because this will **strengthen** the PR experts' opinion.

    (D) This is **incorrect** because it is irrelevant to the argument. Knowing from when the department has been mistrusted does not show whether it can be trusted again.

    (E) This is **incorrect** because some experts' feeling that the image can be changed is not concrete. Also, "some" is ambiguous; it can mean 1-99%.

The correct answer is option B.

27. The above argument states that a judge refused to award a flood damage claim to a municipal council because it is the responsibility of the council to consult scientists and ensure that proper anti-earthquake precautions are taken. Also, seismic researchers have now mapped out zones in which, within the next two years, there's a likelihood of an earthquake happening.

    We are asked, from this argument, to make an inference about a situation in which a three-year community centre project is being undertaken in one of the earthquake-prone zones. We can infer that the judge would want proper earthquake precautions to be taken.

    (A) This is **incorrect** because we cannot necessarily say that an earthquake will happen. The argument says that an earthquake is **likely** to happen.

    (B) This is **incorrect** because it's too extreme. A project need not be scrapped only because there's a likelihood of an earthquake happening. Also, the argument provides no support for this conclusion. The judge did not imply that the council should have not done anything in flood-prone area. The project shouldn't be scrapped, but proper precautions against an earthquake must be taken.

    (C) This is **incorrect** because we cannot definitely say no insurance can be received by the project. The insurance will probably be given commensurate to the safety precautions being taken against an earthquake.

    (D) This is the **correct** answer. We can infer that, based on the Arkansas judge's ruling, the insurance claims will be accepted only if the municipal council was prepared for the earthquake and had taken proper precautions against it.

    (E) This option is **irrelevant**. Which insurance company does what is out of scope.

    The correct answer is option D.

28. We are asked to identify the role of the boldface portion in the argument.

    Statement 1: BF1(In a landmark... Sun Insurance : This statement is a situation that happened in Arkansas, in which a judge denied an insurance claim because he felt it was the responsibility of the council to ensure that proper precautions are taken.

    Statement 2:(Seismic researchers ... casualties): This statement shows a situation that could develop into one like the Arkansas situation. It states that today's science can show us the possible places where calamities can occur.

    Thus BF1 is a situation for which the argument eventually provides supporting facts.

    (A) This is **incorrect** because BF1 is not being opposed by the argument.

    (B) This is **incorrect** because BF1 does not provide any evidence against the argument.

(C) This is **incorrect** because while BF1 can lend support to the argument, there is no main conclusion in the argument.

(D) This is the **correct** answer. BF1 is a position that the argument does not nullify, i.e., the argument agrees with BF1.

(E) This is **incorrect** because BF1 is not being negated in the argument.

The correct answer is option D.

29. This question is on Method of Reasoning. Let us understand the arguments made by Imran and Alex.

    Imran: BCCI may increase the penalty amount if players are caught betting, but the penalty won't be harsh enough to discourage players from doing so. **Imran's conclusion:** Betting will not be curbed, but **prediction:** BCCI will increase its revenue through the increase in penalty amount.

    Alex: Alex agrees with Imran that betting will not be curbed. He predicts that the players may instead bet through their agents, implying no increase in revenue to BCCI as predicted by Imran.

    Though Alex agrees with Imran's conclusion that betting will not be curbed, he disagrees with Imran's prediction: BCCI will increase its revenue. Alex cites a scenario through which Imran's prediction is weakened.

    (A) This option is **incorrect**. 'Measure taken' is meant for 'increase the penalty', and 'effect' is meant for 'curb betting' The meaning of the option is that Alex indicated that 'increasing the penalty' is not significant enough to 'curb betting'. This is incorrect, as Alex's contention is that with even just a modest increase in penalty, the players will instead bet indirectly, thus the penalty amount is irrelevant.

    (B) This is the **correct** answer. As per Imran, the 'measure taken' (increasing the penalty) will result in an increase in revenue for BCCI, but Alex disagrees with that prediction. He suggests an alternative path through which the players can still bet through agents and therefore not get caught, resulting in no increase in revenue to BCCI.

    (C) This option is **incorrect**. Alex agrees with the conclusion: betting will not be curbed. He disagrees with Imran over his prediction: BCCI will increase its revenue. There is no reference of any suggestion on how Imran's conclusion can be supported through an example.

    (D) This option is **incorrect**. Alex does not suggest that the possible effect (BCCI will increase revenue) can be increased multifold.

    (E) This option is **incorrect**. Let us first understand the meaning of the option statement. The 'cause' implies 'increase in penalty', and 'certain effect' implies 'BCCI will increase its revenue'. The option implies: Alex shows that BCCI's revenue will not increase only due to the increase in penalty. This is incorrect because there is no question of suggesting an alternative cause to create the same effect.

30. The argument presents a conflict between ethically correct and legally correct. It suggests that some people prefer to do ethical things, though they may by illegal. The argument then presents an example to strengthen the position. Though slaughtering cow is legal, it is unethical.

The correct option must mirror the conflict and have a supportive example.

- **(A)** This is **incorrect**. Jumping a traffic signal and driving a car without having a license are not conflicting scenarios. Though the example cited is analogous to the situation in the option, the situation itself is not parallel to that in the argument.
- **(B)** This is **incorrect**. This is a case of a conflicting situation: Success with help vs. Failure. However the example: "Success with help is a bigger stigma than failure" is opposite of the premise.
- **(C)** This is the **correct** answer. This is a case of a conflicting situation: High pay with a monotonous job vs. a job with less pay and learning opportunities. The example cited is apt; a telemarketing job, though monotonous, is high-paying.
- **(D)** This is **incorrect**. This is a case of a conflicting situation: Overfeed vs. Underfeed. However, the example ('Though a cup of milk more looks like overfeeding, it is better than underfeeding')is opposite of the premise.
- **(E)** This is **incorrect**. Two conflicting situations are not very evident. Also, the example to support the position is missing in the option.

The correct answer is option C.

31. Let us understand the argument. The argument is simple to follow. Because of <cause A>, the <effect B> occurs, and <effect C> was attributed to <cause A>. So there are two effects and only one cause.

Where A, B, and C are: Cause A: Adoption of the road design Effect B: Decrease in the number of accidents Effect C: Control of fast-moving vehicles

- **(A)** This is **incorrect**. Though the devaluation of stock is an effect, its cause is not stated. It simply states that inefficient operations and inefficient control over the market are not the causes.
- **(B)** This is **incorrect**. Cause A: increase in date bandwidth; Effect B: high sales of 3G data plans; Effect C: high revenue; Cause: sale of 3G data plans (effect B). It is not parallel. The cause is changed.
- **(C)** This is **incorrect**. There are two causes (widening of current account deficit and low forex reserves) discussed for one effect – the currency being devalued. The argument is not parallel.
- **(D)** This is the **correct** answer. Cause A: CEO's new restructuring plan; Effect B: improvement in inter-departmental ties; Effect C: improved ties; Cause A: CEO's plan. It is parallel.

(E) This is **incorrect**. There are two causes discussed (blockage in carotid artery and possibility of a ruptured brain tumor). The argument is not parallel.

The correct answer is option D.

32. Let us understand the argument. The argument is simple to follow.

    The structure is If A then B. If B then C. So if A, then C.

    A: You run daily for an hour B: Your heart rate will improve C: You are healthy

    (A) This is **incorrect**. The structure is If A then B. If B then C. So if A then D. 'Reasoning-based questions' is replaced with 'Integrated Reasoning questions'. They are not identical.

    (B) This is **incorrect**. The structure is If (Not A) then B. If A then C. So if (Not A) then (Not D).

    (C) This is **incorrect**. The structure is If A then B. If B then C. So if D then E.

    (D) This is the **correct** answer. The structure is If A then B. If B then C. If A then C.

    (E) This is **incorrect**. The structure is If A then B. If C then D. So if C then A.

    The correct answer is option D.

33. Let us understand the argument. There are two premises: "No scholars can lack logic", and "but students are not scholars". Based on these, there follows a flawed conclusion: "students lack logic."

    However the logical conclusion should have been: "That students lack logic is not justified." We must look for an option that has two premises, and a flawed conclusion based on them.

    (A) This is **incorrect**. If many animals are sluggish, and fish are not animals, then it logically follows that fish are NOT sluggish. However, to make it parallel to the flawed conclusion drawn in the argument, the conclusion of the option should have been: Therefore, it is wrong to conclude that small fish are sluggish.

    (B) This is the **correct** answer. Since every corporation must pay taxes, and NGOs are not corporations, then it logically follows that NGOs should not pay tax. So the flawed conclusion should be: Therefore, it is not rational to tax NGOs, which is the same as given in the option. So the option argument is parallel to the flawed argument.

    (C) This is **incorrect**. There is only one premise and a conclusion. The argument must have two premises and a conclusion. So the option argument is not parallel to the flawed argument.

    (D) This is **incorrect**. Only one premise and a conclusion are not parallel. Moreover, the conclusion brings in new elements – small animals and large ones.

    (E) This is **incorrect**. There is only one premise and two conclusions. This option argument is not parallel.

The correct answer is option B.

34. Let us understand the argument. The argument is simple to follow. The claim made by the company that its brand of tea is healthy is challenged by an cited yet unchallengeable example: Milk mixed with caffeine will not remain healthy anymore.

    (A) This is **incorrect**. Though the counterpoint made through the example (mixing caffeine with milk) can be called a claim to prove a point, the unchallengeable example is more specific than a claim. If other options do not fit well, this is the answer.

    (B) This is **incorrect**. The example (mixing caffeine with milk) is not used to establish a theory. It is used to counter an arguable claim made by the company.

    (C) This is **incorrect**. Like option C, the example (mixing caffeine with milk) is not used to disprove a theory. It is used to counter an arguable claim made by the company.

    (D) This is the **correct** answer. The example (mixing caffeine with milk) is an unchallengeable fact. The counterpoint made leverages on its truthfulness to counter an arguable claim made by the company.

    (E) This is **incorrect**. The example (mixing caffeine with milk) is an unchallengeable claim, not an arguable claim.

The correct answer is option D.

35. Let us understand the argument. The argument is simple to follow. An IT company primarily deals in the cloud computing business. There is an individual IT consultant who primary specializes in IT infrastructure services. The conclusion made is that the individual IT consultant cannot be an associate at the IT company.

    (A) This is the **correct** answer. The argument assumes without any justification that Alex cannot be part of the company, as his primary specialization is not in cloud computing; however, Alex could be a part of the company, as the company may do business in other sectors, too, such as infrastructure services.

    (B) This is **incorrect**. There is no need to explain why the company is interested or not interested in infrastructure services.

    (C) This is **incorrect**.

    (D) This is **incorrect**. There is no need to assume that Alex should have a secondary interest such as cloud computing.

    (E) This is **incorrect**. It is irrelevant. It has no relation to the flaw in the reasoning.

The correct answer is option A.

36. Let us understand the argument. The argument is simple to follow. Brand M is the most preferred brand, yet its competing brands - brand Q and brand D - sell more than brand M.

    (A) This is **incorrect**. We already know that Brand D sells more than brand M. This does not help resolve the paradox.

Critical Reasoning GuideTraining Set Solutions – Critical Reasoning 365

- **(B)** This is **incorrect**. It compares the prices of brand Q and brand D with no reference to brand M. This does not help resolve the paradox.

- **(C)** This is the **correct** answer. Since the study was conducted only in select clusters where the distribution network of brand M is strong, it is likely that people there may prefer band M to other brands; however, the sales figures are nation-wide, so it is possible that brand D and brand Q are preferred more in other parts of the country. This resolves the paradox.

- **(D)** This is **incorrect**. This option is tricky. Though the price of brand M ice cream is higher than that of brand D and brand Q, it is not higher to the extent that it is explainable why brand M sells far less than brand D and brand Q.

- **(E)** This is **incorrect**. This option is tricky. Had the option been '*most* food stores refuse to stock brand M ice cream because the distributer demands that brand M be stocked exclusively', it would explain why brand M sells less than brand D and brand Q; however, the number of such stores is few, so the information might not make a significant impact.

The correct answer is option C.

37. Let us understand the argument. A man does not buy a ticket costing $5. He reasons that the chances of getting fined is 1 in 10, so if he buys a ticket on each of the next 10 journeys he will spend $50. On the other hand, if he does not buy a ticket, he will have to shell out the same amount, $50, on the 10th occasion when he is caught, so whether he buys a ticket doesn't matter.

- **(A)** This is **incorrect**. If the chances of getting caught without a ticket could be even less than what they are currently, say 1 in 20, then it would be more incentive for the man not to buy a ticket, as the chances of getting caught would be less.

- **(B)** This is **incorrect**. If the price of the ticket for that station could increase significantly, say to $7, then for 10 journeys he will spend $70, whereas the fine is $50. It is more of an incentive for the man not to buy a ticket.

- **(C)** This is the **correct** answer. The man bases his decision to not buy a ticket on the assumption that he would only be caught on every 10th occasion, i.e., regular intervals, whereas the fact is that he could be caught 2 or 3 times in the next 10 journeys, shelling out $100 to $150 in fines, which is more than the total expense of buying tickets for 10 journeys.

- **(D)** This is **incorrect**. Speaking mathematically, he cannot save money as $5 x 10 = $50 = the fine.

- **(E)** This is **incorrect**. Like option B, if the price of a ticket increases significantly and the amount of the fine decreases significantly, it is more of an incentive for the man not to buy a ticket.

The correct answer is option C.

38. Let us understand the viewpoints of Suzy and Brian.

   Suzy: Her stand on numerology is clear – it's a myth. Her opinion is that the destiny cannot be altered. She strengthens her point by saying that the conduct of a person

© 1999-2016 Manhattan Review   www.manhattanreview.com

cannot change with the interplay of letters in a spelling.

Brian: We must understand Brian's stand on numerology. Though he thinks that with the interplay of letters in a spelling, the conduct of a person changes and the person succeeds in life, he attributes the influence to self-confidence gained because the person presumes that his problems are taken care of. Brian does not seem to suggest that numerology is NOT a myth.

- **(A)** This is **incorrect**. As discussed above, we cannot conclusively infer Brian's opinion on whether numerology is a myth.
- **(B)** This is the **correct** answer. As per Suzy, behavior patterns of a person cannot change, while Brian says the opposite.
- **(C)** This is **incorrect**. We cannot infer anything on 'destiny', as Brian did not voice his opinion on it.
- **(D)** This is **incorrect**. Suzy may disagree with Brian on this, but we have to choose an option showing Brian disagreeing with Suzy.
- **(E)** This is **incorrect**. This is a tricky option. We cannot infer anything on 'destiny' as Brian did not voice his opinion on it.

The correct answer is option B.

39. Let us understand the argument. The argument is simple to understand. The per-carton price of Alphonso mangoes ranges from $80 to $100. Much of the Alphonso mango crop has been affected due to rain in the western part of the country, where 80% of these mangoes come from. Despite this trouble, the price of Alphonso mangoes has remained fairly typical, though some had worried it might go as high as $120 per carton.

The paradox is why the price remained almost normal.

- **(A)** This is **incorrect**. At the most, it suggests that up to a maximum of 20% of Alphonso mangoes is unaffected. However, this would not have a major impact on the price across the country.
- **(B)** This is **incorrect**. This will actually worsen the discrepancy. It simply means that there has been almost no change in the number of these mangoes coming from elsewhere, thereby making it impossible for us to infer that more Alphonsos might have been available for domestic consumption, which then could have led to normalcy in the price.
- **(C)** This is the **correct** answer. Since the "Langda" mango, popular, similar-tasting and even cheaper than Alphonsos, had record-breaking production, it is explainable that people might have chosen this mango in lieu of Alphonso, and so the price of Alphonsos did not shoot up unreasonably.
- **(D)** This is **incorrect**. It is focused on the northern part of the country. Had the option stated this fact for the whole country, it would have been the correct answer.
- **(E)** This is **incorrect**. By reading information that the three leading beverage companies invested heavily in fruit beverages not requiring a mango base, it may seem

like they have reduced consumption of Alphonso mangoes; however, we cannot assume this.

The correct answer is option C.

40. Let us understand the argument. The argument is simple to understand. Many articles written by editors are far below a certain scope. These articles do not qualify to be published in the newspaper.

    (A) This is **incorrect**. All that we know is that articles falling **below** the scope are not qualified to be published in the newspaper. We cannot infer that some of the articles written by editors must be **above** the scope outlined; even all the articles may be **marginally below** or **within** the scope, yet are qualified to be published.
    (B) This is **incorrect**. We cannot infer that all the articles that do not qualify to be published in the newspaper lie far below the scope outlined. There may be articles that lie within the scope, yet are not published due to some other reasons.
    (C) This is **incorrect**. With the same reasoning as used in option A, we cannot infer that the newspaper publishes only those articles that lie **above** the scope outlined; even all the articles may be **marginally below** or **within** the scope, yet qualify to be published.
    (D) This is **incorrect**. There is no solid basis to assume this.
    (E) This is the **correct** answer. Since the quantity word "many" ranges from 1%-99%, we can properly infer that there is at least one such article not qualified to be published in the newspaper.

The correct answer is option E.

41. We have to weaken the conclusion.

    Conclusion: The acquisition of the magazine must be allowed. The tycoon will not influence the editorial policies of the magazine.

    (A) This option is **incorrect**. It is not relevant to the conclusion.
    (B) This option is **incorrect**. Though it is against the position of the tycoon, it cannot be pitted against the conclusion to be weakened. Firing the senior journalists of the failing newspapers does not mean that he will influence the editorial policies of the target magazine.
    (C) This option is a **strengthener**. Since newspaper proprietors refrain from meddling in editorial matters, the claim that the tycoon will not influence the editorial board is strengthened.
    (D) This is the **correct** answer. The content will be taken from a news bank serving all his media interests, not only suggesting that he will be interfering with editorial content, but also that he will be in a position to manipulate public opinion by using all his media outlets to disseminate anything he fancies.
    (E) This option is **irrelevant**. Challenges in acquisition due to law are irrelevant to the conclusion.

The correct answer is option D.

42. We have to strengthen the conclusion.

    Conclusion: The acquisition of the magazine must be allowed. The tycoon will not influence the editorial policies of the magazine.

    (A) This option is **incorrect.** The national dailies owned by him not being very influential does not mean that the target magazine will also not be; however, it does not relate to the conclusion.

    (B) This option is **incorrect.** The option may erroneously try to make you infer that since the senior journalists of the target magazine are very competent, they will not allow the media tycoon to have his way easily; however, there is no strong basis to assume this.

    (C) This is the **correct** answer. Since under the acquisition contract, the existing board members will have powers equal to the new board members, it can be assured that the media tycoon cannot force his way and influence the editorial policies at his will. This option is a **strengthener.**

    (D) This is **out of scope.** Drawing any parallel to the editorial board of a political magazine he owns in a neighbouring country is out of scope unless the option states that the neighbouring country is very similar to the country of the target magazine with respect to political affairs and the media business.

    (E) This option is **irrelevant.** Challenges in acquisition due to law are irrelevant.

    The correct answer is option C.

43. Let us consider the appreciation and depreciation of a currency and its impact on exports and imports. If imports exceed exports, there is a trade deficit for that country, since in the case of exports, the country receives dollars, and the in case of imports, it loses its own currency.

    In the current scenario, the value of the euro is declining. This is good news for exporters in European countries, since they will now get more euros for a dollar earned through export. The opposite is true for the importer, as for the same amount of the item imported, the European importer will have to shell out more euros.

    Since the bank raised concern over the decline in the value of the euro, rising imports would be part of the concern.

    The conclusion that needs to be strengthened is that, despite the booming economy of Germany and France, the euro is so undervalued that intervention by the ECB may be required to arrest the euro's further decline.

    (A) This option is **incorrect.** The option focuses on the positive aspect of the decline of the euro. We have to seek an option that focuses on its negative aspect.

(B) This is the **correct** answer. Since the EEC has become a net importer of a wide range of staple products, it is understood that to reduce the trade deficit (Import – Export), the value of the euro vis-a-vis the dollar should not be high. This option is a **strengthener**.

(C) This option is **incorrect**. Like option A, this option, too, focuses on the positive aspect of the decline of the euro. We have to seek an option that focuses on its negative aspect.

(D) This option is **incorrect**. Like options A and C, this option, too, focuses on the positive aspect of the decline of the euro. We need an option that focuses on its negative aspect.

(E) This option is **out of scope**. It talks about a future scenario which has no bearing on the status quo.

The correct answer is option B.

44. This is a question on inference.

(A) This option is **incorrect**. We cannot infer this. Based on the fact that France and Germany benefit due to the decline of the euro – implying more exports than imports – does not mean that all European countries other than these import more than export.

(B) This option is **incorrect**. We cannot infer in what way the ECB might intervene after six months.

(C) This is the **correct** answer. Significant means sizable, which may range from few to many. The issue of the ECB's **starkest warning** if the value of the euro doesn't increase by at least 3% over the next six months implies that a significant number of European countries are suffering due to a decline in the value of the euro.

(D) This option is **incorrect**. We cannot infer that the imports of Germany and France are less than that of all other European countries. Just because Germany and France benefit due to the decline in the euro, implying more exports than imports, does not mean that their imports must be less than that of ALL other European countries.

(E) This option is **incorrect**. With the same reasoning as used in option D, we cannot infer this, either.

The correct answer is option C.

45. As per the move of local communities being made responsible for generating and funding everything they need from health, welfare, education, emergency services, and housing, services will improve. Although such a move would mean that densely populated areas (implying areas having a greater tax base) would be better off in generating funds for themselves, rural communities (implying areas having a lower tax base and thus not being as able to generate funds) could be given top-up subsidies from federal sources.

Conclusion: Rural communities could be given top-up subsidies from federal sources.

This is a question on weakening the conclusion.

(A) This option is **incorrect**. It suggests that although the rural tax base is smaller, expenses are less. The option does not focus on the capability of generating funds.

(B) This option is **irrelevant**. The aspect of state is irrelevant.

(C) This option is **incorrect**. The option implies that that local funding doesn't have to cover all expenses. Like option A, this option, too, does not focus on the capability of generating funds.

(D) This is the **correct** answer. This option shows that rural communities are capable of generating taxes on their own, which will make them independent and without need of federal help.

(E) This option is **incorrect**. Like option C, this option, too, implies that local funding doesn't have to cover all expenses.

The correct answer is option D.

46. This is a question on inference.

(A) This option is **incorrect**. We cannot infer that the expenses for rural communities are less than those for metropolitan communities. We can, at most, infer that rural communities would have a lower tax base compared to metropolitan communities, thus implying lower potential for **fund generation**; hence, they could be given top-up subsidies from federal sources; however, the same cannot be inferred for expenses.

(B) This is the **correct** answer. As discussed in option A, this is the reason the author argues that rural communities could be given top-up subsidies from federal sources.

(C) This option is **incorrect**. It comes from the fact that metropolitan communities are densely populated areas, but that does not mean that rural communities are sparsely populated areas.

(D) This option is **incorrect**. This is a tricky option. Though the argument states that metropolitan communities have a greater tax base, implying more earning, we cannot necessarily infer that employment opportunities in metropolitan communities are more than those in rural communities. It could be true, but doesn't have to be true. Employment opportunities is not a very definite term; we cannot translate it as earning opportunities. Moreover, compared to option B, this option is certainly not a choice. Also, the cities don't need federal help because the number of taxpayers is higher and, therefore, the tax generated is higher. It could be that employment opportunities are just as numerous in rural areas, but the number of people is lower and thus the tax generated is lower. This cannot be an inference because we will have to assume that the lower tax generated in rural areas is because fewer people work there because of fewer job opportunities. However, why less tax is generated in rural areas is not given in the argument. Thus, this cannot be inferred.

(E) This option is **incorrect**. This option talks about the degree of top-up subsidies from federal sources to be provided. We cannot infer anything like this.

Critical Reasoning Guide Training Set Solutions – Critical Reasoning   371

The correct answer is option B.

47. PIP wishes to introduce a central policy of mandatory fiscal transparency and is upbeat that it will undoubtedly be popular with the electorate as, according to a recent Morri Poll, 82% of the electorate placed the abuse of expense accounts as the major complaint they have against politicians from mainstream parties.

   Most politicians from all parties are aware of the Morri Poll results, and have accepted the fact that fiscal transparency must ultimately be executed to retain the credibility of the government.

   However, surprisingly the PIP's mandatory fiscal transparency proposal was rejected without even a reading during yesterday's session of Parliament.

   The paradox: Despite acceptance from most politicians of all parties that fiscal transparency must be undertaken, the proposal for the same was rejected.

   (A) This option is **irrelevant**. It does not answer the question why, despite acceptance from most politicians of all parties that fiscal transparency must be undertaken, the proposal for the same was rejected.

   (B) This is the **correct** answer. As the governing party intended to introduce its own fiscal transparency law, it would be logical for it to reject such a proposal from an opposition party.

   (C) This option is **incorrect**. An increase in the membership of PIP means that more and more voters are joining PIP, but this does not explain why PIP's proposal was rejected without even reading.

   (D) This option is **irrelevant**.

   (E) This option is **incorrect**. We already know this information. This does not help resolve the paradox.

   The correct answer is option B.

48. This is a question on inference.

   (A) This option is **incorrect**. There is no basis to infer this. According to a Morri Poll, 82% of those polled placed the abuse of expense accounts as the major complaint against politicians from mainstream parties. In no way could it mean that the majority of voters will vote for PIP.

   (B) This option is **incorrect**. According to a Morri Poll, 82% of those polled placed the **abuse of expense accounts** as the major complaint against politicians from mainstream parties. We cannot generalize that, according to voters, **widespread corruption is the major issue** in the country.

   (C) This option is **incorrect**. This is an extreme option. A financial transparency bill was proposed by the PIP to bring about financial transparency; however, the government may have certain other measures to halt the abuse of expense accounts and retain credibility.

© 1999–2016 Manhattan Review   www.manhattanreview.com

- (D) This option is **incorrect**. There is no basis to infer this. According to a Morri Poll, 82% of those polled placed the abuse of expense accounts as the major complaint against politicians from mainstream parties. This does not mean that the remaining 18% of the electorate are staunch supporters of the ruling party.
- (E) This is the **correct** answer. Since all parties are concerned about the abuse of expense accounts as the major complaint against politicians, and this is supported by Morri poll data (82%), it must be inferred that a significant number of politicians in Parliament abuse their expense accounts to increase their incomes.

The correct answer is option E.

49. A psychologist claims that too much time in front of a computer causes insomnia. Two groups of adults participated in this study. Group 1 adults spent 3 hours or less a day working on a computer, and Group 2 adults spent 6 hours or more doing so. More Group 2 adults had trouble falling asleep during the period of the study than Group 1 adults.

    This is a question on weakening the argument.

    Conclusion: Spending too much time in front of a computer causes insomnia.

    What is the basic assumption made by the study? That both groups are starting out at the same point. If the psychologist wants to determine whether a certain situation creates a certain pattern in people, he needs to test two groups of people with the same pre-existing conditions.

    - (A) This option is **irrelevant**. This option differentiates the characteristics of the members of group 2 within themselves; there is no reference to group 1. The given information is of no value.
    - (B) This option is **irrelevant**. With the same reasoning as used in option A, it is irrelevant.
    - (C) This option is **incorrect**. This option does not differentiate between the two groups. The given information is of no value.
    - (D) This option is **incorrect**. Like option C, this option does not differentiate between the two groups. The given information is of no value.
    - (E) This is the **correct** answer. It suggests that there may be another cause for the different rates of insomnia between the two groups. This consequently undermines the psychologist's conclusion.

    The correct answer is option E.

50. This is a question on strengthening the argument.

    Conclusion: Spending too much time in front of a computer causes insomnia.

    - (A) This option is **incorrect**. This fact is applicable for both groups. The given information is of no value.

(B) This option is **incorrect**. Like option A, this fact is also applicable for both groups. The given information is of no value.

(C) This option is **incorrect**. The given information is of no value.

(D) This is the **correct** answer. Since the same set of people were asked to repeat the experiment and it showed the same results, the conclusion is certainly strengthened.

(E) This option is **incorrect**. We cannot infer anything based on different gadgets used by the two groups. At the most, we can conclude that the conditions for the experiments with the groups were not identical, so, on the contrary, this option will weaken the conclusion rather than strengthen it.

The correct answer is option D.

51. This question is a modified version of a question from the 'Find the Assumption' chapter. This is a question on weakening the argument.

    Conclusion: The Interstate Highways Commission (IHC) claims that such a reform (only vehicles less than ten years old be allowed to use major interstate highways) would dramatically reduce the number of highway fatalities.

    We have to weaken the conclusion.

    (A) This option is **irrelevant**. It focuses on how the law can be passed rather than on the reduction of accidents, and it does not weaken the conclusion.

    (B) If vehicles older than ten years are less reliable than newer vehicles, the conclusion that moving accident-prone vehicles away from major highways will reduce the accidents will become believable. This option is a **strengthener**.

    (C) As in option B, option C strengthens because if major interstate highways are overused, moving older vehicles away from major highways will reduce highway congestion, and, in turn, the rate of accidents will be less. This option is a **strengthener**.

    (D) This option is **inconclusive**. The definition of high-performance vehicles is not clear. We cannot necessarily assume that they are better than newer vehicles.

    (E) This is the **correct** answer. Since the proportion of older vehicles is significantly less, moving them away from major highways will not significantly reduce the highway congestion, and, in turn, the rate of accidents will not be reduced dramatically. This option is a **weakener**.

    The correct answer is option E.

52. This question is modified version of a question from the 'Find the Assumption' chapter. This is a question on role play.

    Icarus Airline Manufacturing Corporation (IAMC) has been making greater profits with single-decker planes. It wishes to introduce double-decker jumbo jets so that it can serve more passengers and receive more profits.

Let us figure out the conclusion of the argument and what role the boldface portion plays in the argument.

Conclusion: Double-decker jumbo jets will continue to make greater profits like single-decker jets have been doing.

Boldface: The boldface portion plays the role of a fact. It says that IAMC has been making profits for years with its quality planes. On the basis of this fact, IAMC plans to introduce double-decker jumbo jets to earn more profits. (A strategy/plan)

- **(A)** The boldface portion is not a general belief, it is a fact. A general belief is attributed to society or a group of people. Also, the argument does not seek to establish the fact mentioned in the boldface part. It assumes the fact to be true and uses that to devise a strategy for future profits.
- **(B)** This is the **correct** answer. It is aligned with our discussion above.
- **(C)** The boldface portion is not conclusion, it is a fact.
- **(D)** There is only one conclusion, and, as stated, the boldface part plays the role of a fact.
- **(E)** Same as option D. It is the wrong description.

The correct answer is option B.

53. This question is a modified version of a question from the 'Find the Assumption' chapter.

This is a question on weakening the argument.

Let us examine the conclusion of the argument.

Conclusion: The Akhlazian opium companies would have to raise the price of opium and the higher price would then discourage buyers on the world market from purchasing Akhlazian opium. As per the question stem, we have to weaken the conclusion that the companies would have to raise the price of opium, making them less competitive on the world market.

- **(A)** If the shipping charges are now significantly less than what they used to be, then it is likely that the companies need not increase the price and will not be less competitive on the world market. This is a **weakener**. It can be the answer. We will hold this option till we go through all the others.
- **(B)** This option is **out of scope**. This is a statement that pertains to seeking approval to do something; however, it does not impact our objective - why the price should not be raised. This option does not provide a satisfactory reason for not raising prices.
- **(C)** This option is **out of scope**. The statement means that the price charged by the closest competitor to Akhlazian opium companies is nearly the same. However, it does not impact our objective - why the price should not be raised.

(D) This option is **out of scope**. It focuses on the usage of money. It is not our objective.

(E) This option is **inconclusive**. It focuses on the usage of opium. Appreciating the benefits of opium does not mean that the market for opium will increase with an immediate effect and, in turn, benefit Akhlazian opium companies.

The correct answer is option A.

54. This question is a modified version of a question from the 'Find the Assumption' chapter. This is a question on finding the flaw in the argument.

    There are two groups of automobile mechanics who own their own garages. One group completed a qualifying course, and the other did not.

    Of group one, 35 percent of the mechanics earn above $80,000 a year, and of group two, only 10 percent of the mechanics earn above $80,000 a year.

    Conclusion: Getting technical education helps in getting a higher salary.

    (A) This is option is **out of scope**. Cost is out of scope. The argument is concerned with the relationship of technical education with higher salary.

    (B) This is the **correct** answer. What if the remaining 90% of group two mechanics who earn less than $80000 earn significantly more than the remaining 65% of group one mechanics who earn less than $80000? [Each of the remaining 90% of group 2 can make as much as $79000, while most of the remaining 65% of group 1 could possibly make less than say, $10000, making the whole comparison shaky.] This will make the average salary earned by group two more than that earned by group one, and the conclusion will be shattered, with the flaw revealed. So, we cannot conclude that technical education helps to get a higher salary.

    (C) The argument concludes that there is a correlation between the qualifying course and a higher salary. It values the course and, therefore, strengthens the conclusion.

    (D) This option is **out of scope**. Competence is out of scope. The argument is concerned with the relationship of technical education with higher salary.

    (E) Comparable minimum salary of both groups does not address the purpose of determining whether the technical education leads to a higher salary.

    The correct answer is option B.

55. This question is a modified version of a question from the 'Find the Assumption' chapter. This is a question on role play.

    Let us dissect the argument and understand the role of the boldfaced portions.

    Main conclusion: Employing older people is good for business. **Statement 1:** (Now that...people) - It is a fact stating there is a growing population of elderly people. **BF1:** **(despite...workers)**— It is a claim/fact. The argument seeks to refute the fact. It is on the opposite side of the conclusion. **Statement 3:** (Age Concern ...retirement) - It is background information. **BF2: (The elder citizens......citizens)**—It is a counter-example or a fact that goes against BF1, and forms the basis for the main conclusion.

- **(A)** While the first part is correct, the second part is incorrect. The second BF is not a conclusion; it is a counter-example or a fact that goes against BF1, and forms the basis for the conclusion.

- **(B)** The description of both the portions is wrong. The correct description is "The first is a fact inconsistent with the conclusion, and the second is a claim that goes with the conclusion."

- **(C)** This is the **correct** answer. It is aligned with our analysis.

- **(D)** This option is incorrect. BF1 is not a conclusion, but BF2 is correct.

- **(E)** BF1 can be seen as an objection that the argument rejects. BF2 is not the conclusion; it is a claim/fact.

The correct answer is option C.

56. This question is a modified version of a question from the 'Strengthen the Argument' chapter. This is a question on finding the flaw.

    Basically, we need to find a flaw in the conclusion - the IT sector is growing stronger - by proving that the IT sector will NOT continue to grow at the current pace. We can raise doubt whether the demand for the nation's IT services is increasing, whether the IT sector growth is based on a solid foundation and will remain unaffected, or whether the national budget itself has been reduced to a great extent.

    - **(A)** This option is a tricky one. Although the argument does not answer whether the investment in the IT sector is growing equally, it is not necessary to know in the first place whether investment is increasing. The answer to this question in the affirmative still does not make the conclusion - the IT sector is growing stronger - flaw-proof. Investment might not increase but the IT sector could grow regardless, say from from self-generated investment.

    - **(B)** The views of other ministries are **out of scope.**

    - **(C)** The prospects of the manufacturing sector are **out of scope.**

    - **(D)** The comparison of taxes from other sectors with those from the IT sector is **irrelevant.**

    - **(E)** This option is the **correct** answer. If the current national budget is significantly lower than that of last year, despite the proportion of taxes from the IT sector being significantly higher (15/8 = 2 times) than that of last year, it is vulnerable to criticism whether the IT sector is indeed growing at all. Let us look at this example. Say the national budget for the last year was $100M, and that for the current year is $50M. This means that taxes from IT were 8% of 100M = $8M, and that for the current year is 15% of 50M = $7.5M, which is less than the figure from last year.

The correct answer is option E.

57. This question is a modified version of a question from the 'Strengthen the Argument' chapter. This is a question on weakening the argument.

    The argument is easy to comprehend. Maddy claims that he would have won the match had the audience not started vocally and loudly supporting his opponent Hogan from the third set onwards.

    Conclusion: Due to the deafening noise, Maddy lost his concentration, causing him to lose the match.

    The case requiring weakening is that it was an unfair match, that instead, Maddy lost through his own mistakes, not because of circumstances set against him. Perhaps the quickest way to solve such questions is to sort the options into positive and negative categories. The correct option, as a weakener for Maddy's case, must show Maddy is responsible for the loss.

    (A) This option favors Maddy. However, having more stamina than the opponent is not the only decisive factor to prove that a player will surely win a match.

    (B) Like option A, this option also favors Maddy. However, a high bet on a player is not a qualification to conclude that the player will win the match.

    (C) This option is **irrelevant**. It simply means that Hogan drank water more frequently than Maddy did during the third set. This option is a distractor.

    (D) This option is the **correct** answer. Maddy's complaint to his physiotherapist of hamstring pain after the second set implies that during the third set he was not capable of playing to the best of his ability. This proves that the deafening noise did not make Maddy lose his concentration. This option is a **weakener**.

    (E) This option is **inconclusive**. We cannot draw any inference from this.

    The correct answer is option D.

58. This question is a modified version of a question from the 'Strengthen the Argument' chapter. This is a question on evaluating the argument.

    This is a pretty simple argument to understand. The argument is about panic created in low-lying areas caused by the rising level of Yamuna River.

    Conclusion: Over 50,000 people from low-lying areas should be evacuated.

    (A) This option is **inconclusive**. If the answer to the questions is – yes, the Yamuna crossed the highest water level mark of the last decade – we do not know whether this mark was dangerous to begin with. It may be quite an ordinary level. This would mean that Yamuna was not ever, and is not now, a threat to life.

(B) This option is **out of scope**. The situation in the neighboring state cannot mirror the situation in this state. The argument does not state whether the two states are similar or that both face danger from Yamuna's rising water levels.

(C) This option tells us about the preparedness of the unit of the Disaster Management Force to address any eventuality. This option does strengthen the conclusion to some extent; however, being prepared to encounter any eventuality does not provide concrete proof that over 50,000 people should be evacuated. Any state, regardless of existing danger, should be prepared with a disaster management unit prepared to help in eventualities.

(D) This is the **correct** answer. A danger-level mark is a qualifying mark to execute some anticipatory action. Although the preventive action may not necessarily be evacuation, among the given options, this one most logically supports the reason that the evacuation exercise should be carried out.

(E) This option tells us how the city government will temporarily accommodate the flood-hit people. Like option C, this option also strengthens the conclusion to some extent; however, planning for setting up relief camps to tackle the threat and the aftermath of a flood does not provide support for a decision that involves over 50,000 people.

The correct answer is option D.

59. This question is a modified version of a question from the 'Strengthen the Argument' chapter. This is a question on weakening the argument.

Conclusion: Once the computer system is up and running, the system will be able to save more than $500M a year.

The claim that needs to be weakened is that the new system will save money by reducing fraud.

(A) This option is a **strengthener**. It means that the system is reliable, thus supporting the conclusion.

(B) This option is **inconclusive**. We do not know how much 20% of the cost of the system amounts to. Secondly, we also do not know whether the calculation of saving $500M takes into account the cost of annual maintenance.

(C) This is an extreme answer. First, the argument never said that the system will stop all fraudulent claims; second, "all" is an extreme word. Even if 90% of the fraudulent claims are stopped, the system may be called a success.

(D) This option is the **correct** answer. If the Medicare staff cannot be fully trained in the handling of the new system, the objective of implementing the system will be lost.

(E) This option is **inconclusive**. The word "some" has a wide range; it may be 1% to 99%. We cannot conclude anything based on this.

Critical Reasoning Guide Training Set Solutions – Critical Reasoning

The correct answer is option D.

60. This question is a modified version of a question from the 'Weaken the Argument' chapter. This is a question on role play.

The argument is easy to understand. To standardize quality of classes, the university will select the 200 best candidates out of 2000 applications, judged so by the quality of their personal statements.

Conclusion: Selecting the best 200 students on the basis of the quality of their personal statements (SoP) will ensure constant standards of quality in students.

Let us discuss what roles each statement plays.

BF1: (Acme... college) – This is a factual statement. The task for the college is to filter 2000 applications to select the 200 best candidates. It does not directly play any role in forming the conclusion – 'The selection process will ensure constant standards of quality in students' – however, the selection process is designed on the basis on this boldface statement. So, this is a fact mentioned in the argument that outlines the direction the argument will take – selection of students from among candidates.

Statement 2: (The university's......year) – This is what the university wants. So, this is a desirable effect/goal for the university.

BF2: (therefore........statements) – This is the selection process. It forms the basis for reaching the above mentioned goal.

- (A) BH1 is a fact, but it does not form the basis for the conclusion; as discussed, it forms the basis for BF2. BF2 is not the conclusion; it forms the basis for the conclusion.
- (B) BH1 is a fact, but the argument does not discuss it; the argument discusses the selection process and how to maintain the constant quality of students. BF2 does not go against the conclusion; it is consistent with the conclusion.
- (C) BF1: This is correct; BF1 is a fact that forms the basis for the second. BF2 is not the conclusion.
- (D) BF1: This is **correct**. BF1 can be treated as a general consideration presented in the argument. BF2: This is also **correct**; BF2 is the strategy (process) to help reach the conclusion. This is the correct answer.
- (E) BF1: This is incorrect; BF1 is a not challenge in the argument. It is a fact that determines some course of action. BF2: This is correct; BF2 is the strategy (process) to help reach the conclusion.

The correct answer is option D.

61. This question is a modified version of a question from the 'Weaken the Argument' chapter. This question is a mix of both finding the flaw and method of reasoning.

    Due to a huge flood in Hunan during the rice-growing season, the price of rice will double. It will make rice cakes more expensive.

    Conclusion: Due to the doubling of the price of rice, consumers in Hunan will now have to pay more for rice cakes.

    Our task is to find the flaw in the reasoning that the price of rice cakes will rise. The author concludes that the huge flood in Hunan will cause the price of rice to double.

    The author seems to imply that the rice used in Hunan is supplied entirely by Hunan growers. What if Hunan is not the only source of rice? Hunan could import rice from other parts of the country, and possibly at an almost normal price.

    We can treat the situation as cause and effect. The effect is the cost of making rice cakes rising, and the cause is the doubling of the price of rice.

    As discussed above, the flaw in the reasoning is that the effect is ONLY produced by ONLY one cause.

    (A) There are only two things discussed; one, the effect – the cost of making rice cakes rising, and two, the cause – the doubling of the price of rice. No other event is discussed.

    (B) There are not many causes, only one cause is discussed.

    (C) There are not many events, only one event is discussed.

    (D) This is the **correct** answer. It is aligned with our analysis. The argument discusses the possibility of a rise in the price of rice affecting the cost of making rice cakes without taking into consideration there might be alternative solutions to the given problem.

    (E) The argument does take into consideration the law of supply and demand, based on which the author assumes that due to a shortage of rice, prices will rise.

    The correct answer is option D.

62. This question is a modified version of a question from the 'Weaken the Argument' chapter. This is a question on role play.

    Argument of the gun lobby: Every citizen has the right to possess a gun to protect himself. It is written in the US Constitution. Their position is – do not ban gun possession.

Argument of opponents: The most recent UN statistics prove that globally there exists a clear correlation between the number of violent gunfire incidents and the leniency of gun control legislation. Their position is – ban gun possession.

Conclusion: Ban gun possession.

Let us dissect the argument and understand the role of the boldfaced portions.

BF1: (Enshrined ...arms) – It is a claim/fact/evidence. It acts as evidence in support of the 'Don't ban guns' position. The argument seeks to refute BF1. It is on the opposite side of the conclusion (of the argument) – ban gun possession.
Second portion of statement 1: (...remains ... handguns) – The latter part of this statement further explains the position of the lobbyists. It should be paired with BF1 to understand its role.
First portion of statement 2: (Their...that) – it introduces the reference of the evidence used by the opponents. It should be paired with BF2 to understand its role.
BF2: (globally ... legislation) – It is counter-evidence or a counter-claim that goes against BF1, and forms the basis for the conclusion – ban gun possession.

(A) BF1: This is correct. BF1 can be treated as a finding whose implications are at issue in the argument, but BF2 is not a claim presented in order to argue for the derived implications from that finding; it is other way round. BF1 and BF2 are on opposite sides.

(B) BF1: This is incorrect. BF1 does not support the main conclusion; it is against the main conclusion (ban guns). BF2: This is also incorrect. In fact, BF2 is a counter-claim that goes with the conclusion.

(C) BF1: This is **correct**. BF1 is the evidence that strengthens a position – Don't ban guns. BF2: This is also **correct**. BF2 is the evidence that strengthens the counter position – ban guns.

(D) BF1: This is correct. BF1 is the consideration that opposes the conclusion; but BF2 is not the conclusion, it forms the basis for the conclusion.

(E) BF1: This is incorrect. BF1 does not form the basis for the conclusion; rather, it opposes the conclusion; BF2 is not the conclusion.

The correct answer is option C.

63. This question is a modified version of a question from the 'Weaken the Argument' chapter. This is a question on finding the assumption.

Milton International School employs competent teachers and teaches through a revamped course curriculum. Still, the social science and geography scores for grade 10 students are not satisfactory.

Conclusion: Social science and geography should be taught in the native language.

(A) This option focuses on the teachers rather than the students. The parents won't be concerned about the comprehension of the teachers; rather, parents would be concerned about explanations from the teachers. Hence, this option is incorrect.

(B) This option focuses on math and science rather than social science and geography. Although the parents can assume that math and science can satisfactorily be explained by teachers and comprehended by students in the English language, they may not necessarily assume that these subjects can be BETTER explained by teachers and comprehended by students in the English language that in the native language.

(C) The parents cannot necessarily assume that the average scores for grade 10 students in subjects other than social science and geography must be significantly above the expected level; they can at least assume that the average scores for those subjects are at a satisfactory level. This is an **extreme** option.

(D) It is not a necessary assumption. Even if there are no English-medium schools in the town where a few subjects are taught in the native language, parents can still propose a change to Milton School.

(E) This is the **correct** answer. It is a necessary assumption. Parents must assume that teaching through the native language will enhance the comprehension of the students significantly to recommend that social science and geography be taught in the native language.

The correct answer is E.

64. This question is a modified version of a question from the 'Weaken the Argument' chapter. This is a question on completing the argument.

Statistics show that children who are beaten usually grow up believing that it is appropriate to beat their children as well. The intermediate conclusion is that this cycle is just one instance of violence perpetuating violence.

But a certain religious sect claims that beating children is a form of discipline, not violence, and that this discipline is necessary to develop certain good habits in children, because ....

The justification provided by advocates of child-beating in the argument is that children must be beaten because they are not able to make logical conclusions and are unable to respond appropriately to their surroundings. The correct option must directly support this assertion. We have to show that child-beating is necessary and that children do not have the requisite amount of intelligence to grow up to be responsible adults.

(A) From the religious sect's point of view, it does not naturally follow that they would justify beating to regulate children's emotions.

(B) This is the **correct** answer. It follows naturally that the people from the religious sect beat the children for their betterment; they believe that by doing so children will become tough and capable of taking on the world.

- **(C)** This is an **opposite** answer. The option advocates instead that children must not be beaten.
- **(D)** It is unlikely that the religious sect would rationalize the reason for beating based on the intelligence of children.
- **(E)** It follows naturally that the people from the religious sect beat the children for their betterment or some similar reason, and not merely to follow a social practice. The sect has a reason, however flawed it may be. 'Child-beating is an acceptable social practice' does not provide a reason, but merely points out a practice.

The correct answer is option B.

65. This question is a modified version of a question from the 'Weaken the argument' chapter. This is a question on inference.

    The UK has hiked taxes on tobacco and alcohol, making it proportionally the world's leading collector of excise tax. The UK has defended the tax rise as being the only effective deterrent against tobacco and alcohol abuse.

    However, critics claim that such policies are flawed, as the vast money gathered annually funds so many governmental activities and expenses. They state that if tobacco and alcohol consumers were really discouraged, the government would collapse.

    - **(A)** We can only infer from the argument that the high taxes fund some activities and services in the country, but we cannot necessarily infer that one of those services would be medical service.
    - **(B)** Quoting from the argument: "which now makes the UK proportionally the world's leading collector of excise tax", the statement means that the proportion of taxes on tobacco and alcohol is the highest in the world, but that does not mean that the taxes are highest in absolute terms, too.
    - **(C)** This is real world trap option. In the real world, it is reasonable to assume that extreme tobacco and alcohol use is common in many countries, but we cannot infer such an inference from the argument.
    - **(D)** Like option A, we cannot infer that incremental tax rises compensate for the gradual decrease in tobacco and alcohol use and the derived revenue; there may not be such a plan.
    - **(E)** This is the **correct** answer. Quoting from the argument: "as being the **only** effective deterrent against tobacco and alcohol abuse", we can infer with the usage of the word 'only' that the UK government considers that a quantitative measure such as high taxation more effective than a qualitative measure to control tobacco and alcohol abuse.

    The correct answer is option E.

66. This question is a modified version of a question from the 'Weaken the argument' chapter. This is a question on role play.

Country Y wants sanctions against it lifted. Earlier, the sanctions were imposed for repeated use of torture in military prisons and the failure of the ruling military junta to hand over governing to democratically-elected civilian leaders. Country Y intends to return to civilian rule. It blames any continuing instances of torture upon corrupt officers.

Conclusion: Sanctions should be lifted.

Let us dissect the argument and understand the role of the boldfaced portions.

BF1: (Country Y...lifted) – It contains a claim and the conclusion. 'The sanctions have severely curtailed vital exports' is the claim made by Country Y, and '(the sanctions) should be lifted' is the conclusion.
The argument discusses the claim in the argument.
Statement 2: (The sanctions...leaders) – It is background information, and the reason why the sanctions were imposed on Country Y.
First portion of statement 3: (As a basis...rule) – It is a claim that goes with the conclusion, and is consistent with BF1.
BF2: (blaming...officers) – The role of BF2 is tricky. This question is similar to the 'CEO' question in the practice questions of the 'Role Play' chapter. The portion – **blaming...officers** – is something claimed by Country Y that goes against the conclusion, but it believes that it does not weaken its case to advocate for lifting the sanctions.

(A) BF1: This is incorrect; although BF1 is a claim, the argument does not contest it. BF2: This is inconclusive; at face value, it seems that BF2 goes against the conclusion, but as discussed above, it is a prediction made by Country Y, which believes that it does not weaken its case to advocate for lifting the sanctions. BF2 is actually present because Country Y anticipates the objection anyone might make against its request/claim and chooses to deal with the objection. So, BF2 is not really acting against the main claim/BF1.

(B) BF1: This is **correct**; BF1 is a claim which the argument discuses. BF2: This is also **correct**; we also discussed that BF2 is a claim that Country Y believes does not go against the conclusion.

(C) BF1: This is correct; BF1 is a claim that contains the conclusion. BF2: This is incorrect; although BF2 is a prediction, it is not consistent with the claim made in BF1. Both the claims are on opposite sides.

(D) BF1: This is incorrect; although BF1 is a claim, it does not contest the conclusion. It is consistent with the conclusion. BF2: This is correct; as discussed above, BF2 is a prediction that goes against the claim made in BF1.

(E) BF2: This is correct; BF1 contains the continuance of the implications (severely curtailed vital exports) if a certain policy (continuance of sanctions) is not lifted. BF2: This is incorrect; BF2 is neither a fact, nor do its implications form the main point of discussion.

Critical Reasoning Guide Training Set Solutions – Critical Reasoning

The correct answer is option B.

67. This question is a modified version of a question from the 'Weaken the Argument' chapter. This is a question on inference.

    The computer manufacturers' share of industry revenues has declined from 75 percent three years ago to 60 percent today. But for the same period, the revenue share of companies selling computer parts increased from 15 percent to 25 percent, while that of service companies increased from 10 percent to 15 percent. The total revenue for the computer industry is made up of revenue from manufacturers, computer parts, and service companies. It is to be noted that all the data points given are in percentages. Let us list the scenario for today and for three years ago.

Scenario	Today	Three-Year-Before
Computer Manufacturers	60	75
Computer parts companies	25	15
Service companies	15	10
Total Revenue (%)	100%	100%

    From the table, we cannot infer the absolute value of revenue three years ago and today. We can only infer that the percentage revenue share of computer manufacturers is declining, while that for computer parts and service companies is rising. Hence, for all we know, the computer industries revenues may have declined or may have gone up. Mere percentage shares imply no absolute information.

    (A) 'The amount of revenue' is an absolute value; as deduced above that percentage shares imply no absolute information, we cannot conclude that the amount of revenue has declined. Say the revenue of the computer industry was $1000M three years ago, and is $50M today. In this scenario, though the percentage share of revenue for computer parts and service companies rose, the amount of revenues for manufacturers, part-sellers, and service companies declined with respect to that of three years ago.

    (B) As discussed in option A, the revenues for each the three companies – computer manufacturers, computer-part sellers, and service companies – may even decrease.

    (C) This is **out of scope**. We cannot infer anything for the years in between.

    (D) This is the **correct** answer. This option talks in terms of percentage share. We can surely infer that the collective percentage share of computer-part sellers and service companies in the industry has increased from 25% (15%+10%) to 40% (25%+15%).

    (E) This is **out of scope**. We cannot infer anything about the scenario four years ago.

    The correct answer is D.

68. This question is a modified version of a question from the 'Weaken the Argument' chapter. This is a question on finding the assumption.

The wholesale price of mustard has increased substantially in the last six months, whereas that of groundnut has decreased.

Conclusion: The retail price of mustard oil at grocery shops will increase.

(A) The 'retail price of groundnut oil' aspect is **out of scope**. It has no impact on the retail price of mustard oil.

(B) This option is **not relevant**. It compares the wholesale prices of mustard oil and groundnut oil.

(C) This is the **correct** answer. The meaning of the statement is that though the cost of processing groundnut oil has decreased in the last year, the cost of processing mustard oil has NOT decreased. It implies that the processing cost is either constant or has increased. It is a necessary assumption that the cost of processing mustard oil has not decreased, or else the prediction that the price will increase will be less believable.

(D) This option is **irrelevant**. The harvesting of mustard is an activity prior to wholesale trading. We are concerned about the effect on the price of mustard oil after the mustard was harvested.

(E) This is a tricky option. It means that the proportion of the consumption of mustard oil with respect to groundnut oil has increased significantly. If the consumption of mustard oil increased significantly, it is likely that the retail price of mustard oil will increase following the law of supply and demand; however, this option is **inconclusive**. What if the consumption of groundnut oil decreased drastically, whereas that of mustard oil decreased marginally, making the ratio of the consumption of mustard oil and groundnut oil equal to 2. The word 'double' may mislead you; in this scenario, the consumption of mustard oil also decreased. So, we can't say necessarily that the price of mustard oil will go up.

The correct answer is option C.

69. This question is a modified version of a question from the 'Find the Flaw' chapter. This is a question on role play.

When students do not find their projects challenging, they become less interested and in turn they achieve less than their abilities. On the contrary, when students find their projects very challenging, they give up and so again achieve less than what they are capable of achieving.

Let us dissect the argument and understand the role of the boldfaced portions.

Conclusion: No student's full potential can ever be realized.

BF1: (When...allowed) – It cites one scenario: Project is not challenging – accomplishment is less. It forms the basis for the conclusion.

BF2: (when...accomplishing) – It cites the other scenario: Project is too challenging – still the accomplishment is less. It also forms the basis for the conclusion.

The correct answer is option E. Both portions are consistent with the conclusion; they form the basis for the conclusion. They are not mutually contradicting claims; in both scenarios the outcome is unrealized full potential.

The correct answer is option E.

70. This question is modified version of a question from the 'Parallel Reasoning' chapter. This is a question on finding the assumption.

    It is said that, in the next decade, demand for a certain type of car will go down. Companies generally order their steel plating 5 years in advance to get the maximum discount. It follows that the companies would have ordered steel plating for this car type years in advance when the cars were popular. Now, after they learn that the demand will go down, they want to cancel the orders for steel plating they made for cars they would have made in the future, but now won't, because of decreasing demand.

    (A) The aspect of vehicles other than large and family-sized is outside the scope of the argument. We cannot even infer that other types of cars need steel plating.
    (B) This is not a 'must be true' kind of inference. Even if the major automobile companies manufacture few large and family-sized vehicles, they can still cancel the orders for steel plating.
    (C) This is the **correct** answer. As per the argument, orders for steel plating are usually placed five years in advance of delivery to obtain maximum price reduction. It can be inferred that if the companies order now, it will cost more than it would have five years ago.
    (D) The aspect of small-sized vehicles is outside the scope of the argument. Maybe the companies discussed in the argument only manufacture large and family-sized vehicles.
    (E) Even if the proportion of the cost of steel plating is not the highest among other components in a large and family-sized vehicle, they can still choose to cancel the orders for steel plating.

    The correct answer is option C.

71. A magazine shows that 75 percent of its readers want to invest in a new fishing boat. However, fishing boat manufacturers can only produce enough boats to satisfy 30 percent of total potential buyers. The author wants people to invest in fishing boats.

    This is a question on resolving the paradox.

    The paradox: While 75% of a magazine's readers want to invest in a new fishing boat, fishing boat manufacturers can only produce enough boats to satisfy 30 percent of total potential buyers.

This question deals with different reference points.

How can the figure of 75% of a magazine's readers relate to 30% of total potential buyers?

This inequality can hold true if 'total potential buyers' are significantly more than 'a magazine's readers'. Say the number of potential buyers = 1000, and the number of the magazine's readers = 100, then 75% of 100 = 75, and 30% of 1000=300; it is quite evident that 75 < 300. Option D correctly states it.

The correct answer is option D.

72. This is a question on weakening the argument.

    The argument is simple to understand. A manufacturer makes 100 models of mobile phones, but it stocks only the top 10 best-selling models. It plans to increase its stock for the top 12 most popular models to sell more and increase profits.

    Conclusion: Increase the stocking policy from the top 10 best-selling models to the top 12 most popular models.

    We have to weaken the decision to increase the stocking of of the 12 most popular models rather than only the 10 best-selling models.

    (A) This option is **irrelevant**. It talks about the top four models, whereas we are concerned about two additional models.
    (B) This is the **correct** answer. If the top nine out of ten models bring all the money, an additional two models will not make any difference. This weakens the decision.
    (C) This is **opposite**. It talks in favor of stocking less-known brands.
    (D) This option is tricky. It does have an undertone of weakening, though the option does not support stocking less popular models. It talks about stocking additional models that are most popular. Less popular models are out of scope of the argument.
    (E) Like option D, this option, too, talks about less popular models, which are out of scope of the argument.

    The correct answer is B.

73. This is a question on weakening the argument.

    In a certain country, party members earn twice as much as non-party members do. Party members happen to work in businesses that generally have higher wages. Some non-party members who also work in these businesses earn almost the same as party members do. This implies that higher incomes and a connection to the party are not

Critical Reasoning GuideTraining Set Solutions – Critical Reasoning 389

related.

Conclusion: Higher incomes do not necessarily result from a connection to the party.

(A) This option is **inconclusive**. We are concerned about wages; we cannot consider other benefits the same as wages. Had 'other benefits' been significant in wage terms, this could have been the answer, as it would have established that, owing to proximity to the party, party-members earn more compared to non-party members.

(B) Though the option is inconclusive, if it is to be taken at face value, it would validate the conclusion.

(C) This option is **out of scope**. It does not address any differentiation between party workers and non-party workers.

(D) This is the **correct** answer. This option conclusively proves that due to connections with party members, non-party members often receive favors.

(E) This option is tricky. Just by becoming a member of the party within a given industry or business does not prove that higher wages are guaranteed and are because of the connection to the party.

The correct answer is option D.

74. This is a question on weakening the argument.

The Hale Burton Oil Pipeline Construction Corporation has had a bad quarter. Instead of laying off workers to cut costs, , it will simply hold salaries for 30 days and put the money in a mutual fund to earn interest to cover expenses. By doing this, the company and its employees will avoid the negative consequences often associated with earnings shortfalls.

Conclusion: Deferring salaries for 30 days and holding the money in a mutual fund to earn interest to cover expenses will avoid the negative consequences of earnings shortfalls for both the company and its employees.

(A) This option is **irrelevant**: It does not address the issue at all.

(B) This option is out of scope. Understaffing has nothing to do with the current situation.

(C) This is the **correct** answer. If some employees have to borrow money and pay interest on these loans, the negative consequences of the plan would be borne by the employees.

(D) Though some employees will not be affected by the rollover because they have savings, we do not know about others. Hence, this neither strengthens nor weakens.

(E) This option is **out of scope**.

The correct answer is option C.

75. This is a question on weakening the argument.

    Some countries legalized drug X because a significant percentage of the population had been using X on a daily basis without any apparent harm. But since drug X's legalization, there has been an increase in manic depression, suicide, and certain kinds of cancer in those countries. Andovia is a country that is surrounded by those countries and has not yet legalized X. So to avoid any ill effects because of broad usage of drug X, it should close its borders and not issue visas to any tourists from the countries where drug X is legal.

    Conclusion: Andovia should close its borders and not issue visas to avoid spread of the usage of drug X.

    (A) This is a **strengthener.** If trained canines fail to identify drug X users, Andovia should pursue its plan of restricting tourists.

    (B) This is a **strengthener,** too. Even if the detrimental side effects of drug X only become visible after several years of usage, Andovia should pursue its plan of restricting tourists.

    (C) This option is **out of scope.** This option focuses on how effectively Andovia can secure itself from illegal entry. The issue is not whether Andovia should effectively protect its border, but whether the move to restrict the entry of tourists is effective or not?

    (D) This option is **out of scope.** Other drugs are out of scope. The argument is concerned with drug X.

    (E) This is the **correct** answer. Since drug X is very easy to extract chemically from certain consumer products, this demonstrates a condition whereby such restrictions on tourists would prove ineffective.

    The correct answer is option E.

76. This is a question on weakening the argument.

    The argument is simple to understand. The goal of the Flerenchian government is to increase chocolate sales by decreasing competition through import that is hurting the local chocolate industry.

    We can predict a criticism: what if Flerenchian-made chocolate is either low in taste or quality, or both, and not preferred by natives. In that case, the import restriction will not help improve its domestic sales.

    Conclusion: Limiting the import of chocolate will cause a large increase in domestic sales of chocolate produced in Flerenchia in the near future.

    (A) This option is **out of scope.** Foreign investment in the chocolate industry has nothing to do with the current situation.

(B) This option is **irrelevant**.

(C) This option is tricky. If worldwide orders for Flerenchian-made chocolates dropped by more than 15%, it may be inferred that Flerenchian-made chocolates are not preferred by customers; however, we cannot assume that a phenomenon occurring worldwide will necessarily be replicated in Flerenchia, too. Perhaps other countries are banning imports like Flerenchia is.

(D) This is the **correct** answer. If substantial inventories of foreign-made chocolate was stockpiled in Flerenchia during the past year, Flerenchian-produced chocolate will continue to face competition from foreign-made chocolate until the stockpiles are depleted. It is very important to understand that the analyst predict that sales will boom in the near future. "Near future" is the key phrase in the conclusion in relation to this option. This option shows that even in the near future, Flerenchian chocolate will face stiff competition and probably not have as much sales.

(E) This option is **irrelevant**. Aspects of other countries are out of scope of the argument.

The correct answer is D.

77. This is a question on evaluating the argument.

(A) This option is tricky. It is implied that Flerenchian companies are capable of producing sufficient chocolate to cater to the domestic need; however, due to competition from foreign-made chocolate, they are probably not able to sell all that they produce.

(B) This option is **out of scope**. This option talks about the mechanism of limiting imports, which is not relevant to the argument.

(C) This option is **irrelevant**. With regard to exporting chocolate or producing foreign chocolate locally, in either case, it will hurt domestic chocolate makers.

(D) This option is **out of scope**. A consideration of foreign policy is not relevant to the argument of whether domestic chocolate sales will rise.

(E) This is the **correct.** answer. It is important to know whether natives would like Flerenchian-made chocolate in lieu of foreign-made chocolate. If Flerenchian-made chocolate is not welcomed by natives, domestic sales will not improve in the near future.

The correct answer is option E.

78. This is a question on weakening the argument.

Emergency response officials claim that more fires are not occurring, it's just that more fires are being reported. Something that weakens their claim will be something that demonstrates that, in fact, more fires actually are happening.

(A) This option is **irrelevant**. The argument is not concerned about the location of publicity of the fire incident.

(B) This is the **correct**. answer. It identifies a situation in which more fires do happen at certain times.

(C) This is a **strengthener**. If news organizations do not have any guidelines to help them decide how severe or close a fire must be for it to receive coverage, they will report incidents which are not of serious proportion, and, hence, the claims of emergency response officials would be justified.

(D) This option is **inconclusive**. We cannot draw any inference out of the option statement. News sources may report severe or non-severe fire incidents if it is advantageous to them. This does not imply that they report those fires that don't happen.

(E) This is a **strengthener**. Since the number of fires in Springfield is almost the same every month, more reports in some particular months implies that the media does report more though there may not be more incidents of a serious nature.

The correct answer is B.

79. This is a question on weakening the argument.

What is Save-a-Tot's claim? It is that the new safety seats are indeed safer. Something that challenges that claim will demonstrate that the seats are, in fact, not safer.

(A) This is the **correct** answer. It demonstrates that the plastic in the seat turns brittle, rendering it unsafe. It is the best answer.

(B) This option is **out of scope**. So what if the government demands that Save-a-Tot produce these child safety seats to very strict specifications? Save-a-Tot may or may not comply with that.

(C) This option is **out of scope**. Issue of sales is not relevant.

(D) This option is tricky. At first glance, it seems like it is weakener; though enhanced weight to bicycles is a negative aspect, the argument is not concerned about the weight; it is concerned about the safety. Additional weight is not necessarily anti-safety.

(E) This option is **irrelevant**. Issue of cost and price are not relevant.

The correct answer is option A.

80. This is a question on weakening the argument.

There is a logical link missing in the argument of the management. What most weakens their claim is that link. The management says water sources themselves are polluted.

The first thing you should ask yourself is 'why are the water sources polluted?' If it is possible that the plant is somehow polluting water sources, then that would substantially challenge the management's argument.

(A) This option is **irrelevant**. The argument is about the claim that the plant is not responsible for the pollution, and not about differentiation between types of pollution.

(B) This option is **irrelevant**. This option just shows that communities are not affected by the changes in the water, regardless of pollution. They are continuing what they have done.

(C) This is the **correct** answer. It is the best instance of linkage whereby the pollution source can be connected to the plant.

(D) This option is tricky, but it is not conclusive. Though the plant uses and produces nuclear waste that causes mutations, this fact does not bridge the missing link of whether the plan itself is the cause of the pollution in the water in the valley.

(E) This is a **strengthener**. This clearly favors the management by proving that the waste from the plant is not the cause, rather it is the pollution in the water source that is the cause of the mutations in fish.

The correct answer is option C.

81. This is a question on strengthening the argument.

The argument is simple to understand. Despite sending students to special extra courses, the language exam scores of these students were lower than those of students who did not attend the special courses.

Conclusion: The special extra courses are a waste of time and money.

(A) This is the **correct** answer. Despite knowing the exams better than the schools that do not send their students for the special courses, the high schools in question did not fare better. This clearly supports the argument that these special extra courses are a waste of time and money.

(B) This option does not compare the scores of course-takers and non-takers. It merely presents a fact that the scores of course-takers have not dropped since 1995. We do not know whether the scores are excellent or poor.

(C) This option is **out of scope**. Cost is out of scope.

(D) This option is **irrelevant**. The reasons for ineffective courses are not relevant to the argument.

(E) This option is **inconclusive**. We do not know who these students are: course-takers/non-course-takers or both; it does not differentiate between the number of course-takers and that of non-course-takers, hence we cannot compare them.

The correct answer is A.

82. This is a question on resolving the paradox.

The argument is simple to understand. Despite anticipating that after the installation of safety traffic equipment the number of red-light runners would decrease, it increased.

We have to select an option that explains why such a contradiction occurred.

- **(A)** This option does not help explain the contradiction. It compares the situations in two intersections in the city; we have to understand why the increase in violations took place in the main intersection.
- **(B)** With the same reasoning as in option A, this option does not help to explain the contradiction.
- **(C)** This is the **correct** answer. Since the ability of the system to catch traffic violators is more than the earlier system six months back, more reporting of red-light runners occurred. Previously they were unnoticed due to the absence of the new system. This option helps to explain the contradiction.
- **(D)** This option does not add any value. It merely endorses the fact that a six-month period was sufficient time to study traffic violations; however, it does not help to explain the contradiction.
- **(E)** This option is **out of scope**.

The correct answer is C.

83. This is a question on strengthening the argument.

Experts in the Sepharian Federation fear that if Kalistan imposed a ban on the export of one kind of petroleum derivative, it would drive up its price by 20 times. Few countries have that particular derivative. With an embargo, Sepharia might have to turn to sources that offer unproven substitutes for this derivative.

Conclusion: Sepharia might have to depend on yet unproven synthetic fuel technologies to acquire a reasonable substitute for the derivative.

- **(A)** This is **irrelevant.** The argument is concerned about sourcing the derivative, not about Kalistan's economy.
- **(B)** This is **irrelevant.** This is a futuristic scenario; it does not resolve the current crisis.
- **(C)** This is **irrelevant.** This is a futuristic scenario; it does not resolve the current crisis.
- **(D)** This is the **correct** answer. As only a small portion of Sepharia's import expenditure is devoted to acquiring the derivative, it is mandatory for Sepharia to experiment with a reasonable substitute for the derivative to be sourced from other countries.
- **(E)** This is a **weakener.** The ability of Sepharia to purchase the derivative for only 1/4th more would weaken the premise of the threat.

The correct answer is D.

84. This is a question on inference.

- **(A)** This is **incorrect**. We cannot infer that Kalistan is the most dependable supplier; others could also be dependable suppliers but they may be processing petroleum though unproven synthetic fuel technologies.

(B) This is **incorrect**. We cannot infer that among all the countries in the region, ONLY Kalistan's aforementioned petroleum derivative is processed with scientifically proven technologies. There may be other countries that do the same, however the Sepharian Federation may not wish to buy from them due to a reason that is out of scope of the argument.

(C) This is **incorrect**. The Sepharian Federation's selection of Kalistan to buy the aforementioned petroleum derivative from is based on their scientifically proven fuel technologies and not on price.

(D) This is the **correct** answer. Experts fear that due to the embargo, the regular price of the aforementioned petroleum derivative from Kalistan may shoot up by 20 times and this may lead the Sepharian Federation to try a reasonable substitute from another country; this implies that the price of a reasonable substitute from other countries must be less than 20 times the regular price of the aforementioned petroleum derivative from Kalistan.

(E) This is **incorrect**. This option is irrelevant.

The correct answer is D.

85. This is a question on completing the argument.

The argument is simple to understand. The argument highlights the positive points of technological developments in the workplace, yet explains that workers feel dissatisfied because they realize that their particular skills are not crucial any longer. We have to select an option that could complete the conclusion.

(A) The argument is all about technological advancement and its impact on workers. The aspect of efficiency in production does not naturally follow as a conclusion.

(B) This option is **out of scope**. The salary aspect does not figure into it; it's the low sense of achievement with the work that disillusions workers.

(C) This option is **out of scope**. We cannot infer what managers will feel.

(D) This is the **correct** answer. Technological developments make workers key expertise less critical in the workplace.

(E) This option is **out of scope**. Laying off workers is not discussed in the argument.

The correct answer is D.

86. This is a question on finding the assumption.

The argument is simple to understand. Introverts seek belonging, so they frequently immerse themselves in online social activities, through which they feel happy and make online friends. However, when they get bored with online activities, they again become introverts.

Conclusion: Committing oneself solely on to an imaginary world is not a fruitful approach in an attempt to be social.

The premise: "However, when they get disillusioned by the virtual world, they go back into their shells" is important to discuss. Going back into their shells despite making cyber-friends implies that when introverts stop interacting with these "friends" online, the friendship vanishes.

The conclusion that the practice of developing cyber-friendships to become social is not effective is based on an assumption that cyber-friendship is flimsy, and that, to be social, one needs enduring friendships.

- **(A)** This option is **out of scope**. Other approaches are out of scope of the argument.
- **(B)** This is not an assumption; it is an inference. However, we cannot even infer this.
- **(C)** This is the **correct** answer. It is in line with our analysis done earlier.
- **(D)** This is not an assumption; it is an inference. However, we cannot even infer this.
- **(E)** This is **incorrect**. During the process of making cyber-friends, introverts don't have to feign being extroverts. Within the scope of the argument, we cannot assume this.

The correct answer is C.

87. This is a question on finding the assumption.

    The argument is simple to understand. MG did "A". He did not do "B". Anyone who does not do "B" does "C". Where A: Viewing hardships as opportunities; B: Compromise on principals: C: Leads a life of contentment.

    To draw a logical conclusion, we must assume that outcome of "C: Leads a life of contentment" is because of "A: Viewing hardships as opportunities." There was a logical gap between "C" and "A" and option B correctly fills that.

    The correct answer is B.

88. This is a question on method of reasoning. Let us deconstruct the arguments of Jack and Mary.

    Jack: Jack thinks that the reason for the poor showing of the ruling party is because they did not project a Prime Ministerial nominee as well as the opposition party did. The PM nominee of the opposition connected with the people of the country well and this is why they won the election by a great margin.

    Mary: Mary attributes the opposition's success in the election to the charisma of its leader, who was able to charm the people.

    Mary is in agreement with Jack's argument that the leader of the opposition was the reason for the opposition's win. She further strengthens this argument by providing the additional information that his charm won the heart of the people. Let us examine the options one by one.

(A) This is **incorrect**. Mary does not deny the stated premises of Jack's argument. She agrees with Jack's argument.

(B) This is **incorrect**. Mary does not demonstrate that Jack's conclusion is not consistent with the premises he uses to support it. She puts forth her viewpoint, which is consistent with Jack's viewpoint.

(C) This is the **correct** answer. This falls in line with our analysis.

(D) This is **incorrect**. Mary does not question Jack's argument.

(E) This is **incorrect**. Mary does not draw a conclusion. She further explains why Jack's conclusion is correct.

The correct answer is C.

89. This is a question on finding the assumption. Let us understand the argument.

The CT agency predicted 340 total constituency seats with a deviation of + 5. It means the actual total constituency seat figure was 335. The author disagrees with the deviation figure of +5. In his opinion, the deviation should be calculated considering the deviations in all 28 states in the country. CT's figure for each state's deviated from +7 to -10, so CT's total absolute deviation figure comes out to 42 rather than 5. The author concludes that, based on this parameter, the NDTV survey's prediction was better than CT's.

Conclusion: The NDTV survey's prediction was better than CT's based on the calculation of the absolute deviations of seats in each state.

As per the author, absolute deviation calculated from all 28 states should be the parameter. Since CT's figure is 42, it must be assumed that NDTV's figure must be less than 42. This is the necessary assumption.

(A) This option is **irrelevant**. Though it is true, this assumption does not fill the logical gap to reach the conclusion.

(B) This option is **out of scope**. The prediction by Times Now does not affect the conclusion in any way.

(C) This is the **correct** answer. This follows our analysis.

(D) This is **incorrect**. Moreover, this is not an assumption needed. We cannot infer that the NDTV survey is the most accurate in predicting constituency seats in **each** state in the country. The key word here is **each** of the 28 states.

(E) This is **incorrect**. This is not a necessary assumption. We can certainly say this for CT, but not for NDTV.

The correct answer is C.

90. This is a question on finding the assumption. Let us understand the argument.

The school wishes to install large-sized, Techo-make digital white boards in classrooms, and the boards satisfy the school's 'value for money' criterion. So, the school must plan to buy new large-sized, Techo-make boards, as the school should always make a decision that satisfies this criterion.

The concluding sentence implies that the large-sized, Techo-make digital white boards satisfy the 'value for money' criterion. Let us see the options one by one.

- (A) This is **incorrect**. This is an extreme option. It is a mandate. It is fine to say that the large-sized, Techo-make digital white boards qualified to be bought, but we cannot assume that the school should buy them.
- (B) This is **incorrect**. Value for money does not mean cost-effective; a comparatively expensive item may also qualify the 'value for money' criterion. Secondly, saying "indispensable" for the school is beyond the scope.
- (C) This is **incorrect**. We cannot assume that investing in new large-sized, Techo-make digital white boards makes a better 'value for money' choice than many of the **other options** open to the school. We have no information about "other options". Many of the other options may also satisfy the criterion, but may be small-sized, and not Techo-make.
- (D) This is **incorrect**. Like option B, value for money does not mean affordable; a comparatively expensive item may also satisfy the criterion.
- (E) This is the **correct**. answer. At most, we can necessarily assume that the school **needs** new large-sized, Techo-make digital white boards.

The correct answer is option E.

91. This is a question on finding the assumption.

The argument is simple to understand. A party must have some women with lower caste backgrounds (LCB). But no women from poor economic classes (PEC) are in the party. So, the party is not honoring its manifesto.

Conclusion: The party is not currently complying with its manifesto.

The violation of the manifesto is understood by the fact that the party does **NOT** have a single woman with a LCB. An additional premise saying – no women from a PEC are in the party – must be linked with women with a LCB. It follows that: Women with a LCB must belong to a PEC.

- (A) This option is **incorrect**. It is a rephrase of the premise. It is not an assumption.
- (B) This option is **incorrect**. It is the mandate, not an assumption.
- (C) This is the **correct** answer. This is in line with our analysis.
- (D) This option is **irrelevant**.
- (E) This option is **incorrect**. There may be some women from poor economic classes not registered and who do not have a lower caste background.

The correct answer is C.

92. This is a question on evaluating the argument.

The argument is simple to understand. This is a very relatable real life scenario. Though small containers of products cost less, their per-unit cost is higher when compared to the per-unit cost of a larger size of the same product. For example, a 100 ml bottle may cost 200 dollars [2 dollars/ml] but a 1000 ml bottle might cost only 1200 dollars [1.20/ml] instead of 2000 dollars, because the argument states that there is a 40% reduction for 1000ml packs.

Conclusion: Bigger sizes are more value for the money, and, therefore, should be chosen.

We have to choose an option that DOESN'T need to be considered when choosing shampoo bottle size.

(A) This aspect must be considered. If the time limitation regarding quality of the shampoo is too short for your usage rate, it makes more sense to stick with a smaller bottle. If there is no quality time limitation, buying a larger bottle and getting the lowest price per milliliter is the best decision.

(B) This aspect must be considered. If the per ml. price of shampoo going to come down significantly in the near future, buying a smaller bottle is a good idea to tide you over until you can take advantage of the price break. Otherwise, a larger bottle is best, as explained above.

(C) This aspect must be considered. If the brand of shampoo is one that you know from experience that you like, buying a larger bottle is the best idea. If it's a new brand to you, start with a small size to check and experiment with first.

(D) This is the **correct** answer. This aspect doesn't need to be considered. It is irrelevant whether the brand of shampoo being considered is a product of a reputable company. A product of a reputable company does not always mean that it is a quality product.

(E) This aspect must be considered. This option can be understood this way. Say, for example, to penetrate the low-end market a company launched a 5 ml sample bottle priced at 50% of the per ml price of the 1000 ml. bottle. It makes better sense to buys hundreds of the tiny bottle than a 1000 ml bottle. Similarly, say, for example, a 200 ml bottle is being offered at a considerably lower price as a combo-pack with another product, then buying a non-standard size/smaller bottle makes better sense.

The correct answer is D.

93. This is a question on completing the argument.

The argument is simple to understand. The analyst complains that the company cheats artifact collectors by selling some artifacts labelled 'antique'. It reasons that those artifacts, in fact, are relatively common, and accessible on the market at significantly lower prices. We have to anticipate the defense of the company as the company executive starts with —"That is incorrect".

- **(A)** This option is **incorrect**. Being the largest artifact dealers in the world does not form a great defense. The largest company may also cheat.
- **(B)** Though this option is **incorrect,** it is tricky. Authentication of artifacts and being antique are two different things. An authentic artifact may not be antique.
- **(C)** This option is **incorrect**. A licensed artifact dealership may also cheat.
- **(D)** This is the **correct** answer. If the company buys artifacts which are tagged antique by the National Archeological Department, they cannot be called cheaters, as the onus of declaring an artifact antique lies with a government agency.
- **(E)** Though this option is **incorrect,** it is tricky. Though the National Archeological Department is the only authorization agency that tags artifacts as antique, it does not mean that the company buys artifacts from them.

The correct answer is D.

94. This is a question on strengthening the argument.

Moterra Motor Company (MMC) launched its bike in 2005; it claims that among the most fuel-efficient bikes on the market, its 125 cc bikes make up 42% of that total. The same figure for the market leader is approximately 21%.

Conclusion: The highest percentage of the most fuel-efficient motorbikes on the market is MMC's 125 cc bike.

- **(A)** This option is **incorrect**. Buying advanced engine technology from a leading Japanese motor company does not mean that the bike is the most fuel-efficient.
- **(B)** This is **incorrect**. The statement means that the highest proportion of total bikes, classified in terms of capacity (100cc, 125 cc, 150 cc, and 200 cc), is 100 cc bikes and they are comparatively less fuel-efficient than 125 cc bikes. However this option is applicable for all the manufacturers, and not only for MMC. The argument does not state that only MMC manufactures 125 cc bikes.
- **(C)** This option is **irrelevant**. Greater length of free servicing is no logic to infer that the bike would be more fuel-efficient.
- **(D)** This option is **out of scope**. The price aspect is out of scope.
- **(E)** This option is the **correct** answer. The option means that 125 cc bikes are the most fuel-efficient among all bikes and the highest proportion of this kind are manufactured and sold by MMC; this clearly implies that MMC must be a dominant player in the most-fuel efficient bike category. It is a strengthener.

The correct answer is E.

95. This is a question on strengthening the argument.

This is a question on cause & effect.

Effect: The current slump in the realty sector in this region. However, the primary cause of the current slump is not a decrease in purchasing power. This is the conclusion.

Cause: 1. Buyers have not experienced any improvements in infrastructure services in the region.
2. The amenities promised to buyers for their apartments have not been provided.

We need to strengthen one or more parts of this. Let us see the options.

- (A) This option is **incorrect**. First, this option tries to strengthen the effect, not the cause. Second, the option is written with clever word play. It talks about the 'investment' aspect, which may be different from the 'buying' aspect. 'Investing' is a sub-set of 'buying'. Third, we do not know whether only a few invested in the properties in the past. A little more on this number will make the current figure insignificant. Just because people are buying more than their budget dictates does not mean their purchasing power is not reduced.
- (B) This is a **weakener**. If many buyers would not have bought the apartments under the current economic scenario, it tries to weaken the premise. However, the primary cause is not the decrease in purchasing power.
- (C) This is a **weakener**.
- (D) This is a **weakener**.
- (E) This is a **strengthener**, and the **correct** answer. "Poor commuting facilities" is a part of infrastructure services, and "indoor security" is a part of amenities. This information strengthens the causes and also the effect/conclusion.

The correct answer is option E.

96. This is a question on finding the assumption.

The argument is simple to understand. When the economy is booming, people are more inclined to develop skills, but when it slows down, they prefer to earn degrees. However, when the economy worsens, people's eagerness to develop new skills goes down.

Conclusion: The anticipation of the economy turning to shambles dampens people's enthusiasm for learning new skills.

- (A) This is **irrelevant**. It neither addresses the conclusion nor can it be inferred.
- (B) This is **incorrect**. It neither addresses the conclusion nor can it be inferred.
- (C) This is the **correct** answer. When people anticipate that the economy is slowing down, they focus more on earning degrees than on learning new skills, and this trend increases when anticipation of the economy turning to shambles peaks. So, the chance of people preferring to develop new skills depends on the extent to which the economy is flourishing.
- (D) This is **irrelevant**. It neither addresses the conclusion nor can be inferred.

(E) This is **irrelevant**. It is illogical to say that people's anticipation of economic is slowing down depends on how many people are inclined to earn college degree. State of economy cannot depend on how many people are willing to earn college degrees.

The correct answer is option C.

97. This is a question on completing the argument.

    We have to determine a reason why CBSE students would be more knowledgeable that state school students.

    (A) This is **incorrect**. A teacher with a higher salary cannot be construed as one who can necessarily make students more knowledgeable.
    (B) This is the **correct** answer. It correctly fills the logical gap. Teaching resources encompass all resources – teachers, books, infrastructure, and other things; this option also states that all the resources that make students knowledgeable are more effective in CBSE schools than in state schools.
    (C) This is **incorrect**. Expenditure on infrastructure and students' capability to acquire knowledge are unrelated.
    (D) This is **irrelevant**. Motives for running schools and students' capability to acquire knowledge are unrelated.
    (E) This option is **inconclusive**. Teaching students privately does not mean that the teachers can make students more knowledgeable, too. Moreover, we do not know whether teachers of state schools are also known to teach students privately.

    The correct answer is B.

98. This is a question on finding the assumption.

    The argument is that efforts to stop betting during the World Cup did not succeed. If it had been successful, the traditional lottery business would not have experienced a boom during that time.

    (A) This option is a **weakener**. If many first-timers preferred betting on teams during the World Cup rather than on traditional lotteries, the lottery business should not have boomed.
    (B) This option is opposite. It implies that, due to the practice of betting on traditional lotteries, people also bet during the World Cup matches. It does not address why the lottery business boomed during the World Cup.
    (C) This is the **correct** answer. This explains that betting on teams during the World Cup was done by the people who run the lottery business, and this led to a boom in the lottery business.
    (D) This is **irrelevant**. It compares the number of sports bookies to that of lottery bookies. It is not relevant.

(E) This option is tricky. Though lottery bookies did more business than sports bookies, it does not mean that the business done by lottery bookies boomed, too. It might even have declined during the World Cup, but could still be more business than what the sports bookie did.

The correct answer is B. C

99. This is a question on evaluating the argument.

    The argument is simple to understand. The basis of the subsidy is: A fixed amount per student admitted without fee. The minimum number of students to be admitted from a lower economic class without any fee: 25% of the total student body. It can be deduced from the premise that big schools in urban areas have to shell out some money on their own, as the amount of the subsidy per student received is less than what they have to spend to educate 25% of their student body who do not pay anything. We do not know anything about this aspect for small schools in rural areas.

    Conclusion: Small schools in rural areas are in fact earning money from the subsidy outlay.

    (A) This is **incorrect**. The minimum value of a ratio of students without fees to regular students is 1:4. It may vary, as the stipulation is: admit a minimum 25% of students from a lower economic class. This follows that comparing "the amount of total subsidies" and "the total fee collected by the school from regular students" will make no sense.

    (B) This is **irrelevant**. It can be inferred from the argument that the average fee per student charged by big schools in urban areas is more than that by small schools in rural areas; however, this comparison does not relate to the conclusion. Say the fixed amount of the subsidy per student is: $100; the fee per regular student charged by a big school is: $150: and the fee per regular student charged by a small school is either $90 or $120. In each case, the fee per regular student charged by a big school is more than that by a small school, however, if a small school charges $90, it is earning $10 because of the subsidy, and if it charges $120, it is losing $20 because of the subsidy. So, this option does not help.

    (C) This is **irrelevant**. With the same reasoning as used in option B, this option, too, does not help.

    (D) This is the **correct** answer. If the amount of the subsidy per student received by a rural school is more than the fee collected by the school per regular student, it is earning something on account of the subsidy, otherwise not.

    (E) This is **irrelevant**. Comparing the numbers of students does not help. There is no mention of fees in the option.

    The correct answer is D.

100. This is a question on finding the assumption.

     The argument is simple to understand. A potential buyer opines that too many bike-makers dilute the aspects of mileage and power – the most important purpose for owning a bike – when they advertise, and focus too much on other non-primary features. He cites an example of watching a TV commercial of a bike claiming itself to be an uber-cool bike with an ergonomically-designed body. He then makes up his mind that this particular bike is not worth buying.

Conclusion: A bike being touted for purely superficial features is not worth buying.

- **(A)** This is **incorrect**. It does not address why the bike is not worth of buying.
- **(B)** This is a tricky option; however, it is **incorrect**. The potential buyer's intent is that bike-makers should focus more on mileage and power, but their bike does not have to be a leader in mileage and power among all bikes.
- **(C)** This is **out of scope**. Cost is not an issue here.
- **(D)** This is a tricky option; however it is **incorrect**. The potential buyer's intent is NOT that bike-makers should focus either on mileage and power or on style. The potential buyer thinks that those who focus on advertising style instead of utility are being illogical. They are not necessarily mutually exclusive.
- **(E)** This is the **correct** answer. This option correctly summarizes the assumption in the potential buyer's mind. The option means that any bike which ignores the aspects of mileage and power is unlikely to be considered for purchase.

The correct answer is option E.

Chapter 16

Talk to Us

Have a Question?

Please email your questions to info@manhattanreview.com. We will be happy to answer you. Your questions can be related to a concept, an application of a concept, an explanation of a question, a suggestion for an alternate approach, or anything else you wish to ask regarding the GMAT.
Please mention the page number when quoting from the book.

GMAC – Quants Resources

- *Official Guide 2017*: It is the best resource to prepare for the GMAT. It is a complete GMAT book. It comes with a Diagnostic test, which helps you measure your capability beforehand. It features Verbal, Quantitative, and Integrated Reasoning questions types. The book contains an access code to avail GMATPrep Software, Online Question Bank and Exclusive Video.

- *GMATPrep Software*: If you buy the OG, you get a free online resource from the GMAC—the testmaker. Apart from practice questions and explanation, it also has two genuine Computer Adaptive tests; you can also buy four additional CATs and few practice questions upon the payment.

Manhattan Admissions

**You are a unique candidate with unique experience.
We help you to sell your story to the admissions committee.**

Manhattan Admissions is an educational consulting firm that guides academic candidates through the complex process of applying to the world's top educational programs. We work with applicants from around the world to ensure that they represent their personal advantages and strength well and get our clients admitted to the world's best business schools, graduate programs and colleges.

We will guide you through the whole admissions process:

- ✓ Personal Assessment and School Selection
- ✓ Definition of your Application Strategy
- ✓ Help in Structuring your Application Essays
- ✓ Unlimited Rounds of Improvement
- ✓ Letter of Recommendation Advice
- ✓ Interview Preparation and Mock Sessions
- ✓ Scholarship Consulting

To schedule a free 30-minute consulting and candidacy evaluation session or read more about our services, please visit or call:

 www.manhattanadmissions.com   +1.212.334.2500

Made in the USA
San Bernardino, CA
04 September 2016